Art and music: the

This comprehensive introduction to art therapy and music therapy in the UK will dispel many misconceptions about the nature of research in these disciplines. Edited by Andrea Gilroy and Colin Lee, both pioneers of research in their respective professions, it is the first publication to give an overview of research in art and music therapy and to give those interested in research an insight into the pitfalls and possibilities.

The contributors combine the usual framework of literature review, research design, methodology, data analysis, findings and discussion; they also include the additional element of the researcher's personal narrative. They draw research models from art history and music analysis, going well beyond the parameters of psychological and medical research generally used in clinical work. Research projects described include music therapy with offenders and with people living with HIV and AIDS, and art therapy with people with learning difficulties and with clients with a psychotic illness.

Informative and reassuring, *Art and Music: Therapy and Research* provides invaluable guidelines for those interested in doing research. It will also be an essential reference book of interest to all members of multi-disciplinary teams in mental health care, including psychiatrists, counsellors, social workers and nurses.

Andrea Gilroy teaches at the Art Psychotherapy Unit of the University of London, Goldsmiths' College. **Colin Lee** is a music therapist at Sir Michael Sobell House Hospice, Oxford.

Art and music: therapy and research

Edited by Andrea Gilroy and Colin Lee

London and New York

First published 1995
by Routledge
11 New Fetter Lane, London EC4P 4EE

Simultaneously published in the USA and Canada
by Routledge
29 West 35th Street, New York, NY 10001

Typeset in Times by J&L Composition Ltd, Filey, North Yorkshire
Printed and bound in Great Britain by
Biddles Ltd, Guildford and King's Lynn

British Library Cataloguing in Publication Data
A catalogue record for this book is available from the British Library.

Library of Congress Cataloging in Publication Data
Art and music: therapy and research/edited by Andrea Gilroy and
  Colin Lee.
      p. cm.
    Includes bibliographical references and index.
    1. Art therapy.   2. Music therapy.   I. Gilroy, Andrea.
  II. Lee, Colin.
  RM931.A77A76   1995
  615.8'5154–dc20   94–9637

ISBN 0–415–10044–5 (hbk)
ISBN 0–415–10045–3 (pbk)

Contents

Part III Context and culture

Illustrations

Notes on contributors

Malcolm Adams qualified as a clinical psychologist in 1974. He has worked in the field of learning difficulties since then, and has also worked in adult mental health settings. He has been involved in clinical psychology training since 1976 in the Universities of Glasgow, Leicester and Cambridge. He has taught extensively on research methods in psychology and has supervised over 50 Master's level research dissertations, including two in music therapy. From 1978 to 1988 he worked in the learning disabilities service in Cambridge where his research project was carried out. In 1988 he established the present East Anglian training scheme in clinical psychology on which he currently works as clinical tutor.

Andrea Gilroy teaches at the Art Psychotherapy Unit of the University of London, Goldsmiths' College, and has recently been involved in the development of art therapy education at the University of Western Sydney, Australia. She co-edited *Pictures at an Exhibition: Selected Essays on Art and Art Therapy* (Routledge, 1989) and *Art Therapy: A Handbook* (Open University Press, 1992), and was one of the principal organisers of the first Arts Therapies Research Conferences in 1989 and 1990. Her doctoral work considered the occupational motivation and career development of art therapists, focusing on the influence of professional education and clinical practice on their work as artists. Her present research interests include the processes of art therapy groups and single case research design.

Helen Greenwood obtained an honours degree in the history of art from Manchester Polytechnic in 1976. She trained as an art therapist at Birmingham Polytechnic in 1978. She has worked as an art therapist in adult psychiatry for fifteen years, firstly in Birmingham and presently in Wakefield, West Yorkshire. She completed group psychotherapy training at the West Midlands Institute of Psychotherapy in 1981.

John Henzell was born in England but grew up and studied art in Australia. Returning to England in 1959 he practised art therapy in many settings, including Napsbury Hospital where Laing and Esterson were conducting radical enquiries into schizophrenia. He was a founder member of the British Association of Art Therapists and an initiator of art therapy education. Subsequently he has directed postgraduate art and psychotherapy trainings, most recently at the University of Sheffield, and has been invited to teach at universities in Australia and Canada.

Sarah Hoskyns is Course Director of the postgraduate music therapy diploma at Guildhall School of Music and Drama, London. Her clinical interests are work with adult offenders, neurological patients and with young handicapped children and their families. She was Research Fellow in Music Therapy at City University, London from 1985 to 1988. She is a member of the Advisory Panel of the Association of Professional Music Therapists.

Katherine Killick is an analytical art therapist with a private art therapy and psychotherapy practice in St Albans. She has practised as an art therapist in adult psychiatric settings since 1979, and developed a special interest in psychotic and borderline states of mind. She is currently engaged in further training in analytical psychology.

Colin Lee has worked for many years in palliative care, initially at London Lighthouse and currently at Sir Michael Sobell House Hospice, Oxford. He also works in postgraduate music therapy education in England and Germany. He was Research Fellow in Music Therapy at City University (1988–1991), during which time he initiated the formation of the Arts Therapies Research Committee and, whilst Chairman, was the principal organiser of the 1989 and 1990 Arts Therapies Research Conferences. His doctoral thesis focused on the processes contained within therapeutic improvisation with clients living with HIV and AIDS. Present research interests include the influence of musical aesthetics on the processes of music therapy.

David Maclagan is a lecturer at the Centre for Psychotherapeutic Studies at the University of Sheffield, where he is involved with a number of courses dealing with art and therapy. He has published many articles on art therapy, outsider art and the links between aesthetic and psychological experience. He is a practising artist, as well as an art therapist in private practice.

Amelia Oldfield has worked as a music therapist in the fields of learning disabilities, child development and child and family psychiatry for the past thirteen years. She obtained her M.Phil. in 1986, based on the work described in this volume. She is an approved supervisor and past Chair of the Association of Professional Music Therapists. She has given numerous workshops and lectures in music therapy both in Great Britain and abroad, and has published widely. She is co-author of *Pied Piper: Musical Activities to Develop Basic Skills* (Cambridge University Press 1991). She is currently establishing a new music therapy training course in Cambridge at Anglia Polytechnic University.

Mercedes Pavlicevic has worked as a music therapist with people with learning difficulties of all ages, within psychiatry and with cancer patients. Her doctoral thesis examined improvisation in music therapy, its communicative meaning and application with people who have a schizophrenic illness. On completing her PhD she returned to South Africa, where she now lives and works. Her particular interests are in the emotional effects of on-going violence and social instability, and the transformation of anxiety and despair into self-improvement through music therapy.

Mair Rees is a psychology graduate and an experienced art therapist. She has worked for over ten years with people who have learning difficulties and additional mental health or behavioural problems. She has also contributed to postgraduate art therapy education. At present she manages a combined arts therapies service in the Cardiff area.

Joy Schaverien is an art therapist and psychotherapist in private practice. She worked for many years in NHS psychiatry and psychotherapy and taught art therapy at Hertfordshire College of Art and Design (now the University of Hertfordshire), where she was course leader of the Master's programme. She lectures and conducts art therapy workshops in this country and abroad. A founder member of Analytical Art Therapy Associates, she has published widely. Her book *The Revealing Image: Analytical Art Psychotherapy in Theory and Practice* was published by Routledge in 1991. She is currently working on her second book to be published by Routledge in 1995.

Julie Sutton obtained a music degree and postgraduate certificate in education at London University. She qualified as a music therapist in 1982 and worked in London for five years before moving to Northern Ireland. Her clinical and research interests include music therapy in child psychiatry, speech- and language-impairment, Rett's Syndrome and Parkinson's Disease. She is currently the Head Music Therapist and Advisor with the Northern Ireland Music Therapy Trust and is completing her M.Phil. thesis.

Sue Van Colle drove a milk float after her music degree at Reading University. She has worked one way or another using music ever since, first as a teacher and then in fringe theatre as a performance-composer and music director. She then worked in a mental health day centre using music therapeutically, before studying music therapy at the Roehampton Institute. In her music therapy work she has specialised in work with cerebral palsied children: this led to her present research which will form part of a thesis to be submitted for a PhD.

Diane Waller, an art therapist and group psychotherapist, is Head of the Art Psychotherapy Unit of the University of London, Goldsmith's College and President of the British Association of Art Therapists. Her PhD, on which the book *Becoming a Profession: The History of Art Therapy in Britain 1970–82* (Routledge, 1991) is based, dealt with art therapists' struggle towards becoming a profession between 1940 and 1982. Between 1970 and 1989 she periodically lived and worked in Bulgaria and in former Yugoslavia, and now works regularly in Rome establishing art therapy training for staff in a United Nations-sponsored centre for the treatment of drug addiction. Her other major interest is in Balkan ethnography.

Tim Williams is a clinical psychologist working with children for the West Berkshire Priority Care Services NHS Trust. Before studying psychology for his first degree he spent a summer studying with Konrad Lorenz in Bavaria. He subsequently completed a doctorate on teaching methods for autistic children using ethological methods to analyse the function of behaviour. His research interests are wide-ranging and significantly enhanced by an Honorary Research Fellowship at Reading University.

Juxtapositions in art therapy and music therapy research

Andrea Gilroy and Colin Lee

Research is a way in which clinicians can subject their practice to critical analysis within a particular theoretical and practical structure. Through attention to the similarities and differences in art therapy and music therapy research, we hope in *Art and Music: Therapy and Research* to extend our understanding not only of our work, but also of the nature of research itself. The work represented in this book is pioneering in nature and, we believe, gains from juxtaposition and comparison. The validity of research depends on its replicability; shared experiences and parallel conclusions described by independent researchers in allied areas are powerful validation procedures from which consensus and understanding may emerge.

We have tried to assemble a collection of art therapy and music therapy research that is rigorous academically but which includes descriptions of the process of research and the individual's experience of it. Our aim is to reflect the variety of research in art therapy and music therapy, to describe the research process, and to illustrate the various methodologies that have been employed to address different research questions. Outlining the usual structures of research – its academic backbone – will hopefully enable the reader to obtain a sense of the routines of research. Descriptions of the process highlight the person of the researcher and add a narrative element that is often absent in standard research texts. Asking contributors to address not only their research but also their personal processes, their successes and failures, means that we have asked for an unusual degree of openness. We hope the honesty of the descriptions will reassure and encourage would-be researchers to embark on an area of work which is not as tidy or as logical as it may at first appear.

Our collaboration on this publication arose not only from the need to document the research in our respective professions, but also from a wish to address a readership beyond art and music therapists – to reach artists, musicians and members of multi-disciplinary teams. Our aim is to dispel some of the myths and stereotypes about research, in particular those that are prevalent in clinical practice; for example, that research is inevitably about quality control and psychological measurement. We wish to draw attention to research traditions equal to the norms of clinical research orthodoxy (e.g. those in sociology and music analysis) which may be of interest to colleagues who do not have a background in the humanities, whilst also informing artists and musicians of paradigms in clinical research which may widen their exploration of musical and artistic processes.

To set the scene we outline the historical links between our two professions and describe the development of this book. We briefly review the published art therapy and music therapy research literature in this country, considering the progress to date and giving suggestions for future work. Motivation, methodology and the practical realities of research are discussed. The last part of this chapter outlines the structure of the book as a whole.

SETTING THE SCENE

Both art therapy and music therapy are small, specialised and rapidly developing professions. Art therapy has its origins in the mid-nineteenth-century interest in the so-called 'art of the insane' and the subsequent concept of 'art as healing' which emerged in Britain shortly before the Second World War (Waller 1991). During these early days the emphasis was on the use of art as an inherently healing process or as an occupation, largely in 'open sessions' where patients made images in a studio-based environment (Hill 1945, 1951; Adamson 1984). The practice of music as therapy in this country began in the 1950s; it too was characterised by an emphasis on 'music as healing' which emerged from the use of music as diversion and entertainment (Bunt 1994). The pioneering work of Nordoff and Robbins (1971) focused on the therapeutic properties of music using pre-composed and improvised elements within a session; they always used the instrumental combination of percussion and piano and worked exclusively with children. Alvin (1965) used a wider range of instruments, paying attention to the structure and elements of music within the therapeutic relationship.

Current practice in art therapy explores the making of images within a therapeutic relationship, either individually or in groups of various kinds, and draws on various schools of psychoanalytic thought (e.g. Dalley et al. 1987; Case and Dalley 1990; Schaverien 1991; Waller and Gilroy 1992). In 1989 a general definition covering the diversity of clinical practice was offered by the professional association, the British Association of Art Therapists (BAAT):

The focus of Art Therapy is the image, and the process involves a transaction between the creator (the patient), the artefact and the thera-

pist. As in all therapy, bringing unconscious feelings to a conscious level and thereafter exploring them holds true for Art Therapy, but here the richness of artistic symbol and metaphor illuminate the process . . . the expression and condensation of unconscious feelings that art-making engenders are at the heart of Art Therapy.
(Standing Committee of Arts Therapies Professions 1989, p. 5)

Improvisation forms the core of present music therapy practice in this country. A direct musical link between client and music therapist is embodied through the improvisation, the therapist's musical reflections enabling a dynamic interplay to develop within the therapeutic alliance, be it in group or individual work. Some music therapists work within a clearly defined psychodynamic frame (e.g. Priestly 1975, 1980; Bartram 1991; John 1992; Rogers 1992; Sobey 1993), whilst others focus on the music and the non-verbal communication contained within it (e.g. Nordoff and Robbins 1977; Pavlicevic 1990). The definition by the Association of Professional Music Therapists (APMT) states that music therapy:

provides a framework for the building of a mutual relationship be-tween client and therapist through which the music therapist will communicate with the client, finding a musical idiom . . . [which] . . . enables change to occur, both in the condition of the client and in the form the therapy takes. By using skilled and creative musicianship in a clinical setting, the therapist seeks to establish an interaction – a shared musical experience – leading to the pursuit of therapeutic goals.
(Standing Committee of Arts Therapies Professions 1989, p. 6)

The first contacts between art therapists and music therapists were in 1949 at an art therapy conference sponsored by the British Council for Rehabilitation, and through the National Association of Mental Health Working Parties (Waller 1991). Thereafter the histories of the two profes-sions are somewhat different. The British Society for Music Therapy was founded as a charity in 1958 and later, in 1976, the Association of Professional Music Therapists was formed, taking on the trade union function. The British Association of Art Therapists, formed in 1964, took on a learned society and trade union function from the beginning; a charitable wing was founded in 1992. A close association between the two developed in the late 1970s when both professions joined the trade union ASTMS (Association for Technical, Managerial and Scientific Staff; now MSF, Manufacturing Science and Finance) and sought recog-nition for their postgraduate training and distinct professional identities in the National Health Service. From the publication of the Personnel Memorandum PM/82/6, which gave art therapists and music therapists their own career and salary structure and identified approved courses, they have liaised over all major professional issues, the latest being the recognition of their qualifications by the National Joint Council of Local Authorities (Woddis 1992), and State Registration with the Council of the Professions Supplementary to Medicine. They have similar requirements for training – i.e. a degree in music or art as a prerequisite for a post-graduate diploma. Since 1989 there has been both an Art Therapy Advisor and a Music Therapy Advisor to the management side of the Whitley Council of the Department of Health.

Art and Music: Therapy and Research represents the first occasion on which art therapists and music therapists have worked on a joint text, although it is not uncommon for us to work alongside each other in clinical practice. The editors' collaboration came about through their work on the Arts Therapies Research Committee, formed in 1988. Andrea Gilroy (art therapist) and Helen Payne (dance movement therapist) were invited to attend the Fourth Music Therapy Research Conference. At the Conference the formation of some kind of venue for the exploration of shared issues in research was discussed, but it was not until Colin Lee (then Music Therapy Research Fellow at City University) established the links later that year that the Arts Therapies Research Committee came into being.

Research can be an isolating undertaking so it is not surprising that the initial period of the Arts Therapies Research Committee was spent dis-cussing our individual researches. We discovered we had much in common as we struggled to initiate research into the elusive and imaginative realms of the arts therapies. The relief of talking to like-minded people about the difficultes we each encountered led the members of the first Committee to organise two Arts Therapies Research Conferences. It was hoped that through these events we could begin to disseminate information about, and share, our experience of research through our four professions (art therapy, music therapy, drama therapy and dance movement therapy: see Gilroy *et al*. 1989; Kersner 1990).

At subsequent meetings the editors went on to discuss the histories of research in our respective professions, our different clinical practices, and to compare the processes of art-making and music-making. Despite the differences between the two professions there were common threads in our individual experience as therapists and researchers. We found that in our respective clinical practices we believed in the primacy of the musical and artistic process; we had both retained an involvement with our artistic and musical selves, believing it to be a significant factor in the continuing development of the therapist and in the life of our respective professions. Our individual researches focused on the artist in the art therapist (Gilroy 1992b) and the music in music therapy (Lee 1992), and we shared the view that research methodologies more common in art and art history and music and musicology were as valid as those of psychology and psychiatry when addressing research questions in art therapy and music therapy. We felt that these issues could usefully be addressed in a publication in which both new and experienced researchers discussed their work.

We decided to confine this book to art therapy and music therapy research principally because they are parallel in terms of their development and present position as professional groups. Both are ready to tackle research as a significant part of professional and clinical practice, now that they have become established within the state services. There is a body of research that is sufficient to enable a review of the research histories of art therapy and music therapy, and to consider the way forward. Our feeling is that art therapists and music therapists could usefully consider the methods, problems, successes and failures of each other's research, so similar are the issues we face as we endeavour to establish our own research traditions.

Literature review

Reviewing the research in art therapy and music therapy in Britain further sets the scene for this book. We have limited the review to work that has been published in this country, and consequently have excluded a number of interesting studies which have yet to appear (see the 'Directories of Art Therapy and Music Therapy Research' in Gilroy et al. 1989). None the less research in our professions is in its infancy, due perhaps to a mixture of inhibition and inexperience exacerbated by a lack of opportunity within the present state services (Gilroy 1992a; Edwards 1993).

Published research in music therapy can be broadly categorised into process and outcome studies. Initial publications focused on outcome protocols in work with clients with learning difficulties: Bunt (1986) through ethological observation, and Oldfield (Oldfield and Adams 1983; 1990) via videotape analysis. Developments were extended through outcome studies considering the efficacy of music therapy with autistic children (Muller and Warwick 1987, 1993) alongside more general questions about the future of research (Bunt and Hoskyns 1987) and the personal processes contained therein (Hoskyns 1987; Warwick 1988). Concurrently, Pavlicevic (1988) took the first steps towards process-oriented enquiry through examination of 'critical moments' in music therapy with schizophrenic clients, whilst Hoskyns (1988) investigated the application of Kelly's Personal Construct Theory and videotape analysis to music therapy research with offenders.

Lee (1989, 1990) began to develop process-oriented research through the analysis of musical and therapeutic components in improvisations with a client with learning difficulties. Pavlicevic amalgamated process and outcome work in her investigation of the musical assessment of psychiatric states (Pavlicevic and Trevarthen 1989) whilst other music therapists continued to focus on outcome research, all with clients with learning difficulties who benefited from music therapy (Wigram 1989; Hooper and Lindsey 1990; Hooper *et al.* 1991; Hooper 1993). Recent trends in music therapy research are towards a greater diversification of procedures and research questions, for example, Rogers' (1992, 1993) use of collaborative enquiry to examine the symbolic use of instruments by sexually abused clients.

Early research-oriented papers in *Inscape* (the journal of the British Association of Art Therapists) indicated possible areas for research in art therapy and art education (Gummerson 1976; Yomans 1978), and questioned assumptions about naive art (Waller 1976). Holtom (1977) was the first art therapist to address professional issues in his survey-based study of multi-disciplinary team members' perceptions of art therapy, and Dalley (1979, 1980) used self-evaluation questionnaires in her case study-based research. These two areas of study – issues surrounding art therapy as a profession and case study-based research addressing clinical practice, in contrast to the process/outcome debate in music therapy research (Bunt 1990, 1994) – can be said to contain the majority of published art therapy research to date. The preference in both areas of art therapy research has been for qualitative methodologies, with outcome studies absent from the literature.

Historical and sociological research on the establishment and development of art therapy as a profession, both in Britain and Europe, has been conducted by Waller (1983, 1987, 1989, 1991). Maclagan has also used a historical model in his research on psychoanalysis and Surrealism (Maclagan 1992, 1993). Surveys of the profession have addressed art therapists' use of themes in group work (Liebmann 1981), issues surrounding art therapy in private practice (McNab and Edwards 1988), conditions of service of art therapists (Teasdale 1988) and the art practice of art therapists (Gilroy 1989). More recent case study-based research has, unlike Dalley's early work, focussed on phenomenological methods and, in the detailed descriptions of case work alongside rigorous attention to allied theory, contributed to the development of the theoretical bases of art therapy (Greenwood and Layton 1987, 1991; Schaverien 1987, 1989, 1991, 1993; Killick 1991, 1993). Other researchers have used the detailed observational constructs of ethology to explore the art work of clients with severe learning difficulties (Dubowski 1982, 1984; Rees 1984, 1989). Recently, collaborative research and clinical practice in acute psychiatry have been brought together in the work of McClelland (1993).

Three other published studies are worth noting, two of which used experimental designs. Russell-Lacy, Robinson, Benson and Cranage (1979) – a team of researchers, one of whom was an art therapist – explored the validity of using the images of schizophrenic clients in diagnosis and found the procedure unreliable, and Luzzatto (1987) was able to address the disturbed object relations of substance misuse clients through their imagery. Nowell Hall interviewed clients who had attended art therapy and explored their retrospective views of its value, demonstrating how the process of image-making and the resulting artefact can act as a bridge between various aspects of therapy (Nowell Hall 1987).

It can be seen that the two professions have distinctively different research histories. Music therapy has, until recently, concentrated upon outcome studies using quantitative methodologies, mainly with clients with learning difficulties. Research which addresses therapeutic processes and utilises qualitative research models is a recent development. It is striking that music therapy research does not include any work on the profession, its history and development, training, the person of the music therapist, their workplace and so on. It seems that the aim of many music therapy researchers has been to demonstrate the efficacy of their practice through standard psychological research procedures. Art therapy researchers have preferred 'softer' research methodologies and have neither used the more quantitative methodologies nor addressed the outcomes of their work. Professional issues have been paramount, perhaps at the expense of more clinically-oriented research.

Art therapists in Britain have avoided research which 'measures' the art work in terms of outcome or as a diagnostic aid, attractive though this kind of attention to the concreteness of imagery may be to some researchers (e.g. Cohen *et al.* 1988). This may, in part, explain the absence of outcome studies in art therapy; perhaps the obvious thing to do, i.e. 'measure' the art work as evidence of change, is resisted by the artist in the art therapist who would not consider such an exercise outside the therapeutic arena. Within art history, however, the analysis of imagery is iconographical, drawing on the socio-cultural and symbolic references of the artist rather than the quantity of certain pictorial elements, such as line and colour (see Gantt 1986). A similar dilemma about the measurement of music is not apparent in music therapy; researchers have instead focused on evaluating the *behaviour* surrounding the musical act, or process, within the session. Music itself does not seem to have quite the same potential for diagnosis and evaluation as does art, perhaps because of its inherently transient qualities. Thus the nature of the primary disciplines of art and music may explain, in part, why our respective professions' research histories have developed in the way they have (a phenomenon worthy of research in itself!). Reviewing our work clearly indicates the areas that need to be addressed and how we may learn from each other's research questions and methodological procedures.

It is important that art therapists and music therapists who are beginning research pay attention to the boundaries between research and the norms of clinical practice. It is easy for the clinician to ignore the integral structures of research: the essential academic building blocks, the methodological procedures, the customary and precise routines that research requires. This can lead to work being construed as research when it is, in our view, insufficiently rigorous in its procedures and descriptions. Young (1993) illustrates similar difficulties in psychoanalytic teaching and research, describing the differences between 'knowing' (the clinician) and 'knowing about' (the researcher). The essential difference lies between 'knowing' personally and experientially, and 'knowing about' within a broad context that is provided by locating research within the relevant literature, hence existing knowledge, and employing non-sectarian academic conventions (Young 1993). This is not to say that research should lose its ability to evoke and illuminate clinical material in favour of a dusty, academic rhetoric; rather that it should be contextualised within art therapy and music therapy literature as well as in broader historical and social frameworks.

Motivation and methodology

Quality control and clinical audit create considerable pressures for art therapists and music therapists to engage in research. The change to Trust Status for many hospitals and the moves towards community care require practitioners to monitor and evaluate their work so that its efficacy can be proven and jobs preserved. Although political and institutional pressures are compelling reasons for taking the initial steps they rarely provide sufficient motivation for good research. The question 'does art therapy/ music therapy work?' can lead to research that is meaningless in terms of clinical practice. It is an impossibly imprecise *research* question. Unfortunately it is one which we are increasingly asked, and to fall victim to it is to collude with misunderstandings about both research and therapeutic practice.

This is not to say that empirical research which considers the outcomes of therapeutic interventions is unnecessary. Indeed outcome studies are essential if we are to demonstrate that our practice *is* effective, or to explore the appropriateness of one model of work compared to another with a particular client group. It is important to avoid research which compares treatments competitively, but to engage in research which seeks to distinguish between the suitability of varying approaches in art therapy and music therapy to different situations and client groups. Krupnick and Pincus (1992) draw attention to the paucity of research on the cost-effectiveness of psychotherapy and identify a similar need for research which specifies client populations and problems which benefit from psychotherapy.

The need to explain and validate our work often comes from observing or experiencing a phenomenon. An awareness of something new can lead to a wish to make sense of what is happening, to understand it intellectually and then to be able to communicate it effectively to others. Longstanding preoccupations about one's work can provide fruitful material: simple curiosity about why, how, and when something occurs is the seed of research which is intrinsically interesting for the individual. Research that stems from the individual clinician/researcher, that gives rein to the 'bee in the bonnet' that we all have, will be satisfying for the researcher and relevant to the clinician and thus have the potential to significantly influence clinical practice. Such research can have its origins in the most personal of interests.

This polarisation of motivations – from pressures coming from outside our professions to questions that arise from the interests of the individual practitioner – influences the research questions that are asked and hence the methodologies used. *What* one does in research and *how* one does it often reflects *who* the research is for. Research that asks 'what is the effect of this specific kind of art therapy/music therapy intervention with this particular client group?' can be conducted through the standardised procedures of experimental psychology and the medical model. It is usually oriented towards a sceptical audience. This is not to say that more qualitative methodologies are extraneous, particularly with the 'Patients' Charter' which asks the customer their views of the service or treatment they have received. Even within an ideology which is founded upon number-crunching there is perhaps room for the client's voice to be heard in a way that will not be dismissed as simply anecdotal.

Research questions that stem from the personal interests of the clinician/ researcher are unlikely to be those which ask 'does art therapy/music therapy work?' because continuing clinical practice demonstrates that indeed it does! Following one's individual preoccupations is likely to lead to research questions that centre on artistic, musical and/or thera-peutic processes that may be addressed only through non-quantitative methodologies. Such methodologies, drawn from sociology, philosophy, art history and musicology, will probably be more immediately familiar and comfortable to those from a background in the humanities. Hence art therapy and music therapy researchers may return to the research para-digms of their primary disciplines of art and music as do Schaverien (1991) and Lee (1992), and as has been discussed by Gilroy (1992a). However, quantitative and qualitative methodologies are by no means mutually exclu-sive; limiting our horizons to any one approach is to ignore the global research needs of our professions – we need to address both process and outcome (see Bunt 1990, 1994; and Gilroy 1992a for further discussion).

The realities of research

So far we have reviewed our research histories and outlined some of the issues that may be encountered when art therapists and music therapists consider embarking on research. In this section we trace an elementary research pathway and describe the available methodologies.

Dictionary definitions of 'research' and 'science' are interesting starting points: adjectives such as 'careful', 'close', 'specific', 'critical', 'discovery' and 'scientific' are used to describe a procedure which is rigorous, method-ical and precise. But the rogue word 'scientific', with all its attendant stereotypical meanings, is what seems to intimidate would-be research-ers. However, the definition of 'science' is: systematic and formulated knowledge; branch of knowledge; organised body of knowledge that has been accumulated on a subject (*Concise Oxford Dictionary* 1964). Thus the essence of research is that it is disciplined, structured and careful; all of this can be so within the framework of medical and psychological research as well as within historical and anthropological research.

The first task is to establish the focus of the study and eliminate all extraneous issues so as to formulate a clear, concise research question. Some studies postulate hypotheses, either drawn from the existing litera-ture or based on what could be described as an 'informed prediction'; the hypothesis is then tested. Other studies begin without an hypothesis but with an objective (to study x, y or z) or a research question which is then investigated. The literature review assists the refining of the research question or hypothesis, and contextualises the study as a whole. Biblio-graphic searching, organising, describing and summarising the existing work and subjecting it to a critical analysis highlights relevant issues and points to gaps in the literature which research could address. The literature may well suggest appropriate methodologies, that is to say, the tools with which data may be collected and analysed.

It is important that those beginning their research study the diversity of methodologies available at the same time as conducting their subject-specific literature review. Their chosen area of study may influence the methodology; for example, a sociological study can involve data derived from documentary sources alongside structured interviews, or be solely based on participant observation. As already suggested, qualitative and quantitative methods are not mutually exclusive; questionnaires can incor-porate rating scales and open-ended questions whilst descriptive case studies can include quantitative measurement from client and therapist. The practical constraints of time, money and availability of respondents also have to be considered, as does the replicability of the entire study.

Methodologies are clustered in a variety of ways by differing authors (e.g. Cohen and Manion 1980; Bell 1987; Hitchcock and Hughes 1989; Sapsford and Abbott 1992). Broadly speaking they can be classified as follows:

- Documentary: historical, archival material using secondary sources.
- Experimental: controlled trials, correlational studies.
- Descriptive: ethnographic, developmental, *ex post facto*.
- Interactive: action research, collaborative enquiry.

The tools of data collection may fall within several of the above categories according to the overall research design. For example, a case study could be documentary (Chapter Twelve, this volume); experimental, using a strict ABA design (Hooper *et al.* 1991); descriptive (Schaverien 1991); or interactive (Lee 1992; McClelland 1993). The nature of the data collection will inevitably influence the methods of data analysis – large surveys and experimental case designs demand the use of statistics, whereas documentary material and interviews require content analysis. Whatever data analysis techniques are employed the data will form patterns which constitute the findings. These may or may not follow the chronology of the data collection or the indications which arose from the literature review; they may illuminate different patterns and give the research an unexpected coherence and richness. We would refer the uninitiated researcher to the bibliography at the end of the book for guidance on research methodology texts from a number of different disciplines.

The task of writing up the research is to present the work as a coherent whole so that ideas found in the literature give rise to the research questions or hypotheses, which are addressed through the methodology, answered in the findings and discussed at the end. The ordered presentation of the final piece may not reflect the process of either writing or gathering and analysing the data. The process described here is sequential and logical, but there are inevitably overlaps, backtrackings and imaginative leaps which are part of the research process, including the writing-up. It is important to keep hold of the narrative element, the story of the research (whatever the methodology), and to retain the voice of the art therapist or music therapist.

Thus the ideal pathway is by means of a clear research question which is contextualised within the literature; a methodology is found, data is collected and analysed, and presented in a clear and concise manner. Unfortunately experience has taught us that the reality is often otherwise! Research is more like a maze than a pathway. One begins with many questions, most of which are too vague and all-encompassing. There is either no literature at all which is relevant, or so much that an enormous amount of reading is required to limit the area of study. One is then confronted with a gamut of mysterious and unsympathetic methods which do not seem to fit one's individual interests. Having found methodologies with which to create a 'good-enough' design the data collection provides an overwhelming amount of material – this is both exciting and daunting when one is faced with the data analysis. Finding the patterns in the data can be tedious and time-consuming, but also a creative period when original material begins to emerge. The cyclic nature of research then requires reflection on the entire process, from the literature to the data analysis, so that a piece of cohesive and coherent work finally enters the public arena. This sometimes chaotic and messy procedure, which constantly moves between a process which tightens and focuses to one which broadens and loosens, will be a familiar experience for artists and musicians – research is a truly creative process (see Gilroy 1992a for further discussion).

MAPPING THE BOOK

Art and Music: Therapy and Research falls into three parts. The first part describes and debates research practice in terms of practical and philosophical procedures and personal processes. Chapters in the second part are all clinically based studies with various client groups, essentially exploring the effects of art therapy and music therapy in differing settings. The third part of the book has a more discursive tone which highlights the significance of the cultural and theoretical contexts within which research can be based.

Joy Schaverien (Chapter One) describes a research journey from an initial observation of a phenomenon to the presentation of a doctoral thesis some years later. She illustrates how a single case study can be the basis for disciplined, retrospective reflection which leads to the eventual formulation of a new theory. Colin Lee (Chapter Two) outlines his entire doctoral project, focusing on musical and therapeutic processes in improvisation alongside countertransference issues that arise when researching collaboratively with people who are dying. He also explores the use of outside validators in the evaluation of highly emotive material. Mercedes Pavlicevic (Chapter Three) examines the nature and form of communication within a specific theoretical and practical approach in music therapy, and illustrates how one might begin to define a vague idea into something sufficiently precise in order to begin research. Andrea Gilroy (Chapter Four) describes the dilemmas of the researcher who uses a quantitative model to assess the changes in an ongoing experiential art therapy group. She shows how, despite the difficulties engendered by the research design, thought-provoking conclusions were none the less reached.

Sue Van Colle and Tim Williams (Chapter Five) illustrate the evolution of a research project through sympathetic supervision. Their chapter demonstrates how research is a series of building blocks which has problems, pitfalls, moments of inspiration and continuing fascination. Katherine Killick and Helen Greenwood's work (Chapter Six) shows how research can arise directly from clinical practice, become part of it, and indeed be the means through which the researcher sustains the clinician. They demonstrate how careful description of new phenomena, and the matching of practice to theory described in the literature, enabled them to formulate new theory in a way which could be tested empirically. Mair Rees (Chapter Seven) shows how detailed examination of clinical work, using the descriptive paradigms of ethology, can provide valuable insights into art therapy with people with severe learning difficulties. She also illustrates how circular research can be: one begins with an idea and eventually returns to the same place with increased insight and understanding. Sarah Hoskyns (Chapter Eight) presents the development of research with offenders using a sequence of rating scales to assess changes in activity during a period of music therapy. She illustrates how collaborative and evaluative methodologies can be combined. Julie Sutton's cautionary tale (Chapter Nine) illustrates the considerable changes that a research idea may undergo – the initial enthusiasm leading to over-ambition, followed by a paring-down to the essentials and, in this case, a move to an allied area of research. The work of Amelia Oldfield and Malcolm Adams (Chapter Ten) is a classic experimental study which demonstrates the efficacy of therapeutic interventions through attention to detailed behavioural responses, using control groups and videotape analysis.

In Chapter Eleven, John Henzell draws attention to the underlying assumptions in art, psychotherapy, science and research and argues that research models should fit the kind of knowledge that is being sought. David Maclagan (Chapter Twelve) questions the boundaries between collaborative research and collusion. He discusses the countertransference feelings not only of the therapist/researcher who allows their work to enter the public domain, but also those of the historical researcher who uncovers significant material. Maclagan describes an early instance of art work being actively used in a psychoanalytic process which was as much 'artistic' as 'therapeutic'. This chapter explores a controversial collaboration in which therapeutic, artistic and moral issues overlapped. Diane Waller (Chapter Thirteen) describes an ambitious, evaluative project designed to initiate the practice of art therapy in Eastern Europe. The overall research design is outlined together with some of the fieldwork experiences, through which Waller demonstrates how the person of the researcher becomes intimately involved with their research journey and how 'real life' intervenes.

There are other links between the chapters to which we would like to draw the reader's attention. Some chapters use standard research procedures which measure behaviour as indicators of change (e.g. Gilroy, Hoskyns); these 'hard' research methods contrast with 'softer' models (e.g. Maclagan). It is worth noting these authors and researchers who have used a mixture of 'hard' and 'soft' methods and gained a mixture of quantitative and qualitative data (e.g. Waller, Lee), and those whose methodology involves accurate and painstaking description of varying kinds: Rees' use of ethological methods, Schaverien's analysis of a single case, Lee's analysis of music, Van Colle and Williams' use of videotape analysis. It can also be seen how, in many of these chapters, the researcher splits him- or herself into the one who observes and describes in an objective way, yet whose subjective experience becomes part of the project, albeit with different emphases which depend on the nature of the research itself (Lee, Gilroy, Waller). Salutary lessons can be learned: research which addresses changes in the client can give significant feedback about the therapist/researcher's clinical practice (Hoskyns, Oldfield and Adams).

It is also important to note that many of the chapters describe work still in progress – Sutton, Van Colle and Williams, Maclagan and Hoskyns – albeit at differing stages of development. Sutton, Greenwood and Killick, and Van Colle and Williams all illuminate the early stages of research, the building of theoretical and research models and the defining and refining of research questions; they also indicate the importance of academic structures for those unfamiliar with research. Others describe bird's-eye views of completed work (e.g. Rees, Lee) and one is made aware how research can take an unanticipated direction (e.g. Waller).

Many of the research processes will be comfortably familiar to practising clinicians and will demonstrate that research may evolve from 'doing what comes naturally', not only as a therapist but also as an artist and musician, from pursuing individual interests in a more defined and rigorous way than hitherto. The different research paradigms the contributors have used are all forms of description which provide the 'hard copy' of art therapy and music therapy. The spectrum of description moves from the subjective and partial to the empirical and numerical. All are ways of exploring the processes and outcomes of art therapy and music therapy, and increasing the understanding of our work.

REFERENCES

Adamson, E. (1984) *Art as Healing*. Coventure, London.

Alvin, J. (1965) *Music Therapy*. John Clare Books, London, revised 1975.

Bartram, P. (1991) 'Aspects of the Theory and Practice of Psychodynamic Music Therapy', In: *Music Therapy and the Individual*. The Scottish Music Therapy Council, Edinburgh.

Bell, J. (1987) *Doing Your Research Project: A Guide for First-time Researchers in Education and Social Sciences*. Open University Press, Buckingham.

Bunt, L. (1986) 'Research in Great Britain into the Effects of Music Therapy with Particular Reference to the Child with a Handicap'. In: Rudd, E. (Ed.) *Music and Health*. J. Chester, London.

Bunt, L. (1990) 'The Artist as Scientist: Is there a Synthesis?' In: Kersner, M. (Ed.) *The Art of Research. Proceedings of the Second Arts Therapies Research Conference*. City University, London.

Bunt, L. (1994) *Music Therapy: An Art Beyond Words*. Routledge, London.

Bunt, L. and Hoskyns, S. (1987) 'A Perspective on Music Therapy Research in Great Britain'. *Journal of British Music Therapy*. 1: 3–6.

Case, C. and Dalley, T. (Eds) (1990) *Working with Children in Art Therapy*. Routledge, London.

Cohen, L. and Manion, L. (1980) *Research Methods in Education*. Routledge, London, 3rd edn.

Cohen, B.M., Hammer, J.S. and Singer, S. (1988) 'The Diagnostic Drawing Series: A Systematic Approach to Art Therapy Education and Research'. *The Arts in Psychotherapy*. 10: 11–21.

Dalley, T. (1979) 'Art Therapy in Psychiatric Treatment: An Illustrated Case Study'. *The Arts in Psychotherapy.* 6: 257–65.

Dalley, T. (1980) 'Assessing the Therapeutic Effects of Art: An Illustrated Case Study'. *The Arts in Psychotherapy.* 7: 11–17.

Dalley, T., Case, C., Schaverien, J., Weir, F., Halliday, D., Nowell Hall, P. and Waller, D. (1987) *Images of Art Therapy.* Tavistock/Routledge, London.

Dubowski, J. (1982) 'Alternative Models for Describing the Development from Scribble to Representation in Children's Graphic Work'. *Proceedings of the Conference ' Art and Drama Therapy'.* University of Hertfordshire, Herts.

Dubowski, J. (1984) 'The Development of Children's Graphic Art Work'. In: Dalley, T. (Ed.) *Art as Therapy.* Tavistock, London.

Edwards, D. (1993) 'Why Don't Arts Therapists Do Research?' In: Payne, H. (Ed.) *Handbook of Inquiry in the Arts Therapies: One River, Many Currents.* Jessica Kingsley, London.

Gantt, L. (1986) 'Systematic Investigation of Art Works: Some Research Models drawn from Neighbouring Fields'. *American Journal of Art Therapy.* 24: 111–118.

Gilroy, A. (1989) 'On Occasionally Being Able to Paint'. *Inscape.* Spring: 2–9.

Gilroy, A. (1992a) 'Research In Art Therapy'. In: Waller, D. and Gilroy, A. (Eds) *Art Therapy: A Handbook.* Open University Press, Buckingham.

Gilroy, A. (1992b) 'Art Therapists and their Art. A Study of Occupational Choice and Career Development, from the Origins of an Interest in Art to Occasionally Being Able to Paint'. Unpublished D. Phil. thesis, University of Sussex.

Gilroy, A., Hoskyns, S., Jenkyns, M., Lee, C. and Payne, H. (Eds) (1989) *Arts Therapies Research. Proceedings of the First Arts Therapies Research Conference.* City University, London.

Greenwood, H. and Layton, G. (1987) 'An Out-patient Art Therapy Group'. *Inscape*, Summer: 12–19.

Greenwood, H. and Layton, G. (1991). 'Taking the Piss'. *Inscape*, Winter: 7–14.

Gummerson, A. (1976) 'The Therapy of Individual Growth'. *Inscape.* 14: 28–32.

Hill, A. (1945) *Art Versus Illness.* Allen and Unwin, London.

Hill, A. (1951) *Painting Out Illness.* Williams and Northgate, London.

Hitchcock, G. and Hughes, D. (1989) *Research and The Teacher.* Routledge, London.

Holtom, R. (1977) 'Measuring Change Attributable to Art Therapy'. *Inscape.* 1: 3–10.

Hooper, J. (1993) 'Developing Interaction through Shared Musical Experiences: A Strategy to Enhance and Validate the Descriptive Approach'. In: Heal, M. and Wigram, T. (Eds) *Music Therapy in Health and Education.* Jessica Kingsley, London.

Hooper, J. and Lindsey, B. (1990) 'Music and the Mentally Handicapped: The Effect of Music on Anxiety'. *Journal of British Music Therapy.* 4: 19–26.

Hooper, J., Lindsey, B. and Richardson, I. (1991) 'Recreation and Music Therapy: An Experimental Study'. *Journal of British Music Therapy.* 5: 10–13.

Hoskyns, S. (1987) 'Productive and Counter-Productive Issues for Therapist and Researcher'. In: Hoskyns, S. and Clarke, E. (Eds) *Starting Research in Music Therapy. Proceedings of the Third Music Therapy Conference.* City University, London.

Hoskyns, S. (1988) 'Studying Group Music Therapy with Offenders: Research in Progress'. *Psychology of Music.* 16: 26–41.

John, D. (1992) 'Towards Music Psychotherapy'. *Journal of British Music Therapy.* 6: 10–12.

Kersner, M. (Ed.) (1990) *The Art of Research. Proceedings of the Second Arts Therapies Research Conference*. City University, London.

Killick, K. (1991) 'The Practice of Art Therapy with Patients in Acute Psychotic States'. *Inscape*. Winter: 2–6.

Killick, K. (1993) 'Working with Psychotic Processes in Art Therapy'. *Psychoanalytic Psychotherapy*. 7: 25–38.

Krupnick, J.L. and Pincus, H.A. (1992) 'The Cost-effectiveness of Psychotherapy'. *American Journal of Psychiatry*. 149: 1295–1305.

Lee, C. (1989) 'Structural Analysis of Therapeutic Improvisatory Music'. *Journal of British Music Therapy*. 3: 11–19.

Lee, C. (1990) 'Structural Analysis of Post-tonal Therapeutic Improvisatory Music'. *Journal of British Music Therapy*. 4: 6–20.

Lee, C. (1992) 'The Analysis of Therapeutic Improvisatory Music with People Living with the Virus HIV and AIDS'. Unpublished PhD thesis, City University, London.

Liebmann, M. (1981) 'The Many Purposes of Art Therapy'. *Inscape*. 5. 1: 26–8.

Luzzatto, P. (1987) 'The Internal World of Drug Abusers: Projective Pictures of Self-Object Relationships. A Pilot Study'. *British Journal of Projective Psychology*. 32: 22–33.

McClelland, S. (1993) 'The Art of Science with Clients: Beginning Collaborative Inquiry in Process Work, Art Therapy and Acute States'. In: Payne, H. (Ed.) *Handbook of Inquiry in the Arts Therapies: One River, Many Currents*. Jessica Kingsley, London.

Maclagan, D. (1992) 'Between Psychoanalysis and Surrealism'. *Free Associations*. No. 25: 33–50.

Maclagan, D. (1993) 'Inner and Outer Space: Mapping the Psyche'. *Cosmos*. 9.

McNab, D. and Edwards, E. (1988) 'Private Art Therapy'. *Inscape*. Summer: 14–19.

Muller, P.A. and Warwick, A. (1987) 'The Linking of Two Disciplines in Research: Psychology and Music Therapy'. In: Hoskyns, S. and Clarke, E. (Eds) *Starting Research in Music Therapy. Proceedings of the Third Music Therapy Conference*. City University, London.

Muller, P.A. and Warwick, A. (1993) 'Autistic Children: The Effects of Maternal Involvement in Therapy'. In: Heal, M. and Wigram, T. (Eds) *Music Therapy in Health and Education*. Jessica Kingsley, London.

Nordoff, P. and Robbins, C. (1971) *Therapy in Music for Handicapped Children*. Victor Gollancz Ltd, London.

Nordoff, P. and Robbins, C. (1977) *Creative Music Therapy: Individualised Treatment for the Handicapped Child*. John Day, New York.

Nowell Hall, P. (1987) 'Art Therapy: A Way of Healing the Split'. In: Dalley, T. *et al. Images of Art Therapy*. Tavistock/Routledge, London.

Oldfield, A. and Adams, M. (1983) 'An Investigation of the Effects of Music Therapy on a Group of Profoundly Mentally Handicapped Adults'. *International Journal of Rehabilitation Research*. 6: 511–12.

Oldfield, A. and Adams, M. (1990) 'The Effects of Music Therapy on a Group of Profoundly Mentally Handicapped Adults'. *Journal of Mental Deficiency Research*. 3.4: 107–25.

Pavlicevic, M. (1988) 'Describing Critical Moments'. In: Hoskyns, S. (Ed.) *The Case Study as Research. Proceedings of the Fourth Music Therapy Conference*. City University, London.

Pavlicevic, M. (1990) 'Dynamic Interplay in Clinical Improvisation'. *Journal of British Music Therapy*. 4: 5–9.

Pavlicevic, M. and Trevarthen, C. (1989) 'A Musical Assessment of Psychiatric States in Adults'. *Psychopathology*. 22: 325–34.

Priestly, M. (1975) *Music Therapy in Action*. Constable, London.

Priestly, M. (1980) *The Herdecke Analytic Music Therapy Lectures*. Klett-Kotte, Stuttgart.

Rees, M. (1984) 'Ethological Constructs of Territoriality and Dominance, and their Implications for the Practice of Art Therapy with Institutionalised Mentally Handicapped Patients'. *Proceedings of the Conference ' Art Therapy as Psychotherapy in Relation to the Mentally Handicapped'*. Hertfordshire College of Art and Design, Herts.

Rees, M. (1989) 'Territories of the Self: The Use of Physical Space by People who have Severe Learning Difficulties and Challenging Behaviour'. *Proceedings of the Conference ' Art Therapy for People with Severe to Marginal Learning Difficulties'*. University of Leicester.

Rogers, P. (1992) 'Issues in Working with Sexually Abused Clients in Music Therapy'. *Journal of British Music Therapy*. 6: 5–15.

Rogers, P. (1993) 'Research in Music Therapy with Sexually Abused Clients'. In: Payne, H. (Ed.) *Handbook of Inquiry in the Arts Therapies: One River, Many Currents*, Jessica Kingsley, London.

Russell-Lacy, S., Robinson, V., Benson, J. and Cranage, J. (1979) 'An Experimental Study of Pictures Produced by Acute Schizophrenic Subjects'. *British Journal of Psychiatry*. 13: 195–200.

Sapsford, R. and Abbott, P. (1992) *Research Methods for Nurses and the Caring Professions*. Open University Press, Buckingham.

Schaverien, J. (1987) 'The Scapegoat and the Talisman: Transference in Art Therapy'. In: Dalley, T. *et al. Images of Art Therapy*. Tavistock/Routledge, London.

Schaverien, J. (1989) 'The Picture within the Frame'. In: Gilroy, A. and Dalley, T. (Eds) *Pictures at an Exhibition: Selected Essays on Art and Art Therapy*. Routledge, London.

Schaverien, J. (1991) *The Revealing Image: Analytical Art Psychotherapy in Theory and Practice*. Routledge, London.

Schaverien, J. (1993) 'The Retrospective Review of Pictures: Data for Research in Art Therapy'. In: Payne, H. (Ed.) *Handbook of Inquiry in the Arts Therapies: One River, Many Currents*. Jessica Kingsley, London.

Sobey, K. (1993) 'Out of Sight – Out of Mind? Reflections on a Blind Young Woman's Use of Music Therapy'. *Journal of British Music Therapy*. 7: 5–11.

Standing Committee of Arts Therapies Professions (1989) *Artists and Arts Therapies*. Carnegie UK Trust, London.

Teasdale, C. (1988) *Conditions of Service of Art Therapists*. MSF, London.

Waller, D. (1976) 'Naive Artists or Naive Critics: Part One'. *Inscape*. 14: 33–7.

Waller, D. (1983) 'Art Therapy in Bulgaria: Parts One and Two'. *Inscape*. Spring and Autumn.

Waller, D. (1987) 'Art Therapy in Adolescence: A Metaphorical View of a Profession in Progress'. In: Dalley, T. *et al. Images of Art Therapy*. Tavistock/Routledge, London.

Waller, D. (1989) 'Musing Cross-culturally'. In: Gilroy, A. and Dalley, T. (Eds) *Pictures at an Exhibition: Selected Essays on Art and Art Therapy*. Routledge, London.

Waller, D. (1991) *Becoming a Profession: The History of Art Therapy in Britain 1940–82*. Routledge, London.

Waller, D. and Gilroy, A. (Eds) (1992) *Art Therapy: A Handbook*. Open University Press, Buckingham.

Warwick, A. (1988) 'Questions and Reflections on Research'. *Journal of British Music Therapy*. 2: 5–8.

Wigram, T. (1989) 'Vibro-acoustic Therapy: The Therapeutic Effect of Low Frequency Sound on Specific Physical Disorders and Disabilities'. *Journal of British Music Therapy*. 3: 6–10.

Woddis, J. (1992) 'Art Therapy: New Problems, New Solutions?' In: Waller, D. and Gilroy, A. (Eds) *Art Therapy: A Handbook*. Open University Press, Buckingham.

Yomans, M. (1978) 'Art and the Return Journey'. *Inscape*. 11. 3: 13–18.

Young, R.M. (1993) 'Psychoanalytic Teaching and Research: Knowing and Knowing About'. *Free Associations*. No. 29: 129–37.

Part I

The practice of research

Chapter 1

Researching the esoteric
Art therapy research

Joy Schaverien

In this chapter I will discuss research from a personal point of view with the aim of attempting to demystify the process. The chapter is based on the evolution of my own PhD and my experience of supervising and teaching students doing a Master's course in art therapy. The MA is a course with a taught year followed by a year in which a research-based thesis on a topic of the student's own choice is developed. The student often comes with a question that needs research but there is frequently a real inhibition about embarking on the thesis.

It often seems as if the whole notion of research is alien to the intimate conditions of the psychotherapeutic approach to art and music therapy. The way that we work is private, boundaried and confidential. How can we discuss and analyse the processes which take place in the closeted privacy of the art therapy studio? Isn't it enough to say it works? The intitiates, the therapist and the patient, know it works and so why intrude with the penetrating gaze of the 'scientific' research method? The 'esoteric' of the title of this chapter refers to the amorphous area characterised by the often intimate relating of two people and a picture. Thinking about it beforehand, it can seem that to attempt to apply the spotlight of research to such an area will be an ungainly intrusion into a sphere of delicacy. It can be viewed as a potential theft of something precious; rather like researching love or religious experience, it seems an affront to the nature of the work that we should attempt to apply measures and methods.

Research is often seen as especially alien to the artist; it is usually viewed as a science and so research methods are understood as the territory of the scientist. Before commencing research the art therapist is often already engaged on a struggle within her/himself regarding the uncomfortable tension between these two modes of relating. Art therapists are often employed, in hospitals, as a member of a multi-disciplinary team. Here they work beside colleagues, particularly those with medical training, who understand mental distress as illness. Nurses and psychiatrists are trained in scientific method with an emphasis on the relief of symptoms.

The art therapist comes from a different background; she/he is trained firstly as an artist and secondly as an art psychotherapist. Here the interest is in the meaning of the symptom, what it is expressing. Although the differences are seldom as stark as this might seem to imply, it may mean that we meet the patient from different viewpoints. This diversity is the richness, as well as the struggle, of the multi-disciplinary approach. Elsewhere (Schaverien 1989) I have written about the uneasy relationship between the artist and the medical-model approach. The thought of research seems to highlight this divide. Art therapists are often very suspicious of what is being asked of them when they embark on research.

Despite initial objections it is clearly necessary that we overcome them and conduct research. It is then that we realise that it can be rewarding to do so and that it is possible to find methods which are complementary to the work that we do. Far from taking away from the process, they can enhance the work by making us much more conscious of how it is effective. A quote from Bachelard offers a way of realising that perhaps the intuitive approach of the art therapist actually offers a good place to begin. It may be that we do not have to emulate the scientific method but rather find methods which may be more appropriate for our discipline.

> A philosopher who has evolved his entire thinking from the fundamental themes of the philosophy of science, and followed the main line of the active, growing rationalism of contemporary science as closely as he could, must forget his learning and break with all his habits of philosophical research, if he wants to study the problems posed by the poetic imagination.
>
> (Bachelard 1958, p. xi)

Thus perhaps the art therapist who is working with 'the poetic imagination' in the daily course of her/his work is excellently placed to begin to research. Like art psychotherapy itself, research brings to consciousness that which was previously unconscious. Research is rather like a torch which brings light to a selected area in the darkness. Through its beam that which was intuitively known becomes more easily discernible; a pre-conscious awareness is brought to consciousness. Like psychotherapy too there is a resistance to consciousness for fear that something will be lost. And, just as in the consulting room or studio, resistance is lifted by analysing the defence, so too with research. It is necessary to understand the defence and what it is defending in order to free the potential researcher.

I have found it helpful to realise that research is fundamentally, and simply, an investigation of what happens. It is a formalised way of regarding and questioning what it is that we actually do and the effects of that action. If, as a profession, we are to find ways and means of talking about and justifying our practice it is essential that we should become familiar with talking about it. It is no longer sufficient to say that we know it works; we need to be able to state, with confidence, to our colleagues and managers why and how it works.

PART-TIME STUDY

At present the majority of art therapists undertaking research do so on a part-time basis. This was the case with my own PhD, which was registered at Birmingham Polytechnic in 1985 and was completed in the summer of 1990. I registered for the PhD in the year following the completion of my MA (Schaverien 1984). Both these degrees were completed part-time, the PhD taking five years.

Part-time study raises particular practical problems if the researcher is otherwise employed for the rest of the week. It is often difficult to find time to do the required reading and writing, and it certainly eats up weekends and vacations. However, there are also benefits in part-time research, particularly if the employment is complementary to the research. It may be an asset to be working as an art therapist when involved in art therapy research. This is because some aspect of that practice is usually the foundation of the research. The benefit of a part-time research degree may be that there is a continuous interplay between theory and practice, with the chosen topic always in mind. This leads to a particular type of Master's thesis in which there is a balance between theory and practice. As course leader of the MA at St Albans, I have noticed that external examiners often comment on the commitment and originality of thought in the Master's degrees of art therapists. The weakness is often in a lack of self-confidence and an underestimation of the significance of the thesis.

My aim in this chapter is to illustrate one type of approach which suited me. I do not aim to tell anyone how to do research but rather to tell my story, in the hope that others may gain the confidence to find ways to pursue a topic of central interest to them personally.

A personal investment in the topic is essential; if you are to spend five years of your life with a topic it has to be one in which you have more than a passing interest. Very few art therapists embark on research for the sole purpose of gaining a degree; it is more frequently from a need to under-stand better some aspect of the work in which they are engaged, and the degree is a secondary consideration. This is an exciting time for art therapy; I meet an increasing number of people in the profession who are becoming experts in particular areas of the practice. This chapter has the aim of encouraging them to overcome their diffidence and to write and investigate their own area of special interest.

HYPOTHESIS

An hypothesis needs to be founded on one main idea. Any research is based on some motivating force or interest from which an hypothesis is derived. The title of my thesis is 'Transference and Countertransference in Art Therapy: Mediation, Interpretation and the Aesthetic Object' (Schaverien 1990). It was founded on a question that had interested me for some years prior to the research. I was curious about the ways in which the transference and countertransference in art psychotherapy were affected by the pictures made by the patient.

I selected the topic – or rather it selected me – from an early stage in my work as an art therapist. I found that I experienced intense feelings in the therapeutic situation for which I could not fully account. In an attempt to find some explanation for my experience I investigated art therapy literature and psychoanalytic theory. The literature regarding transference and countertransference in psychoanalysis and psychotherapy offered some insight, but I was left with the sense that there was an element which was not accounted for by these theories. This was the effects of the feelings evoked, in both therapist and patient, by the pictures. This led me to my hypothesis. This was that there were some, as yet unspecified, effects of pictures within the therapeutic relationship and that these seemed to be linked to aesthetic appreciation. In order to explore this I needed to investigate the aesthetic effects of the picture within the therapeutic relationship and, specifically, their effects on the transference and the countertransference. Thus the hypothesis – *what* is being investigated – leads to the question of *how* to investigate it: the need for a method emerges.

METHOD OF ENQUIRY

Art therapists, in my experience, tend to retreat or flounder in confusion when asked to describe their research method. This is frequently because they have not been asked such a question before. When doing a degree in fine art, which is often the original training of the art therapist, the method of research is not defined as such but is, in fact, mainly painting or making objects. The artist may consider that this is not really research in the scientific sense. Thus, on unfamiliar territory, the mature student feels ill-equipped and unequal to the task. This is a great underestimation of their experience and areas of expertise. 'The artist is just as much a discoverer of the forms of nature as the scientist is a discoverer of facts or natural laws' (Cassirer 1944, quoted in Cassirer 1955a p. 29). What is actually required is a new way of formulating the processes in which the art therapist is involved every day. The art therapist is often an expert in her or his particular area of work but undervalues that expertise because of the effects of the dominant scientific culture.

> Is all reality accessible to us only through the medium of scientific concepts? Or is it not evident, on the contrary, that a thinking which like scientific thinking moves only in derivations and in derivations from derivations can never lay bare the actual and ultimate roots of being? This does not cast any doubt on the existence of such roots. Everything that is relative must after all be rooted in an absolute. If this absolute persistently evades science, the evasion only shows that science lacks the specific organ for knowing reality. We do not apprehend the real by attempting to attain it step by step over the painful detours of discursive thinking; we must rather place ourselves immediately at its center. Such immediacy is denied to thought; it belongs only to pure vision. Pure intuition accomplishes what logical and discursive thought can never achieve, what indeed, once it recognises its own nature, logical thought will never even attempt.
>
> (Cassirer 1957, p. 35)

Although it was clearly not his intention when writing this, I consider that here Cassirer is giving the art therapist permission to start research from the point where she/he is placed. The involvement with our clients and their art work places us 'immediately at the centre' of that which we aim to research. This should give us confidence, following Cassirer, to attempt to find a language which is appropriate for investigating our own discipline.

On a personal note, the MA (Schaverien 1984) was an important foundation for the PhD; it offered a theoretical base for further research and also gave me some confidence about writing. In 1982 I published a paper entitled 'Transference as an Aspect of Art Therapy' (Schaverien 1982). This was a precursor of my PhD topic and it came from my work for the MA. The response that I received to this paper gave me confidence; and I realised that this topic might be of general, as well as personal, interest.

When registering for my PhD I encountered the usual question from the academic authorities regarding which method of research I would apply. My supervisor intervened at this point; he is a philosopher and had no problem in explaining that the method would be 'thinking hard'. I was impressed by this and liberated, too, from a feeling that I had to justify my work in alien terms. Thus it was that I set about thinking hard and observing what happened in my practice as an art psychotherapist. Initially this included noticing everything that my colleagues said when referring to transference and everything I read about transference. To avoid any misapprehensions of my meaning here I should add that this 'thinking hard' was a disciplined and considered approach which developed into a systematic analysis.

The research method which I used was a mixture of philosophical analysis influenced by Wittgenstein (1921), Wollheim (1968, 1984, 1987), Langer (1957, 1967), Cassirer (1944, 1946, 1955a, 1955b, 1957), and phenomenological approaches: Merleau-Ponty (1962), Sartre (1957), Bachelard (1958). It was also a single case study approach, based on art-historical biographies (Kuhns 1983; Spitz 1985) and psychoanalytic case studies, to which I refer below.

READING AS RESEARCH

An important aspect of any philosophical investigation must be reading to discover what others have said on the topic. However, this reading needs to have a structure and a purpose. The aim is to test the hypothesis in relation to what others have written. Library searches enable the beginner to locate previous work in the field. This is very different from the casual reading that we do to inform our practice. This is a disciplined approach; reading with the intention of testing the hypothesis and finding out if it has previously been investigated. This is reading from a critical stance during which we are alert to nuances which may unexpectedly relate to our topic or lead to a new direction. An example of this follows.

I was guided to read Cassirer (1955/57) by my supervisor. Whilst reading I happened upon a passage which struck a chord (Cassirer 1955b, p. 56). This passage has been quoted elsewhere (Schaverien 1987, 1991) and so, rather than repeat it, I will refer to it. It concerned the scapegoat which Cassirer referred to as subject to a 'transference of attributes and states'. This apparently bore no relation to the concept of transference in the traditional psychoanalytic meaning of the term, and yet this passage captured my imagination. I felt sure that what I read related to my search to understand transference in art psychotherapy and yet I could not formulate how. I kept it in mind and gradually came to understand the meaning of my interest; this passage became the basis of one aspect of my enquiry. At this point my hypothesis firmed up, the field narrowed, and I became totally engaged with the topic.

Thus an apparently chance discovery led me to explore this theme both in my practice and in the work of other writers. It led to a purposeful enquiry in which I read further in an attempt to understand what it was that had captured my imagination. To this end I widened the scope of my reading. I found that here, in this one passage, I had a key to a way of understanding the phenomena I had encountered in my own art work and also that of my patients. This was a beginning; from this the idea that the picture is a kind of scapegoat and possibly subject to similar processes emerged. I then had to find out what had been said about scapegoats. I needed to trace the origins of the scapegoat; its biblical and anthropological antecedents. The theory seemed to weave in with the emergent ideas. A theoretical discourse developed between myself and the sources of my reading. A theory began to emerge out of the continual process of disciplined thinking, observing and writing. Then came a point when I realised that I had to attend to the pictures which I had in my possession. I needed to test, theoretically at least, whether the hypothesis regarding the scapegoat related to the pictures of my patients.

THE CASE STUDY: ANALYSIS OF PICTURES AS RESEARCH

In discussing the processes which occur in art psychotherapy it is necessary to look at the pictures or art objects in order to see how they affect the viewers. Looking carefully seems to be an important element of research in art of any kind , but in a relatively new field such as art therapy this is even more important. The single case study is a recognised method of research (Barlow and Hersen 1978; Sapsford and Abbott 1992). 'New paradigm' (Reason and Rowan 1981) is also relevant in considering the approach to art therapy case studies. However, my influences are from two different fields of investigation. I have described elsewhere (Schaverien 1993) that my base is firstly the work of art historians, who write a biography of the artist, including paintings and life history. Secondly, psychoanalysts who have written case studies about patients who make art work: Baynes (1940), Jung (1959), Milner (1969), Klein (1961), Winnicott (1971) and Edinger (1990).

An art therapy case study is usually based on pictures or art objects made by the patient. These are often implicitly accepted as the foundations for research into the process of art therapy. Although this is not often the stated purpose of keeping them, most art therapists working in a hospital or out-patient setting have many such pictures stored. In the libraries of the colleges where art therapists are trained there are files of case studies written by the students. These follow roughly the same pattern: they have a theoretical section, a description of the setting, and of the patient and the diagnosis; then they describe the process of art therapy with this patient. They are usually illustrated with photographs of the art works made by the patient or (in a group) patients. Thus the potential for this method of research is built in to the initial training of art therapists; they are encouraged to look at the pictures and discuss them. Again, although this is common practice, it is rarely recognised as the potential basis for research.

Art therapy is the only discipline where actual objects created within the frame of the setting exist in a concrete form. They last long after the session is over and even after the therapy is finished. They are a continuing reminder of the atmosphere of any given session and, through them, some sense of this period in therapy can be re-created. In art therapy the single case study method of research is illuminated through the patient's art works.

The retrospective review

Art therapists are usually artists and familiar with the retrospective exhibition in art galleries. This I have discussed elsewhere as having been adapted by art therapists into what is usually known as the review session within the process of art therapy (Schaverien 1991, 1993). This is not a method used by all art therapists, but I am aware of other art therapists who work in this way in particular (my colleagues Nowell Hall, Case and Henzell at St Albans College of Art 1982–6).

The review session is part of my clinical practice, inherited from my own experience as an artist. It is a method I have applied in open and closed group sessions and with group-analytic art therapy groups. I also work in this way with individual patients in analytical art psychotherapy sessions. The review may take place during the process of therapy, or in a session prior to termination. At times it is initiated by the therapist, at others by the patient. In some analytic groups, for example, the review session is built into the boundaries at the beginning, so that there is an expectation that at some point the group will come to a decision to review.

In the review, like the retrospective exhibition in the art gallery, all the pictures that have been made, or all the pictures from a certain period, are assembled and looked at together and in sequence. As a method of clinical practice this can be very helpful for the patient in ways too numerous to list here. It can certainly be self-affirming to see what has been created, but it can also reveal connections and links which had been previously unconscious. Clearly this is not research but there is potential research material in viewing the pictures in this way. A retrospective is literally a 'backward view', a 'survey of past time and events' (*Concise Oxford Dictionary*). The review is to display for formal inspection and also a 'second view'. This is the process to which I subjected the pictures I analysed as part of my research.

When I commenced my research I had several sets of pictures which had been made by patients over the years. One such set of pictures, amounting to over two hundred, had had a profound influence on my thinking. These had been made over a four-year period, between ten and fourteen years previously, by a young man I have called Harry. Harry was, at the time, twenty-four years old and I was an inexperienced art therapist a little older than him. I knew these pictures contained something I needed to understand better so, during the course of my research, I decided to concentrate on these pictures and describe exactly what I saw. I was familiar with them, and thought I had seen them, but I decided to put this to the test and analyse the content. This was done within the framework of testing my hypothesis.

From the whole series I organised the pictures into the sequence in which they were made; they were all dated. Then I selected them according to themes. I had photographs but decided to look at the actual pictures. Photographs are not an accurate record; they distort paintings and drawings in many subtle ways. They distance the viewer from the actual pencil marks and brush strokes; they alter the colour; parts are sometimes ommitted; and the medium used is not always evident.

Having thus organised the pictures I set about the lengthy task of recording exactly what I saw. With each picture I wrote down size, medium, content and style of execution. I noted all the figurative elements in the pictures and their relation to each other. I noted the abstract forms and the colours; I wrote down all the words and noted the dates of each picture. (The patient had in fact dated his work but it is important for the art therapist to date work if the patient does not do so.) Gradually patterns emerged; certain figures were repeated but in altered form or relationship. Themes emerged so I sorted the pictures into themes and common elements and noted how they related to each other.

I discovered that during a nine-month period the patient had made several pictures a day for many days each week, and that gradually the pace of this production had slowed down. The significance of this seemed to be connected to a regression. I had remembered that these pictures related to an early and regressed part of the transference, when he had stayed in the art room, close to me, for most of the time I was in the building. I had previously been unaware that this had gone on for nine months. I found that the style of execution changed when the patient began to relate to others outside the one-to-one relationship with the therapist. Later Harry went through a kind of adolescence and the pictures from this period were often jokey and made more to impress his peers than for the art therapist. There were inner, archetypal images which related to the regression, and others with overt sexual content which related to a still later period. There were other pictures which were based on common pop art themes and again these were made as a step out into the world.

I was suprised to find how much I had previously missed; I thought I had seen these pictures but actually I had only seen a superficial layer. I now began to understand the web that they had woven me into. The pictures related closely to the transference; Harry had been intensely regressed at first and then, later, rather adolescent. There were certain archetypal themes which recurred intermittently, alternating with other more external themes. I began to understand how these pictures with their powerful aesthetic quality had affected the countertransference. What I had seen, as well as the atmosphere of the therapeutic relationship, had woven its spell. I had been absorbed into the inner world of the artist in the most subtle manner.

COUNTERTRANSFERENCE AS RESEARCH TOOL

In art psychotherapy it seems it is possible to use the countertransference to the pictures as a research tool. Clearly this is a real difference from psychotherapy. In researching the transference and countertransference in art psychotherapy the pictures continued to exist. The pictures offer a particular way for the therapist, as researcher, to recapture the atmosphere of a long-past therapeutic relationship.

This became evident through the realisation of the power of the unconscious processes which seemed to engage me again as I looked into these pictures now. It was as if the countertransference was reawakened. I found that the original feelings I had had about the pictures and the person who made them came back to life. The countertransference was thus evoked through the images and what they carried. It became live once again in viewing the pictures in this way. I was living with them and, once again, trying to enter into the world of the young man who had made them. I found he too came to life for me again. This is rather strange because of the time that had elapsed since we had worked together. It was evident that the pictures held the memory of his state at the time.

The pictures were an integrated aspect of the transference and countertransference at the time they were made. When I analysed the pictures this was long past. It could be said that they were like archive material. However, unlike most archive material, I would argue that they were still live because the people involved were both still alive and could become engaged with them again. The atmosphere of the therapeutic relationship came to life for me again through the pictures. It became clear that the pictures had illuminated the transference in a powerful way when they were made. I had to contact the artist to ask his permission to publish his work. He affirmed that they brought the period to life for him again too. Thus the research was based in the pictures but it was also very much about the process of the therapeutic relationship.

Reflection

After recording what I saw I left the pictures on one side and began to reflect on the processes involved. It seemed to me that I was beginning to understand the source of the powerful transference and countertransference as it had manifested itself in the pictures. To reflect is 'to look inward', 'to go back in thought, to meditate and to consult with oneself', 'to remind oneself or consider whence' (*Concise Oxford Dictionary*). This I did with regard to the pictures and psychoanalytic theories of transference and countertransference. I read some more and reflected on what I read in relation to the nascent theory.

When these pictures were made it had been Jung's writings on the transference which connected to my experience of the transference with this patient. At the time I had read *The Psychology of the Transference* (Jung 1946) and recognised in it a correspondence with the relationship between the elements in Harry's pictures. Jung offered no clear explanation of what was happening, but did evoke connections. In this book he uses pictures from an alchemical text to illustrate the unconscious transference and countertransference relationship. The imagery resembled Harry's pictures and led me to understand that there was a collective, as well as personal, unconscious element in the pictures and their effects.

Theoretical analysis and writing up

Another strand of my research now developed; I found I needed to make a distinction between the different stages and different transferences which seemed to be involved in analytical forms of art psychotherapy. It seemed to me that there were two distinct processes which needed to be recognised: these were the stage of painting the pictures, and that of looking at them when they were completed. I realised that each of these stages had different effects. The patient was artist but also viewer, and each of these affected some aspect of the transference and the countertransference.

At this stage I was beginning to feel overwhelmed; the project seemed to be growing beyond itself and I did not see how I could limit it. I knew I had to prioritise and write one chapter before I could write another. I was feeling that the whole project was becoming unmanageable. It seemed to be growing in all directions with no end in sight. None the less I managed to keep going and realise that there was some coherence here if I just rearranged and organised the material. I had no doubt that it all belonged together but it was a matter of establishing priorities.

I decided to write the whole thesis from beginning to end, completing one section at a time. I realised that I could not write one chapter without first exploring a particular theme and so, in a way, the chapters dictated their own order. Gradually a shape emerged and one idea followed another. The process was a constant weaving of theory and practice; of observation and discussion.

Supervision

In any research degree which is registered in an institution the question of supervision arises. The research student/supervisor relationship can be a sensitive one; it is long term and both people have an investment in the student's work. It is common to hear of students who 'fell out' with supervisors because of theoretical or personal differences. Sometimes supervisors leave their posts. Often the loss of a supervisor can seem like a real disaster, but it is surmountable, and many people who have completed their thesis have had several supervisors.

Initially I had two supervisors: one within the institution and one outside it. My internal supervisor, who had supervised my MA, fostered in me a belief that I could complete a PhD. Thus his encouragement was central in enabling me to begin. He left his post in the college when I was three-and-a-half years into my research. At the time I knew where I was heading and my external supervisor, who was out of the country most of the year, provided an intellectual reference point. I was assigned another internal supervisor within the institution, and his help was considerable in bringing the thesis to its conclusion. He knew little about the topic but understood textual organisation and was able to point out structural inconsistencies. Thus for the last year-and-a-half I was mostly on my own with the project; I realise that this had many advantages. By this time I knew what I had to do; there was someone there to give me feedback on what I wrote; there was no interference from anyone else at the writing-up stage.

In any thesis there comes a point where the student has become the expert on her/his topic. It is necessary to leave the comfort of the support of a supervisor and complete the project alone. Many people feel that in the end they are restrained by a supervisor. It is inevitable in such a long course of study. It is important to remember that, in the end, the area of the thesis is the area in which the student has become an expert. In this small area of knowledge the writer of the thesis comes to surpass the supervisor and must stand alone (Elton 1988).

If we use a psychoanalytic analogy we might see the student/supervisor relationship as rather like the mother/child relationship. In the beginning there is dependency and a lack of differentiation. Gradually, through a series of steps, a sense of self emerges and the student/child grows and develops in confidence. The parent/supervisor watches as a reference point in case the student stumbles and needs additional support. Eventually a separation has taken place, and they stand separately as two adults or colleagues.

CONCLUSION

What are the effects of the pictures on the people who look at them in the art therapy context? And what bearing do they have on the chosen topic of research? I consider this to be an essential element of the investigation of art in therapy. Thus the case studies are fundamental and central to art therapy research, but that is not all. They are the basis, the foundation; but something more than the reporting of case studies is required. It is necessary to find ways of thinking about and analysing what happens.

The word research means to 'look back', a 'careful search or inquiry', an 'endeavour to discover new facts' and a 'critical investigation' (*Concise*

Oxford Dictionary). All these seem to encapsulate the process of my research but the method was not consciously formulated prior to beginning. Rather, method developed as it was needed. There are many ways of approaching research and I have merely recounted the one that emerged as I investigated my topic. Each person needs to find a way that is compatible with their idea and interests. The method I applied is characterised by a few key words which begin with the prefix 're'. Research, review, retrospective, record, read, reflect. These words are all about looking back. Perhaps that is the key to research: that it is a looking back at a process, and an attempt to discover what it was that happened. Thus for me practice comes first and research follows it. This gives substance to the quest.

ACKNOWLEDGEMENTS

This whole chapter is a grateful acknowledgement of my supervisors: Dr Anthony Winterbourne, Professor Richard Wollheim and Professor John Swift.

REFERENCES

Bachelard, G. (1958) *The Poetics of Space.* Beacon, Boston.
Barlow, D.H. and Hersen, M. (1978) *Single Case Experimental Design.* Pergamon Press, New York.
Baynes, H.G. (1940) *The Mythology of the Soul.* Routledge and Kegan Paul, London.
Cassirer, E. (1944) *An Essay on Man.* Yale University Press, New Haven and London.
Cassirer, E. (1946) *Language and Myth.* Dover, New York.
Cassirer, E. (1955/57) *The Philosophy of Symbolic Forms.* 3 vols. Yale University Press, New Haven and London.
Cassirer, E. (1955a) *Language.* vol. 1. Yale University Press, New Haven and London.
Cassirer, E. (1955b) *Mythical Thought.* vol. 2. Yale University Press, New Haven and London.
Cassirer, E. (1957) *The Phenomenology of Knowledge.* vol. 3. Yale University Press, New Haven and London.
Edinger, E. (1990) *The Living Psyche.* Chiron, Wilmette, IL.
Elton, L. (1988) 'Report and thesis writing', paper given at conference on research supervision at Brighton Polytechnic.
Jung, C.G. (1946) 'The Psychology of the Transference'. In: *The Practice of Psychotherapy, CW* 16. Bollingen, Princeton.
Jung, C.G. (1959) *Archetypes and the Collective Unconscious. CW* 9 Part 1. Bollingen, Princeton.
Klein, M. (1961) *Narrative of a Child Analysis.* Hogarth, London.
Kuhns, R. (1983) *Psychoanalytic Theory of Art.* Columbia University Press, New York.
Langer, S. (1957) *The Problems of Art.* Routledge and Kegan Paul, London.
Langer, S. (1967) *Feeling and Form.* Routledge and Kegan Paul, London.

Merleau-Ponty, M. (1962) *The Phenomenlogy of Perception*. Routledge and Kegan Paul, London.

Milner, M. (1969) *The Hands of the Living God*. Hogarth, London.

Nowell Hall, P. (1987) 'Healing the Split'. In: Dalley, T. *et al. Images of Art Therapy*. Tavistock/Routledge, London.

Reason, P. and Rowan, J. (Eds) (1981) *Human Inquiry: A Sourcebook of New Paradigm Research*. John Wiley, Chichester.

Sapsford, R. and Abbott, P. (1992) *Research Methods for Nurses and the Caring Professions*. Open University Press, Buckingham.

Sartre, J.P. (1957) *Being and Nothingness*. Methuen, London.

Schaverien, J. (1982) 'Transference as an Aspect of Art Therapy'. *Inscape*. September: 10–16.

Schaverien, J. (1984) 'Word and Image in Art Psychotherapy'. Unpublished Master's thesis, Birmingham Polytechnic.

Schaverien, J. (1987) 'The Scapegoat and the Talisman: Transference in Art Therapy'. In: Dalley, T. *et al. Images of Art Therapy*. Tavistock/Routledge, London.

Schaverien, J. (1989) 'The Picture Within the Frame'. In: Gilroy, A. and Dalley, T. (Eds) *Pictures at an Exhibition*. Tavistock/Routledge, London.

Schaverien, J. (1990) 'Transference and Countertransference in Art Therapy: Mediation, Interpretation and the Aesthetic Object'. Unpublished PhD thesis, Birmingham Polytechnic.

Schaverien, J. (1991) *The Revealing Image: Analytical Art Psychotherapy in Theory and Practice*. Routledge, London.

Schaverien, J. (1993) 'The Retrospective Review of Pictures: Data for Research in Art Therapy'. In: Payne, H. (Ed.) *A Handbook of Inquiry in the Arts Therapies: One River, Many Currents*. Jessica Kingsley, London.

Spitz, E.H. (1985) *Art & Psyche*. Yale University Press, New Haven.

Winnicott, D.W. (1971) *Therapeutic Consultations in Child Psychiatry*. Hogarth, London.

Wittgenstein, L. (1921) *Tractatus Logico-philosophicus*. Routledge and Kegan Paul, London, 1961.

Wollheim, R. (1968) *Art and its Objects*. Cambridge University Press, Cambridge.

Wollheim, R. (1984) *The Thread of Life*. Cambridge University Press, Cambridge.

Wollheim, R. (1987) *Painting as an Art*. Thames & Hudson, London & Princeton.

Chapter 2

The analysis of therapeutic improvisatory music

Colin Lee

INTRODUCTION

This chapter will discuss the core content of a recently completed piece of doctoral research which was concerned with the musical and therapeutic processes involved in therapeutic improvisation (Lee 1992).[1] The questions and subsequent hypotheses evolved from the desire to consider process and outcome equally when researching music therapy. It is my view that the unity and division of both musical and therapeutic avenues will afford music therapists a greater clue to the understanding of the music therapy process itself. Through the analytical and methodological framework of the research I attempted to discover a formula for viewing therapeutic improvisation at both macro and micro levels. Three improvisations with three individual clients living with the virus HIV and AIDS were chosen for the project, the investigation being juxtaposed between specific music analytic procedures and verbal data collected from the client, plus perspectives from three outside validators (a counsellor, musician and music therapist). This chapter will focus on the results of the research rather than the complex components of the analyses themselves. I will discuss the research both academically and personally, highlighting the merits and problems of such an analytical procedure.

BEGINNINGS

Schmidt (1984) was the first music therapist to undertake an analytical investigation into the musical processes within music therapy. The main aim of her study was to examine a Nordoff–Robbins play song, 'Something is Going to Happen', in terms of a Schenkerian analytical model.[2] The need to focus on questions of process, alongside those of outcome, was initially identified in the UK by Steele and Dunachie (1986). They analysed a small section of an improvisation, in an attempt to discover possible connections between musical content and therapeutic outcome. The accuracy of the results were hampered by problems of accurate notation (aural transcription from an audiotape), and the qualitative interpretations of their chosen client (a child with learning difficulties). Rudd (1990) focuses on similar problems of interpretation through the musical study of the opening measures of an improvisation with a child with behavioural problems:

> The question is how we might go in the process of proceeding from the structure of music to possible fantasies, images or associations by the client and therapist. The procedure illustrates how every step of description includes a possible interpretation. We may never be sure that the description of the client's music which therapists suggest is the same as given by the client himself.
>
> (Rudd 1990, p. 18)

These studies highlight the problems of analysing musical content and its influence on understanding the music therapy process when the client is unable to provide personal feedback.

Bunt (1985) and Odell-Miller (1989), in the concluding stages of their research into music therapy outcome, identify the need for process-oriented research. Bunt and Hoskyns (1987) further suggest that a synthesis of the two styles (process and outcome) could provide a more convincing and extensive structure when researching music therapy. Certainly it seems incongruous to isolate one or other approach. To focus on either process or outcome as research procedures, I believe, diminishes the essence of balanced questioning. I further believe that music therapy needs to develop new methods of research in order to address the unique qualities of its theory and practice. Recently completed and on-going process-oriented research projects in the UK (Dunachie 1991; Pavlicevic 1991; Van Colle 1991) suggest that these issues and problems are now being tackled within a variety of methodological frameworks.

The combination of issues from the music therapy literature and my own ideas and beliefs led me into the first stages of the research: two short analytic pilot studies looking at the differing approaches of music analysis[3] and their potential for the investigation of therapeutic improvisation (Lee 1989, 1990). Two improvisations from music therapy sessions with a client with Down's Syndrome were chosen, one tonal in design and the other atonal. The main aim of both papers was to explore the musical components and any potential structure that might lay behind the therapeutic improvised act. The problems encountered during these small pieces of research were:

1 The therapist's/researcher's subjectivity in analysing the improvisation of a non-verbal client.
2 Adapting theoretical models of music analysis to therapeutic improvisation.
3 The inaccuracies of aural notation.

4 Unsubstantiated assumptions with regard to formal musical complexities and their relevance to the music therapy process.

These pilot studies enabled me to develop various methodological confines, and proved crucial in shaping and directing the main body of my research, such that:

1 The analysis of musical material should not be restricted to any one theoretical model.
2 The research methodology should originate from a combination of therapeutic and musical postulates.
3 Verbally articulate clients are essential if elements of the therapist's/researcher's subjectivity are to be decreased.
4 The structural intricacies of the improvisation should be considered as significantly related to the music therapy process only if directly corroborated by outside sources.

THE RESEARCH

The chosen client group were people living with the virus HIV and AIDS. All sessions were held at London Lighthouse, where I worked for one day a week for three years. London Lighthouse is Britain's first major residential and support centre for people living with HIV and AIDS. The centre is committed to providing the best possible care, support and facilities so that people affected by AIDS can live.

Whilst all the data collected was completed by the end of the second year of the research project, it was crucial that I continued my work as a music therapist, firstly for the on-going clients, and secondly to afford a broad overview of therapeutic intervention necessary for the project as a whole. The session content of each week varied depending on the number of long-term clients and the health of the people requiring music therapy on the hospice/palliative care unit (the residential unit). Generally there would be an average of four long-term clients (one-hour sessions) with two hours spent on the residential unit. Due to the health and emotional difficulties of people who were very ill and/or near death, it was decided not to include them as a part of the in-depth analyses.

Hypotheses

The four hypotheses were formulated prior to the main data collection and analysis. They were written, rewritten, considered and reconsidered over an extended period. Their final format was as follows:

1 That in therapeutic improvisation for people living with the virus HIV and AIDS it is possible to perceive a direct link between musical representation and therapeutic development.
2 That the musical components of therapeutic improvisation are as important as the therapeutic evaluations in highlighting and evaluating the efficacy of music therapy for people living with the virus HIV and AIDS.
3 That specific musical themes and/or motifs are employed (consciously or subconsciously) as a generative basis for the therapeutic improvisation as a whole.
4 That the musical preference and culture of both client and therapist have a direct effect upon the musical components incorporated within the therapeutic improvisation. This may consequently affect the therapeutic outcome.

The decision to investigate three individual improvisations originated, in broad terms, from the improvisations that were occurring during my work as a music therapist at London Lighthouse. The quality and content of both the musical and therapeutic avenues appeared to be very dense and concentrated in format. Rather than attempt a broad overview of a whole series of improvisations it was decided to ask each of the three clients involved to select one of four piano improvisations transcribed during a one-month period. The core analyses of the research consisted solely of piano improvisations. Whilst this was not representative of the therapeutic procedure as a whole (percussion instruments being used often), because of the problems of aurally notating extra instrumental lines accurately among the often complex music, it was decided to confine the study to piano improvisations alone.

Data collection

The apparatus used in this project centred around a Yamaha MIDI–Grand Piano situated at City University, London. It is a piano fitted with electronic sensors on every key, with MIDI ports to transmit the information to another MIDI–compatible instrument. The piano was linked via a MIDI cable to an Apple Macintosh computer, and was recorded using the Opcode 2.6 sequencer software. Simultaneous to this, a further recording was made on a DAT tape recorder. The original sequences were converted into 'standard MIDI files', transcribed via the Finale 2.0 software package.

One of the main limitations of this transcriptional format is the notational layout received after the full programme has been completed. The Finale 2.0 software package will receive and transcribe the information only in terms of a pre-determined time signature (for these experiments 4/4 was chosen); thus changes in tempo appear as multi-complex notation (see

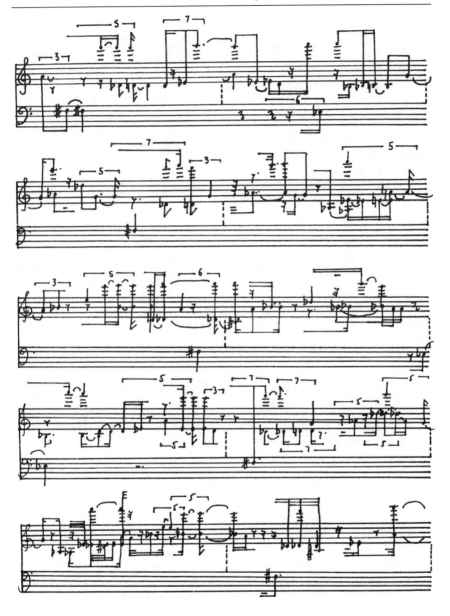

Figure 2.1 Computer simulation of tempo changes

Figure 2.1). This difficulty in relating the 'hard core' data to the audio recording meant that all the music had to be retranscribed aurally from the recordings in order to produce musical notation that would accurately represent the musical content itself. The difficulty in reading the

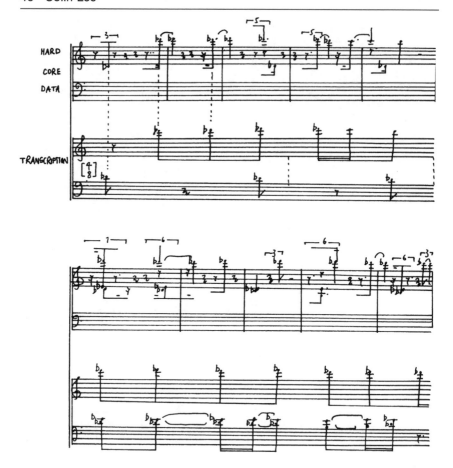

Figure 2.2 Hard core data and transcription

computer printout hard core data can be seen by comparing a section of an improvisation in both transcribed formats (see Figure 2.2).[4]

In order to contextualise the stages of each analysis verbal reflections were collated from the clients and three external validators (a musician, a counsellor and a music therapist). This gave rise to interesting issues around the nature and function of 'blind' assessments. It was impossible to find a music therapist to act as an external validator who was not aware of my work. The responses could therefore include a potential bias compared to the responses of the other external validators. Therapeutic improvisation deals with musical expression, communication and creativity that are essentially personal between client and therapist. This contrasts with the 'second-hand' nature of audio recordings. There are further differences in the verbal reflections from the clients, as well as with the 'blind' assessments from an imbalanced group of external validators. My eventual approach was to incorporate all the information freely and creatively within the overall structure of the research.

The improvisations chosen took the following forms:

Improvisation One:	Piano, four-hands	Client – Treble	Therapist – Bass
Improvisation Two:	Piano, four-hands	Client – Bass	Therapist – Treble
Improvisation Three:	Piano solo	Client	

Special note must be made of the disparity between the different musical roles and the possible effects this had upon the research findings. The fact that the therapist and client took both the treble and bass lines (Improvisations One and Two) would appear to be balanced in format. The differential in the solo (Improvisation Three), however, produces a more noticeable imbalance. Within this analysis there could be no investigation of the active relationship between client and therapist. During the research trials it was made clear to each of the three clients that it would be their decision as to which improvisation was chosen to represent their stage within the music therapy process. Whilst the resulting discrepancy caused many problems it was essential that the client felt empowered to make the final choice. This highlights the problems of collaborative research and the view that, when researching music therapy, the research design should conform to the needs of the client and not the research project itself.

The client was asked to return to the university in order to listen to the chosen improvisation. All comments were recorded and subsequently transcribed. The guidelines for stopping the tape and making observations were based on the simple proviso that the client felt either something important had happened, or that they had something to say in general terms. The assessment was conducted in the form of a discussion between the client and myself. The three validators each listened to all three improvisations and were asked to comment in the same way. They were asked to consider the music they heard from their own professional standpoints, e.g. the musician was asked to comment on the music, the counsellor on the therapeutic relationship and the music therapist on the product as a whole. After all the verbal data had been collected and transcribed it was tabulated in order to find those areas of the highest density of tape stops, and to discover the specific parts of the improvisation that were chosen by all four people.

Data analysis

The methodological structure consisted of five stages. Stage One (an idiosyncratic description) gave an overall picture of the whole therapeutic process, comprising a descriptive synopsis of the complete therapeutic period. It included selected data from the client's own reflections during the therapeutic process as well as information from the research session. The therapist's subjective viewpoints were added where appropriate, and selected comments were taken from the outside validators' data. Stage Two (an integral investigation) consisted of an inventory of musical interrelations in order to obtain an overall catalogue of the musical components.

These two initial stages led into the main core of the investigation (Stage Three – two single analyses). The two sections were selected from the chosen improvisation of each of the three clients, based on the following criteria: a) those occasions during the improvisation where more than one tape pause was recorded (client and/or outside validators' assessment data); b) those periods where there was an evident density of tape pauses (verbal assessment data); c) those sections, contained within the verbal assessment data, where there was the richest amount of material available; d) that the sections chosen for analysis began and ended at points that made grammatical sense; and e) that the client was included as an active participant in the selection stage. The actual length of section that was analysed in comparison with the complete duration of the improvisation is shown below:

Improvisation One   Duration – 14 min. 15 sec.
                     Analysis One –   (7:05 – 8:18) 1 min. 13 sec.
                     Analysis Two – (11:41 – 13:46) 2 min. 5 sec.
Improvisation Two   Duration – 15 min. 6 sec.
                     Analysis One –   (7:07 – 8:07) 1 min.
                     Analysis Two – (11:16 – 14:35) 3 min. 19 sec.
Improvisation Three Duration – 25 min. 43 sec.
                     Analysis One –   (0:00 – 1:51) 1 min. 51 sec.
                     Analysis Two – (12:51 – 14:07) 1 min. 58 sec.

Once the two sections for analysis were chosen it was necessary to collate and categorise the specific verbal assessment data. Analytic procedures were adopted to highlight Stages One and Two, considering specific questions of therapeutic intent, musical invention and process. During this stage specific musical constructions, e.g. harmony, melody and rhythm, were investigated in an attempt to discover the essential building blocks of the improvisation. The verbal assessment data was subsequently compared and contrasted in relation to the therapeutic process as a whole.

Stage Four (evaluation and synthesis) compared and contrasted the findings of Stages One to Three. It developed and discussed the possible connections between the macro and micro analyses and suggested further interpretations about the therapeutic process as a whole for each individual client. Stage Five (review and findings) considered the project as a whole: it evaluated the results of the hypotheses and compared the therapeutic and musical processes analysed in Stages One to Four. It suggested that there are certain musical and therapeutic issues to be found within individual therapeutic improvisations that are specific to people living with HIV and AIDS. Finally it considered the significance of this project in terms of further music therapy research.

THE RESULTS

Evaluation of the processes of therapeutic improvisation for people living with HIV and AIDS in terms of musical content and therapeutic outcome can be addressed at various levels. I will describe the results of the data analysis with reference to the four hypotheses, which acted as anchors throughout the entire project.

Testing the hypotheses

One: That in therapeutic improvisation for people living with the virus HIV and AIDS, it is possible to perceive a direct link between musical representation and therapeutic development.

In testing this hypothesis verbal data was collated from the project as a whole. It showed that there was a connection for the three clients between musical representation and their stage in the therapeutic process. The idea that certain styles of improvisational playing evolved – a) as part of a musically interactive therapeutic relationship (Clients One and Two), and b) as an individual (Client Three) – was studied from all the data concerning the three clients investigated. Client Two, though limited in musical ability, seemed to formulate an improvisational style that was based upon certain musical modes which were directed into simple structural divisions of two contrasting sections. He stated on three occasions that the music was an accurate transcription of his feelings. Client One's musical procedure appeared more complex, avoiding tonality wherever possible and evolving through small sections of divergent textural devices. He was aware of the benefits of relating the musical technique to aesthetic expression as a fundamental component of his development. Client Three's improvisations were diaphanous and limited to the smallest expression of musical components. The clients' reflections supported my initial data analysis.

Two: That the musical components of therapeutic improvisation are as important as the therapeutic evaluations in highlighting and evaluating the efficacy of music therapy for people living with the virus HIV and AIDS.

There is at present no current information in music therapy literature that deals with the significance of musical components in therapeutic improvisation. Music is most commonly referred to as the intermediary object through which the therapeutic process passes. Thus the quality and content of the music itself often take second place to the therapeutic aims. It was the intention, therefore, of this hypothesis to investigate certain improvisations in terms of musical and therapeutic process and outcome. These were researched both in terms of the musical/therapeutic relationship and the individual within the relationship. Whilst the aesthetic quality of the improvisations were not taken as a prerequisite for inclusion within this project, all three clients commented on the need for the therapist's consideration of musical content and aesthetic status:

> When we improvise together in the sessions the expertise of your musical input is vital. I expect your musical inventions to be of the highest order, otherwise I would not have been prepared to travel personally. I remember testing you musically when we first started working together; could you match and meet my quite often intricate musical inventions? I needed that aesthetic musical content before I was ready to move on.
>
> (Client Three)

> I love it when your music is good, it enables me to grow. I depend upon the quality and beauty of your music to say the things I can't say musically myself.
>
> (Client Two)

> The music you provide for me in the sessions is important. Whilst I don't always want beautiful music, there are times when I need you to support me musically through the more complex structures that I can manage. They give me the opportunity to express my feelings at a much higher level. These times for me contain elements of beauty.
>
> (Client One)

These comments seem to suggest that when one is working with people living with HIV and AIDS, equal consideration should be given to the intricacies and quality of the musical as well as therapeutic components. This should be regarded in terms of both the therapist's own musical input and his/her reflections on the client's musical expression.

Three: That specific musical themes and/or motifs are employed (consciously or subconsciously) as a generative basis for the therapeutic improvisation as a whole.

The audio and notational transcriptions of the three improvisations provided an overall view of the complete musical executions. Throughout the analyses, the main area of unity dealt with what is termed the generative cell and seed motif.[5] These terms formed the most crucial and potent musical representation of the association between therapeutic improvisation and expression of the client's psychological state. In the case of Clients One and Two the significance of the cell/seed did not become apparent until the micro analyses. Client Three's incorporation of the cell, however, was instantly unmistakable, although the extent of its contribution to the musical make-up was not fully ascertained until a full cell dissection was made. Each client's use of the cell/seed was unique to his own personal growth within the improvisation and music therapy process as a whole. What was common was the crucial nature of the cell/seed in transferring into musical expression aspects connected with living with a terminal illness:

> The cell for me is the closest representation of how I am feeling. I feel that you don't express the thing by being the thing itself, you express it and communicate it by providing a structure, which in itself is supportive, even though you may be expressing things which are intrinsically not so. The cell thus provides me with a structure in which I can focus my feelings, particularly when exploring issues of death and dying.
>
> (Client Three)

> I was able to express the pain that I was feeling through those few notes, which developed into a simple but powerful melody.
>
> (Client Two)

The concept that a small group of notes provides the basis for a conscious and/or subconscious containment of specific and/or global expressions of therapeutic and musical meaning suggests that therapeutic improvisation can originate from a core which develops through various stages towards a complete unification of musical and therapeutic ideals. Whilst each client's share in this process appeared different, the exploration appeared to travel generally along the same route.

Four: That the musical preference and culture of both client and therapist have a direct effect upon the musical components incorporated within the therapeutic improvisation. This may consequently affect the therapeutic outcome.

Each of the three clients discussed within this project, plus myself as therapist, had clearly identifiable musical influences that may have affected certain aspects of the single improvisation analysed. Client One found that contemporary jazz influenced his musical thinking; Client Three reflected on his love of Liszt, Ravel, Debussy and Prokoviev; and Client Two found that the oriental modes and Spanish music became central to his improvisational expression. My own musical components on one level were guided by the needs of the client, and on another level were influenced by my own culture and preferences as a musician (Tippett, Moeran, Finzi, Bach, Sondheim and Zappa).

To test this hypothesis small sections of the improvisations were placed alongside extracts from pre-composed music that were chosen to show similar musical constructions to those of the improvisations. It was significant to note that in two cases (Client Three comparison – Liszt, Sonata in B minor; therapist comparison – Tippett, *King Priam*) the musical constructions and intricacies between improvisation and pre-composed selection were very similar. Client Three struggled with his own musical influences within the therapeutic framework. He realised the potential of their inclusion within the improvisations, but also acknowledged the potential that they might have to block the therapeutic direction. By the conclusion of our sessions his improvisations had become a much clearer representation of his own musical personality, whilst acknowledging the core from which his expression originated. Clients One and Two utilised their musical influences at a much more fundamental and subconscious level. They did not wish to acknowledge the musical origins of their improvisations beyond their basic recognition. The alternating balance between the client's and therapist's ability to lead and/or follow in general music therapy terms can also be applied to the musical components and direction of the improvisation. If the musical preference and culture of both client and therapist can have a direct effect upon the musical components incorporated within therapeutic improvisation, then what is its effect on the therapeutic outcome? The therapist should therefore acknowledge his/her own musical influences and the potential they have to affect the therapeutic relationship/process.

Personal evaluations

My initial attempts at addressing the personal issues faced whilst working alongside people living with HIV and AIDS developed during the later stages of this project (Lee 1991). Feelings of fear and 'not knowing' served as both potentially positive and negative forces in terms of the research and therapeutic process. In terms of countertransference I considered my reactions in relation to the work of Winiarski (1991). His writings on psychotherapy and HIV and AIDS consider countertransference in terms firstly of the broad spectrum – the reactions to the client, and secondly the narrow spectrum – the therapist's feelings that are idiosyncratic perceptions of the client. Throughout the project these two concepts enabled me to examine a complex and multi-layered set of responses.

The methodology that was necessary to answer the questions of this project could be only loosely based on previous methods of research analysis and investigation. I tried to bridge the gap between art and science: art can be investigated 'scientifically', as indeed can behavioural responses to a therapeutic intervention. The 'not knowing' arose when I tried to extrapolate the appropriate methodological components from each and apply them to my research. On reflection the fear I experienced gave me the impetus to challenge previous methodologies in music therapy research, and search for a more creative approach that could move between the research orthodoxies of art and science.

Alongside the struggle with research methodology was a fear of being unable to evaluate my feelings both with regard to the music therapy itself, and to its development without reference points from other similar work in music therapy and research. This, in terms of the music therapy process, on the one hand, enabled me to proceed slowly and honestly but, on the other hand, was a potential problem when considering the clients' needs within the therapeutic process. Bosnak (1989) has described how the therapist's skills and knowledge can act as a negative force in the therapeutic process with people living with HIV and AIDS. Thus the imbalance between knowledge and fear became central to formulating a therapeutic procedure that was true to myself as a music therapist, and which acknowledged a vulnerability that was essential for the therapeutic relationship. At times, attempting to mould such emotional and stressful issues into an academic study felt futile and irrelevant. The results of the musical analyses were illuminating on an academic level in terms of the micro-musical content and therapeutic outcome, but on another, more personal level gave rise to questions about the validity of such an in-depth study given the reality of the client's situation.

Having reviewed the music therapy literature it seems to me that music therapists need to be more honest about their feelings within the therapeutic setting, both in terms of the generalities of clinical practice and research, and with regard to the more specific considerations of countertransference. Does an academic study preclude the emotions of the researcher? From my own personal experience throughout this project I would answer 'no'. My own inadequacies, dilemmas and sensitivities as a researcher and therapist were integral to the processes and results of the investigation. It was essential that I acknowledged my own vulnerability alongside my knowledge and experience as a musician, researcher and therapist. The death of Clients Two and Three and the physical deterioration of Client One during the writing up of the research added dimensions of emotional intensity that can be identified at all levels of the project.

CONCLUSION

Throughout this research I hoped to develop possible avenues for process-oriented research in music therapy. The results raised more questions than could adequately be answered within the bounds of the project. Further studies need to be undertaken, looking at a complete series of improvisations with both a) an individual client, and b) a whole series of similar or varying clients in order to describe models of therapeutic improvisation. In terms of quantitative and qualitative data and the researcher's interpretation of it, where lies the most appropriate balance that will result in findings which both enhance and inform our clinical practice?

One of the main reasons for choosing the client group described in this chapter was the opportunity it gave for clear, articulate feedback about the music therapy process. The assumption that the empirical examination of verbal material from a person living with HIV and AIDS will provide clear information about the music therapy process can only be significant if it is accepted that the client in question is of sound mind and is unbiased. Of course, it would be foolish to deny the existence of any number of influences which may impinge on a research process. An acknowledgement of the problems, however, may be balanced against the potential for illumination of the music therapy process. Why there is only a small amount of research being undertaken with non-impaired and verbally articulate clients in this country (Hoskyns 1988; Rogers 1991) is an interesting issue. Could it be that the base of information with regard to both clinical practice and research is small, or is it difficult to accommodate the data of verbally articulate clients within the bounds of a strict quantitative study? This leads to the question of 'who is the research for?' It is my view that if the clients needs are not addressed in our research then the findings and results are invalid. Music therapy deals with the *relationship* between therapist and client through music. Is it not possible to redress the number of outcome studies with research that embraces the concepts of collaborative inquiry (Reason and Rowan 1981), doing research *with* rather than *on* people? The terms researcher and co-researcher seem to offer a more balanced and sympathetic approach to researching a process which involves a therapeutic musical interaction between client and therapist, than methodologies where the roles remain firmly those of researcher and subject.

The journey travelled throughout the four years of this research project influenced my concepts of music, music therapy, research and death and dying. That two of the clients were unable to see the fruition of their investment in the research bears testament to both their and my work within HIV and AIDS. To attempt any personal descriptions of my own sense of loss as a therapist, a researcher and an individual without resorting to sentimentality was constantly complex and painful. These difficulties aside, the project enabled me to research music therapy in terms of both music and therapy with equal weight. My belief that behind the exterior aural layers of therapeutic improvisation lies a wealth of musical and therapeutic treasures to be harvested and explored will hopefully begin to gain wider circulation as a result of this research.

ACKNOWLEDGEMENTS

To the Oxford Music Therapy Charity and The Nordoff–Robbins Music Therapy Centre, without whose financial assistance this project would not have been possible. To London Lighthouse and all those people I had the the privilege to know who were, and are, living with the challenge of HIV and AIDS.

NOTES

1 For the purposes of the research the term 'therapeutic improvisation' was chosen to describe music therapy that is based solely on improvisation.
2 Schenker's theory, applicable to tonal music only, investigates analysis from a linear perspective. Taking the tonic note as the basic fundamental, he formulated the hypothesis that the clear cadential principle underlies all musical structure.
3 For a synopsis of the main forms of music analysis see either Cooke (1987) or Dunsby and Whittall (1988).
4 Bar-lines and key signatures were added to the score from the audio recording. They should be regarded as the researcher's subjective representational guide-lines, and thus have been added in brackets and dotted lines. Accidentals were retained on the score as produced via the computer printout (hardcore data). They were not altered to fit any inferred tonal centre and apply only to the notes they precede. Dynamics were incorporated from the audio recordings.
5 The generative cell: the germination of the improvisational procedures from a small group of notes; the seed motif: small musical themes that form the core of the improvisational procedure.

REFERENCES

Bosnak, R. (1989) *Dreaming with an AIDS Patient*. Shambala, Boston and Shaftesbury.
Bunt, L. (1985) 'Music Therapy and the Child with a Handicap: Evaluation of the Effects of Intervention'. Unpublished PhD thesis, City University, London.
Bunt, L. (1990) 'The Artist as Scientist: Is there a Synthesis?' *Proceedings of the Second Arts Therapies Research Conference*. City University, London.
Bunt, L. and Hoskyns, S. (1987) 'A Perspective on Music Therapy Research in Great Britain'. *Journal of British Music Therapy*. 1: 3–6.
Cooke, N. (1987) *A Guide to Musical Analysis*. Dent, London.
Dinnage, R. (1990) *The Ruffian on the Stair: Reflections on Death*. Penguin, London, pp. 191–203.
Dunachie, S. (1991) 'An Investigation of the Improvisations of Mentally Handicapped Adults'. *Music Therapy Research Register*. The Association of Professional Music Therapists in Great Britain.
Dunsby, J. and Whittall, A. (1988) *Music Analysis in Theory and Practice*. Faber Music, London.
Hoskyns, S. (1988) 'Studying Group Music Therapy with Offenders: Research in Progress'. *Psychology of Music*. 16: 26–41.
Lee, C.A. (1989) 'Structural Analysis of Therapeutic Improvisatory Music'. *Journal of British Music Therapy*. 3: 11–19.

Lee, C.A. (1990) 'Structural Analysis of Post-tonal Therapeutic Improvisatory Music'. *Journal of British Music Therapy*. 4: 6–20.

Lee, C.A. (1991) 'Foreword: Endings'. *Journal of British Music Therapy*. 5(1): 3–4.

Lee, C.A. (1992) 'The Analysis of Therapeutic Improvisatory Music with People Living with the Virus HIV and AIDs'. Unpublished PhD thesis, City University, London.

Odell-Miller, H.M. (1989) 'An Investigation into the Effects of Music Therapy with Elderly Mentally Ill People'. Unpublished M.Phil. thesis, City University, London.

Pavlicevic, M. (1991) 'Music in Communication: Improvisation in Music Therapy'. Unpublished PhD thesis, Edinburgh University.

Reason, P. and Rowan, J. (Eds) (1981) *Human Inquiry: A Sourcebook of New Paradigm Research*. John Wiley, Chichester.

Rogers, P. (1991) 'Working with Sexually Abused Clients using a Psychodynamic Approach'. *The Fifth Music Therapy Research Conference*. City University, London.

Rudd, E. (1990) 'A Phenomenological Approach to Improvisation in Music Therapy: A Research Method'. *The Sixth World Congress of Music Therapy*. Rio de Janeiro, 15–20 July.

Schmidt, J.A. (1984) 'Structural Analysis of Clinical Music an Important Tool for Music Therapy Practice and Research'. *Music Therapy*. 4: 18–28.

Steele, P.H. and Dunachie, S. (1986) 'Towards a Musical Process Model of Research'. *The First Music Therapy Research Conference*. City University, London.

Van Colle, S. (1991) 'Music Therapy Process with Cerebral Palsied Children'. *Music Therapy Research Register*. The Association of Professional Music Therapists in Great Britain.

Winiarski, M. (1991) *AIDS-related Psychotherapy*. Pergamon General Psychology, Oxford.

Chapter 3

Music and emotion
Aspects of music therapy research

Mercedes Pavlicevic

Human beings have always imbued music with powers to evoke the Gods, to embrace and embody the vastness of the human spirit and, more recently, to heal. In Western thinking, music's established and secure place in the world of the arts has proved difficult for music therapists, for whom music exists in the world of healing. For music therapists there is a converging question: where and how do music-as-art and music-as-therapy meet, if at all?

This chapter begins by touching on artistic creativity, emotional creativity and creativity in music therapy, as a prelude to a fuller discussion on forming processes in music therapy. I clarify the distinction *and* the link between art form, emotional form and dynamic form in music therapy, and then address what I understand to be key music therapy research issues: what does the musical act in music therapy mean? What inferences can be made about the person from their musical acts? I attempt to clarify these various aspects of research by proposing some hypothetical models in conclusion.

CREATIVITY

Artistic creativity

In Western musical tradition, the creative act usually culminates in a musical composition (or improvisation), and a long and rich tradition of thought presents us with highly developed understandings and descriptions of music's aesthetic value. As music therapists, we are drawn to that particular literature in music aesthetics which makes it clear that the act of creating or composing music has to do with *much more* than creating and organising sound. The musical process, some composers assure us, is imbued with inner, emotional meaning for the composer: the act of composing offers the composer a new synthesis of the Self (Copland 1952; Stravinsky 1974; Tippett 1974; Langer 1979; Cook 1990). The fact that it is composers and musicians themselves who make the link between inner, emotional processes, and the act of musical creation is reassuring for music therapists, whose praxis is based on that very premiss, but whose tradition of thought and research is so much younger and less established.

Emotional creativity

Writers such as Winnicott (1971, 1988) and Storr (1972) have made it clear that creativity exists not only in 'artistic' works, but that it is a feature of being-in-the-world. Creativity has to do with the capacity to exist in the world with a clear sense of a subjective Self, *and* to perceive the world objectively, as both part of, and separate from, oneself. Viewed with this understanding, we see that persons who are able to be in the world creatively exist neither wholly in their inner world, distant and removed from the external world, nor wholly in the outer world, 'out of touch' with their inner, privately subjective world. They have the capacity to be influenced by the external world of objects, and to remain separate from it – i.e. to objectify it. Winnicott calls this the capacity to be 'authentically autonomous'.

Although artistic creativity and emotional creativity are interlinked, emotional creativity also exists as a life process in itself, separate from artistic creativity. Emotional creativity may or may not be expressed through a work of art.

Creativity in therapy

My understanding is that in music therapy it is the person's emotional creativity – or the person's capacity for authentic autonomy – which is tapped, rather than their 'purely' artistic creativity (Pavlicevic 1990). In music therapy emotional creativity is sounded *through* the musical act; music and emotion are 'fused', so to speak. The one presents the other. And yet each of these has its own, separate system of thought. It is my view that, as music therapists, we need to be clear about this pivotal interface between the two if we are to escape confusion in research. This will be elaborated later.

FORMING IS BEING

In music therapy, the act of improvising music with (or without) the therapist enables the person to hear and experience themselves through sound. It is my understanding that the process of *forming*, of moving towards coherent and fluid form, is the therapeutic process. Aldridge *et al.* (1990) put it succinctly:

When we introduce form and order into the creative act then we promote a higher form of human articulation. This is the process of healing – the escape from emotive fragmentation to the creative act of becoming whole.

(p. 195)

To clarify music therapy processes for research purposes, I concentrate here on three aspects of form: artistic form, emotional form and, finally, dynamic form in therapy.

Emotional form

The qualitative ingredients of our communicative acts have been clarified by Stern (1985). These amodal qualities of feeling, which he calls 'vitality affects', are intensity, shape, contour, motion and number, and are common to all modes of expression, be it movement, vocal or facial expression. These exist in our minds as abstracted forms, not bound to any particular gesture or feeling, and are expressed through any of our senses. Thus intensity could be described as the amount of energy in a vocal sound, in a movement, in a smile or in a river which has burst its banks.

Psychologists such as Condon and Ogston (1966), Trevarthen (1980, 1984, 1986), Stern (1985), Brown and Avstreih (1989) and Murray (1989) offer useful insights into emotional form. Although they use different experimental contexts, a common theme in their work is that self-organisation and self-coherence are at the root of being an emotionally co-ordinated human being, with a clear sense of a subjective Self, and with a fully-fledged capacity to engage in the world meaningfully. It is our capacity to form ourselves into coherent human beings, as well as our capacity to respond to the communicative form of another human being, that lies at the root of human communication. It is this self-coherence (which some psychologists call self-synchrony), contained in the integrated quality of our acts, that gives us a sense of subjectivity (Trevarthen 1987).

Those psychologists who have examined in micro-detail the communicative and expressive acts of mothers and newborn babies demonstrate the communicating partners' mutual sensitivity and responsiveness to one another, revealed through constant interpersonal adjusting of the vitality affects of gestural events. Thus, a mother and baby 'know' one another through reading the emotional coherence of one another's gestures (e.g. the intensity of a mother's smile will match the intensity of her vocal sounds, and this will present the intensity of her internal state at the time). A mother and baby respond to one another by constantly adapting and adjusting the intensity, timing, contour and volume of their acts (the baby 'reads' the intensity in the mother's acts and responds to it).

Similarly, highly empathic communicating adults show a sensitivity to one another with regard to the timing, contours and energy of their communicative acts (Beebe *et al.* 1985).

The absence, collapse or severe limitation of self-synchrony results in stilted and limited interactional synchrony. Condon and Ogston (1966) found that people who suffer from severe mental illness not only lack self-synchrony, but show a collapsed or decreased capacity to enter into interactional synchrony with another person. Here, the sense of subjectivity – the subjective experience of selfhood – is dented, collapsed or interrupted.

As communicating beings, humans present themselves to the world as co-ordinated, cohesive beings, and this coherence is a subjective one: it is a feature of being in the world as a unique person, separate from it and linked into it. It is the quality of the internal state (how intense? fragmented? rough? smooth?), revealed by the constantly fluctuating shifts of selfhood that I understand as emotional form. Emotional form does not exist in a solitary vacuum, but is intrinsic to being-in-communion-with-the-world. Emotional form is more than just expressive, it is communicative. Emotional form is revealed through basic human communication – indeed, it might be said that humans need to be in communication with one another in order to 'know' how they are in the world.

Art form

Langer (1979) has argued that artistic form cannot exist devoid of emotional import: art form without emotion is sterile, she says, and the patterns of tension and resolution, inherent in all art, reflect human feeling. Similarly Arnheim (1986), through using different contexts, proposes that both art form and the world of human feelings have a single, inherent dynamic structure. Stravinsky (1974) supports this view by insisting that stylistic form and the conventions of musical tradition are essential to him as a composer. The external structures of musical form contain his artistic impulses – indeed, he writes of needing the boundaries of style so as not to feel terrified by the abyss which its absence would present. The presence of art form, refined and honed over many centuries of musical energy, provides him with secure boundaries for his creativity.

Despite these and other assertions about the emotional content of artistic form, many approaches to musical analysis concentrate on the 'purely musical' (and I suspect potentially sterile?) structure of musical works. Thus, a piece of music could be analysed from various perspectives. The music could be analysed from a structural/perceptual dimension, and questions could be asked about whether the music has a sense of conjunction or disjunction; whether it falls within binary, tertiary or rondo form; how the various themes and motifs are sequenced; how the two players' sequences interact – what is their trigger point. And so on. However, while revealing complex and fascinating aspects of the musical processes, this is far from adequate in revealing something about the emotional import of the music – import which, aestheticians and composers assure us, exists. It would seem, from the immense literature on musical form and analysis, that structural analyses of composed (and even improvised) music satisfies most musical scholars, while leaving the music aestheticians less than satisfied.

Where does this leave music therapists?

Dynamic form in music therapy

Bjorkvold's (1987) angle on musical/emotional form is useful for clarifying the fusion or interface between music and emotion alluded to earlier. It is this interface which I call dynamic form: dynamic form is distinct both from art form and from emotional form, but contains both. Bjorkvold discusses musical form in young (four- to six-year-old) children's spontaneous vocalisations, which he studied in Scandinavia, Leningrad and southern California. These vocalisations are not syntactically or aesthetically refined or sophisticated, as are stylistic art forms. Rather, they are produced as a natural expression of the child's inner dynamic life, and their form, which is highly subjective, is a function of the role of the vocalisation in fulfilling the child's immediate needs. He cites an example of a child playing with a paper aeroplane, whose glissando vocal sounds will accompany the motions of the plane's movements. Spontaneous vocalisations such as solitary song monologues tend to have a fluid, amorphous form, and their role can be to provide the child with access to, or an opportunity to experiment with, his inner world. In this sense they are solitary and intrasubjective, although they can also be used to great effect socially.

Musical speech acts, whose role is to communicate specific social intentions, such as teasing, calling, commanding or relating to another, tend to be brief: Bjorkvold describes specific intervals, such as the falling minor and major third, which he has found in several cultures. Pre-set songs can also have a social as well as cultural function: they imply a group cohesion or structure. They can accompany either solitary or group play activities, and provide a contextual frame, or an emotional back-up to the activity.

This creating of sound form for emotional intent by children is nearer to the concept of dynamic form in music therapy: it is a form whose features are not exclusively musical, but neither are they exclusively emotional. Rather, dynamic form is a consequence of its psychological function, which is to explore, communicate and receive emotion in organised sound. In my view, it is dynamic form that the therapist elicits in music therapy, and dynamic form is at the heart of the therapeutic process in music therapy.

In music therapy, the person organises and experiences the elements of pulse, rhythm, metre, melody, harmony, dynamic and timbre as a statement of themselves-in-the-world. The form of these elements is communicatively, rather than purely musically, meaningful. This musical/emotional form, which is a statement of the self in the world, is what I call dynamic form in music therapy (Pavlicevic 1990, 1991). The essence of dynamic form is emotionally communicative, while its elements are artistic. Its dynamic elements are inherent both to music and to human emotion. Dynamic form reveals the interface of music and emotion, but only where the improvisation has a communicative rather than a purely musical agenda.

The amodality and abstractness of human emotional form, which Stern (1985) described earlier (i.e. intensity, contour, shape, motion and number), are portrayed in musically expressive features and their fluctuating, constantly shifting contours. These expressive features of both music and direct human communication exist as abstract, functional entities in the mind. They are signalled through the quality of our expressive acts and through the expressive quality of musical improvisation in music therapy.

I think it is critical to stress that not just any musical improvisation in music therapy will do: Nordoff and Robbins (1971,1977) pioneered techniques in clinical improvisation which enable a highly intimate and emotionally dynamic relationship to develop between the therapist and the person within the shared musical context. It is my understanding that clinical improvisation techniques enable the sounding of dynamic form: they enable the person to present their communicative features of intensity, contour, shape, motion and number through their spontaneous musical utterances (Pavlicevic 1990, 1991, in press).

Thus, music therapists using these particular clinical improvisation techniques might describe the improvisations in music therapy not in 'purely' musical terms but in terms of dynamic form: they might suggest that unstructured, un-formed musical utterances present the person's unstructured, fragmented Self (much as Condon and Ogston's study (1966) demonstrated the absence of self- and interactional-synchrony in severely mentally ill adults). They will also assert that increasing flexibility of musical inter-utterances over sessions corresponds to, or presents, the process of integration and synthesis within the Self (Nordoff and Robbins 1971; Aldridge 1989).

RESEARCH IN MUSIC THERAPY

Any enquiry into music therapy may address the meaning of the creative act in the therapeutic context. We might ask, therefore, what the creative process in therapy means. Our primary understanding is that the person's musical act is about more than just music: it is the *Self* that is being presented to us, through the medium, and it is the Self which we imbue with meaning. To quote from Aldridge (1989):

> It may be inferred from this playing that one is hearing a person directly in the world as a direct expression of those patterned frequencies in a matrix of time. . . . What can be heard is the person being in the world.
>
> (p. 96)

But this act of being in the world is stated through the act of playing music – which has its own paradigms of enquiry. In terms of an enquiry, then, research emerges with more clarity: how do we distinguish this art form, whose essence is artistic but which carries emotional meaning, from dynamic form whose essence is emotional, but whose elements are artistic? Or, to put the question from a slightly different position, how do these two forms, which carry the same dimensions (i.e. emotion and music) reveal their different emphasis? How can we, on listening to a music improvisation, distinguish between an improvisation which has a 'purely' musical agenda, in contrast to one whose agenda is emotional/communicative?

Do we look to the music utterances and make inferences about the Self? Do we begin with the musical experience during the session (Lee 1989) or do we enter into a broader view, as did Andsell (1991) in his illuminating map, and, if so, how do we connect this to the level of inference? Or, to take another perspective, we could examine three levels of reporting, as set out by Aldridge *et al.* (1990), i.e. those of experience (the phenomenon as it is experienced), of description (in relation to musical idiom), and/or interpretation (the explanation of the musical in terms of psychological processes).

In theory, we can suggest that the intent underlying the improvisation is the distinguishing feature, since creativity in art has as its intent the new formalising of musical/artistic ingredients (a process which, we acknowledge, engages the Self). In music therapy, the intent underlying the form is the Self: to express, present and communicate the Self (a process which, we have seen, uses musical/artistic ingredients).

I would like to attempt to clarify the distinction between 'emotional' and 'purely musical' processes in music therapy by presenting and discussing various hypothetical models. These all approach the issue from slightly different angles.

Model One: polarising perspectives

In Figure 3.1, the musical and personal/emotional processes in music therapy are separated *and* polarised (in contrast to earlier discussion where

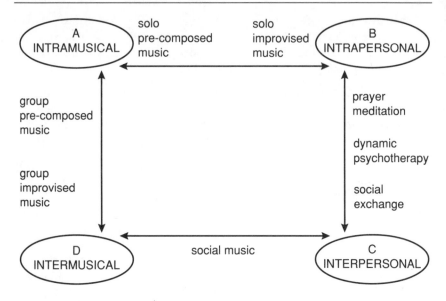

Figure 3.1 Music and personal/emotional processes

they were presented as 'fused'). The four polarities presented here are: A, the intramusical state, i.e. the individual's internal musical experience; B, the intrapersonal state, i.e. the individual's selfhood or processes of the Self; C, the interpersonal state, which is the relating between the Self and the 'Other'; and D, the intermusical state, which is the shared musical experience.

If we examine, first of all, the relationship between B and C (that is, the intrapersonal and the interpersonal processes), we could position any human interaction along this line, on the understanding that the interpersonal influences, and is influenced by, the intrapersonal. Interactions along this spectrum might range from dynamic psychotherapy, which combines the interpersonal with the intrapersonal (the exploration of self in the context of a relationship), to a more socially oriented situation such as a task-oriented gathering, where there would be less emphasis on the intrapersonal and more on the interpersonal. If we move towards the intrapersonal end of the same spectrum, here we might position the state of deep meditation, with its utter focus upon the Self, and less emphasis on the interpersonal. If we now examine the A–B spectrum (that is, the intramusical and intrapersonal processes) we might find the solo act of playing pre-composed music nearer the A polarity (i.e. intramusical) than the B polarity (i.e. intrapersonal). This does not mean that playing solo pre-composed music excludes the intrapersonal, but rather that the emphasis is at the very least on both, if not tending towards the A polarity. If, however, we look at a solo jazz improvisation, we might well place this on the same spectrum,

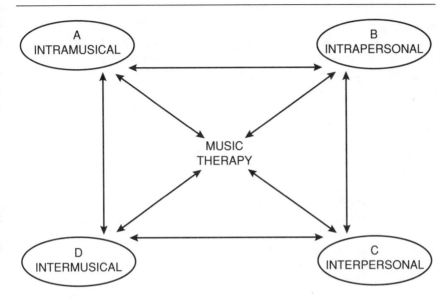

Figure 3.2 Music therapy and the four polarities

but nearer the B polarity of the intrapersonal, arguing that the spontaneity and unpredictability of jazz engages more of the Self than does playing someone else's music. If we now examine the A–D spectrum (the intra-musical and the intermusical) and think about group music-making, we might position the group playing pre-composed music nearer to the inter-musical polarity, while a group jazz improvisation would lean towards the intermusical.

Model One (B): music therapy within the polarities

Here I still choose to maintain the musical and personal as separate and polarised. In terms of attempting to clarify the musical and the personal in music therapy, we could, for argument's sake, position music therapy at the centre of these four polarities and see it as containing aspects of all four polarities, to a greater or lesser extent (Figure 3.2). Thus, the dynamic nature of the musical relationship between the person and music therapist includes the interpersonal, C, as well as the intermusical, D (the intermu-sical reveals the interpersonal); and because music therapy is not just about playing music but about the self, it includes B (intrapersonal) as well as A (intramusical) – though the latter, I would suggest, to a lesser extent.

In terms of research, then, we might choose to examine any of these polarities in isolation. Thus, in examining the music therapy process of a person, we might focus on A (intramusical) and ask: how 'musical' is this person, what is the quality of her musical display? And leave it at that. Or we might examine B (intrapersonal) and ask: what is going on within that person, there and then? We might answer this by ignoring the musical aspect of the session altogether, or by making inferences about the intra-personal through the musical processes. At C (interpersonal) we might examine the quality of the interpersonal relationship between the person and therapist: what are the features of the transference and countertrans-ference? Again this might be inferred from the musical processes, or gleaned directly. And finally at D (intermusical) we might examine the musical relationship between the two players: does their joint playing 'fit'? Or not?

Alternatively, we might choose to examine one spectrum: thus, along A–D (intra–intermusical) we might ask about the intramusical features of the intermusical relationship: what does each player bring to the joint improvisation or to the joint performance of pre-composed music? What does the intermusical reveal about the intramusical? And so on.

This positioning of music therapy among these polarities simply suggests the dimensions that research might take. It also suggests that there is a link between them. Thus, while any one dimension may be seen as valid as a research focus, the overall context cannot simply be ignored. Rather, a convincing argument needs to be presented for choosing that particular dimension.

Model Two: music improvisation and dynamic form improvisation

Another way of attempting to clarify the distinction between the 'artistic' and the 'emotional' aspects of a person's acts in music therapy would be to compare a joint improvisation which has a 'purely' musical agenda (say, a jazz improvisation) to one which has a 'communicative' agenda. The two improvisations could be evaluated from both a musical and an emotional/communicative perspective, i.e. the jazz improvisation would be evaluated for both 'musical' and 'communicative' value, as would the music therapy improvisation (Figure 3.3). If music therapy improvisation is more about dynamic form than artistic form, and if a 'purely musical' improvisation, such as jazz, is more about art form than emotional form, then we would expect the music therapy improvisation to get a lower score than the jazz improvisation for musical/aesthetic value, and a higher score for emotional/communicative value.

This hypothetical model is presented to clarify my own understanding of the distinctions between art form and emotional form, as discussed earlier. Thus, I suggest that an improvisation whose agenda is the creation of artistic form, while containing emotional significance, leans more towards the 'musical': its key focus could be seen as being aesthetic rather than emotional communication. In contrast, an improvisation whose agenda is the sounding of dynamic form, whilst using musical elements, can be seen

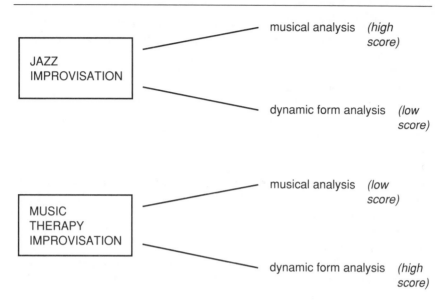

Figure 3.3 Music therapy improvisation

as primarily about direct emotional communication: its musical/aesthetic content might sound rather odd.

But perhaps we could go further in attempting to distinguish between 'musical' and 'emotional' processes. The next model treats them as 'fused' rather than 'polarised'.

Model Three: clinical improvisation with/without illness

In order to tease out the purely musical aspect and the emotional/communicative aspect of communicative musical acts in music therapy, we might compare the clinical improvisations of people with mental illness or learning difficulties (severe enough to disrupt self-synchrony) with the clinical improvisations of people who are 'well'. These clinical improvisations could then be analysed from both the musical and the emotional/communicative perspectives. If dynamic form is indeed evoked in music therapy improvisation, and if the focus of the improvisation really is communicative rather than purely musical (as in clinical improvisation techniques), then we would expect the person's emotional state to interfere with the quality of their musical acts (we have seen earlier that emotion and music are fused in dynamic form, and the musical process presents the emotional process). Thus, we would expect those people with damaged or collapsed capacities for self- and interactional synchrony (e.g. severely mentally ill people), to show a lack of organisation and a limited capacity for dynamic musical interaction with the therapist.

For example, we would select four people (or four groups of people), A,B,C and D, according to the following criteria: A would have substantial musical experience and be free from illness or disability, while B would also have substantial musical experience but suffer from mental illness (e.g. bi-polar depression or chronic schizophrenia). C would have no musical experience and be free from illness, whilst D would also have no musical experience but, like B, suffer from mental illness. Each of these would have a musical improvisation with a music therapist (who would not be briefed on the four people), using clinical improvisation techniques as described earlier. The improvisations would be evaluated by a blind rater for the purely musical aspects of their performance, and then for the emotional/interactive quality of their performance. The four people would then be ranked for both aspects separately.

If assertions about dynamic form and clinical improvisation techniques are accurate, we could expect a difference in the ranking of the four people, depending on whether we were evaluating the 'musical' or 'emotional'.

If we rated their improvisations for their purely musical content, we might expect their ranking to be as follows (see Table 3.1): A, with musical skill but without illness, would show the highest level of musical performance, since their musical skill and experience would enable the improvisation to be musically complex and cover extensive musical ground. We would expect B, with musical skill plus a pathological syndrome, to be next since their musical skill would see them through the musical act. C, with no musical skill and without illness, would probably be ranked third since, despite the lack of musical experience, their inherent expressive flexibility and coherence would give their playing some form; and finally D, with no skill and with illness, would score the lowest: as well as having no skill, their musical acts would lack expressive and subjective coherence and structure because of their inner pathology.

However, if we evaluated the same performances for their emotional/ interactive capacities, rather than their musical ones, i.e. taking into account the communicative and expressive features of their playing (Nordoff and Robbins 1977; Andsell 1991; Pavlicevic, 1991), then we would expect the ranking would be different (see Table 3.2).

Here A, with musical skill and without illness, would probably still show the highest level of interaction; I base this assumption on the fact that they would feel comfortable with the medium itself, and have access to their own

Table 3.1 Ranking for 'musical performance' only

A	Musical skill – illness	1	high
B	Musical skill + illness	2	
C	No skill – illness	3	
D	No skill + illness	4	low

Table 3.2 Ranking for interactive/emotional features

A	Musical skill – illness	1	high
C	No skill – illness	2	
B	Musical Skill + illness	3	
D	No skill + illness	4	low

emotional coherence and flexibility, revealed through dynamically shifting, fluid and expansive dynamic form. However, as distinct from Table 3.1 C, with no musical skill and without illness, might well rank second. This could be explained as follows: despite having no musical skill, she or he would have the capacity to acknowledge and respond to the therapist sensitively and assertively, so that the quality of self-expressiveness and of engagement with the therapist would be reciprocal, despite limited musical vocabulary. We would expect B, who has musical skill plus illness, to be ranked third. This allows for musical skill to carry him or her through the improvisations, while their inner fragmentation and lack of self-coherence would severely limit the fluidity and coherence of their dynamic form, as well as limit the quality of their engagement with the therapist. Finally, D would still rank last, with pathology interfering with the dynamic form whilst, to compound the limited interaction, the absence of any musical experience might interfere with her or his comfort in using the instruments.

The (hypothetical) difference in these rankings is used merely to illustrate that the presence of pathology (and its manifestation in a collapsed sense of subjectivity and a severely limited capacity to interact synchronously) interferes with the sounding of dynamic form in music therapy. This hypothetical situation was, to some extent, borne out by a study (Pavlicevic and Trevarthen, 1989) which showed that psychotic subjects with some musical skill scored better than those with no skill, on a scale which measured the interactive rather than the musical processes; on the whole, however, their scores were lower than either the 'neurotic' subjects' or the 'normal' controls'.

This subtle distinction of emphasis is one that music therapists need to be clear about in research, since it has implications for the making of inferences about the person through their musical utterances in music therapy.

CONCLUSION

Music therapists wishing to embark on research face an abyss of silence. Music therapy research literature is a fairly recent phenomenon and, by and large, experimental studies which are genuinely about music therapy (rather than about music psychology, or music psychology research with subjects who might be mentally ill or mentally handicapped) are thin on the ground. However, a rich tradition of literature exists in allied fields – such as psychiatry, psychology, psychotherapy, neurology, musical aesthetics and musical analysis – and music therapists need to be confident about crossing the great divides, building bridges and venturing into the unfamiliar. This chapter has attempted to offer some bridges by concentrating on the distinction between musical and emotional processes in music therapy. It is a distinction which I believe is critical: without a clear understanding of what it is that makes our work unique, different from *and* similar to that of other, allied professions, we cannot be confident about presenting ourselves as researchers.

REFERENCES

Aldridge, D. (1989) 'A Phenomenological Comparison of the Organization of Music and the Self'. *The Arts in Psychotherapy.* 16: 91–7.

Aldridge, D., Brandt, G. and Wohler, D. (1990) 'Toward a Common Language among the Creative Art Therapies'. *The Arts in Psychotherapy.* 17: 189–95.

Andsell, G. (1991) 'Mapping the Territory'. *Journal of British Music Therapy.* 5: 18–27.

Arnheim, R. (1986) *New Essays on the Psychology of Art.* University of California Press, Berkeley.

Beebe, B., Feldstein, S., Jaffe, J., Mays, K. and Alson, D. (1985) 'Interpersonal Timing: The Application of an Adult Dialogue Model to Mother-Infant Vocal and Kinesic Interactions'. In: Field, T.M. and Fox, N. (Eds) *Social Perception in Infants.* Ablex, Norwood, NJ.

Bjorkvold, J-R. (1987) 'Our Musical Mother Tongue – World Wide: Some Communicative Traits of the Spontaneous Singing of Young Children in Oslo, Leningrad and Southern California'. In: Soderbergh, R. (Ed.) *Children's Creative Communication.* Lund University Press, Lund.

Brown, J.J. and Avstreigh, Z.A.K. (1989) 'On Synchrony'. *The Arts in Psychotherapy.* 16: 157–62.

Condon, W.S. and Ogston, W.D. (1966) 'Sound Film Analysis of Normal and Pathological Behavior Patterns'. *The Journal of Nervous and Mental Diseases.* 143: 338–47.

Cook, N. (1990) *Music, Imagination, and Culture.* Clarendon Press, Oxford.

Copland, A. (1952) *Music and Imagination,* Cambridge University Press, Cambridge, MA.

Langer, S. (1979) *Philosophy in a New Key.* Harvard University Press, Cambridge, MA.

Lee, C.A. (1989) 'Structural Analysis of Therapeutic Improvisatory Music'. *Journal of British Music Therapy.* 11–19.

Murray, L. (1989) 'Winnicott and the Developmental Psychology of Infancy'. *British Journal of Psychotherapy.* 5: 333–48.

Nordoff, P. and Robbins, C. (1971) *Therapy in Music for Handicapped Children.* Gollancz, London.

Nordoff, P. and Robbins, C. (1977) *Creative Music Therapy: Individualised Treatment for the Handicapped Child.* John Day, New York.

Pavlicevic, M. (1990) 'Dynamic Interplay in Clinical Improvisation'. *Journal of British Music Therapy.* 4: 5–10.

Pavlicevic, M. (1991) 'Music in Communication: Improvisation in Music Therapy', Unpublished PhD thesis, University of Edinburgh.

Pavlicevic, M. (in press) 'Interpersonal Processes in Clinical Improvisation'. In: Saperson, B., West, R. and Wigram, A. (Eds) *Music and the Healing Process.* Carden Publications, Chichester.

Pavlicevic, M. and Trevarthen, C. (1989) 'A Musical Assessment of Psychiatric States in Adults'. *Psychopathology.* 22: 325–34.

Stern, D. (1985) *The Interpersonal World of the Infant: A View from Psychoanalysis and Developmental Psychology.* Basic Books, New York.

Storr, A. (1972) *The Dynamics of Creation.* Penguin, Harmondsworth.

Stravinsky, I. (1974) *Poetics of Music.* Harvard University Press, Cambridge, MA.

Tippett, M. (1974) *Moving into Aquarius.* Paladin, St Albans.

Trevarthen, C. (1980) 'The Foundations of Intersubjectivity: Development of Interpersonal and Cooperative Understanding in Infants'. In: Olson, D.K. (Ed.) *The Social Foundation of Language and Thought: Essays in Honor of J.S. Bruner.* Norton, New York.

Trevarthen, C. (1984) 'Emotions in Infancy: Regulators of Contacts and Relationships with Persons'. In: Sherer, K. and Ekman, P. (Eds) *Approaches to Emotion.* Erlbaum, Hillsdale, NJ.

Trevarthen, C. (1986) 'Development of Intersubjective Motor Control in Infants'. In: Wade, M. and Whiting, H.T.A. (Eds) *Motor Development: Aspects of Coordination and Control.* Martinus Nijhof, Dordrecht.

Trevarthen, C. (1987) 'Sharing Makes Sense: Intersubjectivity and the Making of an Infant's Meaning'. In: Steele, R. and Threadgold, T. (Eds) *Language Topics: Essays in Honour of Michael Halliday,* J. Benjamins, Amsterdam.

Winnicott, D.W. (1971) *Playing and Reality.* Tavistock, London.

Winnicott, D.W. (1988) *Human Nature.* Free Association Books, London.

Chapter 4

Changes in art therapy groups

Andrea Gilroy

This chapter describes a part of my doctoral research project. The aim was to explore some of the changes occurring within experiential art therapy groups which are part of postgraduate education in art therapy. This work was at the mid-point of research which explored the processes of occupational choice and career development of art therapists with particular reference to their practice as artists (Gilroy 1989, 1992). I saw membership of the group as a pivotal experience in art therapy students' careers, a place where their personal histories and occupational motivations as artists and art therapists would meet and be mutually influential, leading to change in their subsequent art practice. It seemed that students would either integrate their experiences in the group with previous art practice, withdraw in some way from their art work either in the group and/or later, or continue to engage in an art practice which effectively split 'Art' from art as therapy. The research was largely undertaken at my place of work in the Art Psychotherapy Unit of the University of London, Goldsmiths' College.

Research which explored the processes of occupational choice and career development provided well-trodden theoretical and methodological pathways (Henry *et al.* 1971; Henry 1977; Racusin *et al.* 1981). However, trying to analyse the changes within experiential art therapy groups was uncharted territory. There were a number of difficult issues: conducting research in an on-going group, the dynamic interactions between the students and myself when participation in the group was part of their training, and addressing the art work in the group. It was a complex undertaking which involved consideration of the processes and outcomes of the group as well as evaluation of individual change within it. I used a mixture of qualitative and quantitative methodologies: namely interviews, case study and questionnaires. In the group questionnaire I asked respondents to rate their responses to a number of statements and give open-ended comments to a few questions. Lack of space prevents full presentation of this material. I have chosen instead to focus on the quantitative material because, as an almost innumerate researcher, I had doubts about my ability to work with the quantitative data, and was also concerned about the impact of this kind of data collection procedure on the group.

In this chapter I will describe the evolution of the research design, the nuts and bolts of data collection and analysis, and discuss the main issues I encountered as a researcher, art therapy educator and group conductor.

THE LITERATURE ON ART THERAPY GROUPS

Bibliographic searches revealed an absence of research on experiential art therapy groups. Most of the literature on art therapy groups is general and describes authors' clinical work, addressing issues such as structures and boundaries and the appropriateness of differing approaches for varying client populations (e.g. Denny 1975; Lachman-Chapin 1976; Wadeson 1980; Liebmann 1981; McNeilly 1983, 1987, 1989; Skaife 1990; Strand 1990; Waller 1993). Research on art therapy groups in Britain is limited to Liebmann's survey-based study of theme-centred groups (1981), Greenwood and Layton's case study-based research on a group of psychotic patients (1987, 1991), and Nowell Hall's interview-based follow-up study of an art therapy group (1987). American research includes descriptive studies which address the difficulties of running art therapy groups within acute psychiatry (Buoye-Allen 1983; Vogt and Vogt 1983); an experimental study showing that improvements made in an art therapy group for chronically mentally ill patients were maintained (Borchers 1985); and papers which describe technique-oriented sessions where imagery is used merely as a prompt to verbal interaction (Shatin and Kymissis 1975; Wolff 1975). This literature did not address my particular interests and so I turned to the research literature in group psychotherapy, hoping to clarify my research questions and find some clues about methodology.

GROUP PSYCHOTHERAPY RESEARCH

The research literature on group therapy is considerable.[1] For the sake of brevity I will concentrate on one text, Lieberman *et al.* (1973), focusing on a particular aspect of their research. Yalom states that despite the variety of approaches, theoretical frameworks, goals and leader styles, core methods and 'mechanisms of change' in all groups are similar (Yalom 1975). Further, he argues that the goals of groups which attempt characterologic change will, whatever the theoretical approach, draw on group cohesion and interpersonal action amongst the members. Together with Lieberman and Miles, Yalom explored these 'mechanisms of change' through attention to, amongst other issues, 'psychosocial relationships' in groups. This was part of a large study which involved 210 students at Stanford University who took part in eighteen different kinds of 'encounter' groups over a period of thirty hours with sixteen leaders who had different leadership styles. Psychosocial relationships were measured through a 'sociometric questionnaire' which asked respondents to consider both their own and others' behaviour in the groups. Lieberman *et al.* were able to identify particular group members who played an important role in groups through taking on what they describe as a 'VCIA role', i.e. they were individuals who were Influential and Active and whose Values were Congruent with the goals of the group. Such people were found to take risks, were spontaneous, expressed themselves and were helpful to the group through their influence and activity. There was considerable agreement between the VCIA members' self-perceptions and the perceptions of them by other members of the group, although a VCIA member's self-perceptions changed more during the group than other members' perceptions of him or her. Those who were able to learn about themselves in and as a consequence of the group significantly increased their 'VCIA role', and those who were distresssed by the group significantly declined in their 'VCIA role' (Lieberman *et al.* 1973).

Lieberman *et al.*'s research demonstrated that group members were likely to experience specific changes in their behaviour during the group. This posed a question about whether analogous changes could be found in the behaviour of students in experiential art therapy groups. Would their 'VCIA' roles increase or decline as they became either more or less open, spontaneous and self-aware? Would art therapy students' self- and other-perceptions be congruent, but with self-perceived change being greater than other-perceived change? Lieberman *et al.*'s research enabled me to articulate clear questions about the possible *behaviour* of group members. It also gave me the framework for a methodology with which to explore the changes in behaviour and art work within experiential art therapy groups.

RESEARCH DESIGN

The study overall was based upon data collected from two consecutive academic year groups of art therapy students, together with a survey of registered art therapists (Gilroy 1989, 1992). In the work described here I used a mixture of methods; I kept process notes week by week, discussed group members' expectations and later reflections about the group in interviews, and administered a questionnaire three times. This included thirty-two items which gathered a mixture of quantitative and qualitative data through the measurement of students' perceptions, both of themselves and of each other, regarding behaviour and art work in the group. The questionnaire was directly based on Lieberman *et al.*'s work, with the behavioural descriptors in my questionnaire being directly adapted from their 'sociometric questionnaire' (Lieberman *et al.* 1973, p. 336). The

Table 4.1 Statements used in the Art Therapy Group Questionnaire

Behaviour
1 Expresses own feelings openly and directly.
2 Does a lot to help the group move along with its work.
3 Takes risks, is willing to try things, is not cautious.
4 Is spontaneous, does things freely on the spur of the moment.
5 Is out of the group, not really involved in the group.
6 Listens to feedback from others, does not get defensive.
7 Sees self clearly, does not kid self about his/her own strengths and weaknesses.
8 Shows a contradiction between what s/he says and what s/he does.
9 Is influential in what happens in the group; is able to get the group to do what s/he wants.
10 Seems to be learning a lot in the group.

Art work
11 Is willing to share his/her art work and is open to comment about it from other group members.
12 Generally speaking is aware of the meaning of his/her art work.
13 Works spontaneously with the art materials; is willing to take risks and relinquish what is comfortable in so far as working methods, symbolism and imagery are concerned.
14 Shows a contradiction between what s/he says about his/her art work and what the work conveys to the group.
15 Is fearful, inhibited and threatened by the uncovering of unconscious meanings in his/her art work.
16 Seems to be learning a lot in the group about the meaning of his/her art work.

questionnaire employed a series of statements to which students were asked to respond in differing ways (see Table 4.1). I chose to retain statements from Lieberman *et al.* which I thought relevant to *behaviour* in art therapy groups, e.g. group cohesion, spontaneity and self-awareness, numbering ten items in all, and adapted five items so that they would be relevant to particular behaviours regarding *art work* made in the group (Table 4.1, nos. 11, 12, 13, 14 and 16). I also included an item on fear of the latent, unconscious meanings that may emerge in imagery (no. 15). This was because experience had led me to believe that a growing aware-ness of previously unknown meanings in imagery could be frightening and inhibiting as well as exciting and liberating, and therefore might be a significant area of change in art therapy groups.

In the art therapy group questionnaire there were therefore ten items on group interactive behaviour and six items on art work, all of which asked for self- and other-perceptions. Items 1–16 asked group members to name two people in the group whose behaviour and art work seemed most like, and a further two people who seemed least like, each statement made. Items 17–32 asked group members to rate their own behaviour and art work on five-point scales (with 5 being very true and 1 totally untrue) on the same series of statements as for their perceptions of others. A final two questions asked for open comment on the most significant piece of art work and the most significant event in the group (material not addressed in this chapter). Finding a method for assessing group members' behaviour *per se* and their behaviour regarding their art work, and exploring significant events and images through qualitative description in the questionnaire, enabled me to formulate a research design with 'hard' and 'soft' elements which measured the changes whilst retaining the voices of the students.

The questionnaire was administered to two art therapy groups (in two consecutive academic years) on three occasions; early in the year (after three sessions of the group), at the mid-point of the year, and shortly after the academic year had ended. The students in the group had all fulfilled the usual criteria for admission to the course, i.e. had a degree in art (or allied subject, or a professional qualification from an allied area) plus one year's full-time relevant working experience. The groups had been formed in the usual way, depending on other areas of staff/student contact and seeking a mix of men and women and part-time and full-time students. For these groups there was a slight difference from usual in that they were all fine art graduates, although they had not been chosen specifically for my group(s) and – therefore – for this part of the research programme. They had no option about their membership of my group and therefore their role in the research. However they did have a choice about completing the questionnaires and being interviewed.

Before describing the results I will outline the immediate issues I faced with regard to the groups, the research and my role as tutor/group conductor/researcher. The questions posed to students were often of an intensely personal nature. This was a potential area of difficulty, as was the fact that this part of the study was within a course of professional training in an academic institution. I asked the entire student group of Years One and Two to participate in the first part of the research which explored processes of occupational motivation, and in a (later) general survey of the profession. I assured them that the material would remain confidential and quite outside the course. However, the students knew me as a tutor and supervisor as well as the conductor of one of the weekly experiential art therapy groups: every aspect of my contact with them contained an element of assessment. Within the course this dynamic is constantly explored, particularly in the experiential groups when student self-disclosure is often involved; the research added an extra dimension to an already complex dynamic. I therefore restricted the group-work aspects of the research to the experiential groups that I conducted so that colleagues were not unduly involved in processes generated by it. I drew the research into the group arena, when it seemed appropriate, in an effort to have the research and the group processes mutually enhance one another in the manner described by Firth *et al.* (1986). I restated the boundaries of confidentiality and assessment to the students in the experiential art therapy groups, and added that I would not look at the group questionnaires until after the group and the course had ended. I remained concerned about the impact of the research on the groups' processes but, at the time, could see no other way to access the material.

It is important to remember that the numerical picture that follows is part of a larger picture created by the qualitative data. It provides a particular kind of 'snapshot' of the changes in students' behaviour, and behaviour with regard to their art work, that were measurable: these are like Polaroid images which give quick access to the findings on an individual level, on a group level and on an inter-group level. This is not to say that the process of data analysis was speedy; far from it. The impact of the research on my behaviour as group conductor and apparently on the group's process in Year One was such that I thought seriously about not repeating the exercise in Year Two. I decided to continue, having been encouraged by the work of Firth *et al.* (1986). The following year it seemed to work better, though I did not look at any of the questionnaires for several months after the end of the group, and was unable to begin the data analysis or writing up for several years. It was as if I had to digest and then distance myself from the subjective experience before I could consider the data with the necessary objectivity.

When I finally opened the completed questionnaires I was quite baffled. I knew what to do with the qualitative material contained within them but, despite having some experience of statistical analysis in other areas of the research, had no idea how to go about analysing the self- and other-perceptions. It was during this part of the research that my supervisor (Dr Peter B. Smith, University of Sussex) had to lead me very slowly through the procedures: first you do this, then you do that, then (with luck and correct use of the computer) some numbers emerged. Mostly they were understandable, so long as I kept my supervisor's dictum in my head – 'Let the numbers lead you, they're just giving the skeleton; the rest of the data puts flesh on the bones.' Once I had pieced it together the skeleton in itself was quite fascinating.

RESULTS

The numerical data was analysed as follows. Group members' perceptions of each other were scored according to the number of times a name appeared: a person scored +1 each time s/he was named as 'most like' and −1 for 'least like' each of the sixteen statements offered in the questionnaire. This showed the groups' perceptions of individual behaviour throughout the academic year. The change between the early and post-group scores on each item for every person was then calculated (e.g.

Year One, Respondent Four, item 1: early score = +5, post-group score = 0, therefore the final score = −5). The degree of change for all individuals on the same variable was then pooled, regardless of their sign, to obtain a score showing the amount of change that occurred in the group as a whole. The same procedure was carried out for ratings of self-perceptions, i.e. an early to post-group score was calculated for each individual followed by a final score for each variable in both groups. The final self-perception scores were then multiplied by 7 in order to make them comparable with the other-perception scores (there were eight people in each group). The two groups' scores for each variable were added to give overall scores for self-perceptions and other-perceptions (see Table 4.2).

The data was analysed using independent and dependent T-tests. No significant differences were found between the two groups, but as this was not a comparative study this was to be expected. However, the raw figures show similar, discernible changes occurring within the groups and in individuals, as well as interesting inter-group differences. Although there are changes on all items there are notable differences in the amounts of change. The highest overall change scores are in the self-perceptions, demonstrating that private perceptions of change in these groups not only differ from but are greater than public perceptions of change. Four of the highest scoring overall self-perceptions (nos. 4, 5, 9 and 11) are items to do with the individual in the group, i.e. their openness, spontaneity and

Table 4.2 Other-perceptions and self-perceptions in art therapy groups

	Totals/Other			Totals/Self		
	Yr1	Yr2	Overall	Yr1	Yr2	Overall
Behaviour						
1 Expresses feelings openly	33	19	52	42	14	56
2 Helps group along	31	35	66	21	42	63
3 Takes risks	20	24	44	14	49	63
4 Spontaneous	31	29	60	28	84	112
5 Out of the group	28	27	55	49	63	112
6 Listens, not defensive	20	17	37	21	77	98
7 Sees self clearly	22	14	36	35	42	77
8 Contradictory	21	21	42	28	49	77
9 Influential in the group	29	22	51	56	70	126
10 Learning a lot	21	27	48	21	42	63
Art work						
11 Willing to share	24	25	49	56	84	140
12 Aware of meaning	16	17	33	28	21	49
13 Works spontaneously	31	32	63	49	42	91
14 Shows contradictions	17	28	45	28	28	56
15 Fearful of unconscious meaning	18	28	46	28	77	105
16 Learning a lot	36	25	61	14	35	49

influence within it. Self-perceptions of the fears of unconscious meanings in the art work also score highly, and the lowest score on both self- and other-perceptions is the awareness of meaning in the imagery.

There are interesting inter-group differences to be seen in Table 4.2. Whilst the amounts of change in each group's other-perceptions in the main differ only slightly, the amounts of change in self-perceptions are often higher in Year Two; for example, spontaneous and undefensive behaviour (nos. 4 and 6) and fears of unconscious meaning (no. 15).

It is important to remember that the figures in Table 4.2 refer only to the *amount* of change on each item and not its increase or decrease, whereas Table 4.3 shows the *directions* of self-perceived changes in each group. These figures (in Table 4.3) were calculated through the addition of the degree of change for each individual to obtain a group score for each variable; the overall figure is the sum of both groups' scores. When summarised in this way it is important to remember that these figures are cumulative figures of change which refer to increases or decreases on each variable within the two separate groups *as a whole*. The figures do not refer to individuals but are a summary of relative, individual scores, i.e. respondents did not begin from the same baseline.

Table 4.3 also highlights subtle differences between the two groups. Year One's scores show how they felt they became less open, worked less spontaneously, yet experienced themselves as becoming more 'in' the group and able to see themselves more clearly. The Year Two group,

Table 4.3 Self-perceived directions of change

	Year 1	Year 2	Overall
Behaviour			
1 Expresses felings openly	−4	0	−4
2. Helps group along	1	2	3
3 Takes risks	0	−1	−1
4 Spontaneous	0	2	2
5 Out of the group	−5	−1	−6
6 Listens, not defensive	1	−3	−2
7 Sees self clearly	5	3	8
8 Contradictory	2	1	3
9 Influential in the group	4	6	10
10 Learning a lot	−1	2	1
Art Work			
11 Willing to share	2	−4	−6
12 Aware of meaning	−2	−1	−1
13 Works spontaneously	−3	2	−1
14 Shows contradictions	2	0	2
15 Fearful of unconscious meaning	4	3	7
16 Learning a lot	0	1	1

however, became less willing to share their art work and more defensive, and were more cautious than Year One about how 'in' the group they felt. Yet Year Two also felt they had become more influential within the group, and were more spontaneous in their art work and behaviour than Year One.

The foregoing 'snapshot' shows the changes during two, nine-month, weekly experiential art therapy groups taking place within a one-year course of professional education. To give a different numerical picture, and to illustrate how different people learn different things in the same group, I will briefly describe the scoring of two students from one of the groups.

A was immediately perceived by most of the group as prepared to take risks (2), willing to share (4), helpful to the group (5), and neither defensive (4) nor fearful (−3); his behaviour was not seen as spontaneous (−2), although his art work was (3). (The numbers represent the number of times he was mentioned by others as 'most like', i.e. a plus sign; or 'least like', i.e. a minus sign, for certain statements.) A's early self-perceptions were congruent with the perceptions of others. At the mid-point he was viewed even more positively: A was helpful (5), influential (4) and not at all 'out' of the group (−5), although a few people thought his behaviour was contradictory and one student thought he did not see himself clearly. A's self-perceptions were not so effusive as the group's but remained mostly congruent, except that he thought himself to be behaving unspontaneously and to be fearful of the unconscious meanings in his art work. By the end of the group A was still perceived very positively by the group, yet his self-perceptions indicate reflection; he saw himself as uninfluential in the group, not particularly helpful or open, yet learning about himself and his art work. Overall, A appeared to have a more measured view of himself than the group who, with one exception, heaped increasingly positive VCIA role projections onto him.

A's directions of changes overall were therefore towards greater openness and spontaneity and he remained influential, helpful and 'in' the group and was able to learn about his art work. In contrast, B's directions of change were away from being influential, helpful and spontaneous in the group, decreasing in openness and learning and becoming increasingly contradictory and fearful. Initially, however, B was perceived as open (5) and very helpful (7), influential (6) and not out of the group (−6) and, although she did not see herself quite so positively, B thought she was very much 'in' the group. By the mid-point others' perceptions of her were that she was no longer spontaneous and open in either her behaviour (−3) or her art work (−6), was not taking risks (−4) or learning (behaviour −4, art work −3) and was fearful of the unconscious meanings in her imagery (4). B's self-perceptions were that she had no influence and was not helpful to the group, yet she felt she was very much a part of it. She also felt she was neither behaving nor working spontaneously, but was learning about her art work. The considerable shifts in the group's perceptions of her were maintained at the end of the group. B was seen as very unwilling to share (-7), unspontaneous in her behaviour (-5) and art work (-5), not helpful (-2) yet regaining some influence (1). She was also thought not to be learning about either her behaviour (-5) or her art work (-3), and to be increasingly fearful of the unconscious meanings in her art work (6). B's final self-perceptions were either non-committal or negative, agreeing with the group's view of her as unspontaneous and unwilling to share her art work, yet feeling herself to be remaining very much 'in' the group. Initially it seemed that B was to be, in Lieberman *et al.*'s terms, a group member with a high VCIA role, yet during the life of the group she was perceived by others, and by herself, as decreasing in a VCIA role.

These illustrations of the changing self- and other-perceptions of two individuals highlight how an increase in a VCIA role might correlate, in experiential art therapy groups, with a decrease in fears of unconscious meanings in art work and an increased ability to learn about themselves and their art work, and vice versa. This pattern held for all group members: eleven people were able to increase their VCIA role (or aspects of it), lessen or contain their fears as they got in touch with the issues in their art work and in the group, and hence were able to learn. The fears of five people increased and aspects of their VCIA role declined, implying that the group became a difficult arena in which to learn about group work, their own behaviour and their art work. However, it must be remembered that these scores were not absolute but relative to the individual as everyone in the group did not begin from the same baseline. Individual change is also relative to other group members: scores early on, at the mid-point and at the end reflect members' perceptions of their own and each others' roles in the group at that time. Therefore an individual's role in the group might change rather than, for example, their spontaneity increasing. Alternatively, someone who was unwilling to share their work at the beginning might become more open, whilst someone else who was willing to share their art work initially might withdraw: thus by the end of the group both students could finish at the same point.

DISCUSSION

This chapter illustrates a procedure for the collection and analysis of quantitative data in art therapy groups and presents the findings, but does not describe the research process in its entirety. As suggested earlier there was some researcher/group conductor countertransference. The results tend to emphasise the similarities in the two groups but there were interesting inter-group differences which, although primarily to do with membership constellations and the consequent dynamics of the group, may also have been part of my reaction to the research process.

This was my first experience as a researcher, let alone researcher/group conductor/tutor. In Year One I felt, by the end of the group, that the research had given the group a 'hook' on which to hang their natural anger with me as group conductor (and tutor) and became a defence mechanism against transference issues. I too was defensive and found it difficult to address the feelings provoked by the research; this was because I wished to maintain reasonable relationships with the students so as to continue with the research programme after the group had ended. Within the groups and the research process I also experienced powerful counter-transference issues around betrayal. I was very scared before sessions when the questionnaires were due, so much so that one of my colleagues described me as 'white with fear' before one such group. Hence I believe Year One's experience was not as productive as it might have been as I was not so challenging or able to work with transference as usual, although it did improve as the year went on.

Year Two was in some ways a more 'successful' group both in terms of the group and the research. This is borne out in the numerical data, showing their greater increases in spontaneity and learning about their behaviour than Year One. I was much more positive and active with regard to the influence of the research; whilst acknowledging the group's responses to it on a reality level I did not let them focus on it as a defence; for example, I was intolerant of 'whingeing' about the research, saying 'What's in the questionnaires that's not being said here, and why not?' I believe I was more open, honest, spontaneous and challenging in Year Two than Year One, and that this helped the group to be the same.

Certain dynamics in both experiential groups seemed to me to be unusual and could also have been part of reactivity to the research. Unusually destructive reactions to some art works were perhaps displaced aggressive responses to the questionnaires, which I was both surprised and relieved to find were not destroyed or left incomplete. Both groups experienced an early loss of confidence in my ability to protect and contain them, some of which may have hinged on the research. This can also be viewed as part of the early stages of group development, when there is disillusionment with the leader when members' expectations are not fulfilled (Yalom 1975). Indeed both groups were sometimes characterised by disenchantment, conflict and anger, and were able to move into a period of cohesion and spontaneity only towards the end of the year. Yalom also states that it usually takes nine months to establish an effective group, i.e. one that has been through disorientation, disenchantment, conflict and harmony, and reached the status of an open, honest and therefore effective group (Yalom 1975). It may be that both groups' processes, within the nine months of an academic year, were within the usual time frame of the early development of an analytic group and had the potential for being truly effective as they ended. Similarly Lieberman et al. (1973) discuss the timing of group harmony, saying that late harmony in a group is associated with positive outcomes for the group members. It was striking that both experiential groups experienced late harmony and had a good ending, recalling significant events and imagery from the end in their last questionnaires. Whether these patterns of group development were specific to the research programme, these particular groups and/or my group conductor/researcher behaviour can only be clarified by further research.

Despite all the difficulties there were significant results regarding the changes in experiential art therapy groups which centre around group cohesion, spontaneity, openness and fear. As would be hoped, group cohesion variables show an increase, as did group members' ability to see themselves clearly. It was demonstrated that public perceptions differ, sometimes markedly, from private perceptions and the latter usually perceive greater changes than the former. This echoes Lieberman *et al.*'s (1973) findings that an individual's perception of his/her role changes more than others' perceptions of his/her role in a group. The fact that the areas of change concern group cohesion, spontaneity and openness concurs with the research literature about changes in verbal groups (Yalom 1975; Smith 1980; Bloch and Crouch 1985). This illustrates the parallel processes at work in verbal group analysis and experiential art therapy groups. Further research could assess whether similar parallels exist in art therapy groups with other client populations.

However, there are also changes which are specific to the groups addressed here. There is a particular kind of openness in art therapy groups that centres around the sharing of art work. As the fears of what the imagery might mean either increase or decrease so the willingness to share it may alter: if fears increase so there may be a decrease in openness about it and understanding of it. This may explain why, even though they scored slightly differently and Year Two became more spontaneous than Year One, both groups became more self-aware yet less sure about what their imagery meant, and reacted defensively aganst further exploration.

The apparent correlation, for most group members, between their VCIA role, a change in their fears of unconscious meanings in their art work and their ability to learn could well be associated with the other area of this project to do with occupational motivation (Gilroy 1992). Here it was found that art therapy students had significant experiences of loss in their childhood and adolescence, as well as emotional distress, unhappiness and severe physical illness in their adult lives. This made their occupational motivation similar to that of psychotherapists (Henry *et al.* 1971; Henry 1977; Racusin *et al.* 1981). Also, at the time they applied to art school, half the art therapy students were using art as a means of self-exploration and to escape from unhappy circumstances at home or school. Thus it could be that unresolved issues around loss in childhood and other distressing experiences in adult life, alongside a growing awareness of the nature and content of personal imagery in art, were touched on through the imagery and the processes of the experiential art therapy groups. All but three of the sixteen group members had experienced early losses, separations or illnesses, and all but two had personal experience or close contact in adult life with emotional distress or severe physical illness – no one had escaped unscathed.

Experiential art therapy groups may be an affirming or disquieting experience, depending on the individual. The realisation that painful issues are present, albeit unconsciously, in imagery made in a group can be frightening enough at the best of times, but must surely be aggravated by the experiential nature of the groups described, as well as through being the subjects of research. These were not therapy groups, but groups in which the students were expected to gain an understanding of the theory and practice of group art therapy through experience of it. The emergence of personal material is inescapable, given the nature of the art therapy process, but an experiential group is not the place to explore personal material fully. It is therefore understandable that fears might increase, although worrying that it may present students with difficulties in learning. This indicates the importance of personal therapy for trainee art therapists so that painful personal issues which arise may be safely contained and explored outside the context of their professional education.

Becoming aware of some art therapy students' fear of the unconscious, latent content of their imagery is a salutary lesson. Usually the fears lessened or were contained as the group progressed, but art therapists would be well advised to be cognisant of the power of imagery and the fear that might be generated in art therapy groups with vulnerable clients who do not have the ego strength of trainee therapists.

Two issues remain: how else might this research have been designed, and what, finally, were the influences of the groups on the students' art practice? With regard to the research design, it would be difficult to give students a choice about whether or not to enter the group, ergo the project, given the parameters of the other areas of staff/student contact on the course. Ideally, a researcher/group conductor should make plain the research element in a group as part of the assessment so the client has a choice about taking part; the circumstances I was in precluded such a process. Hence, were I to use this design again, potential participants would be given a choice about joining the group and the research. Also, I would not hesitate to intervene when the research was a dynamic in the group so that the whole experience remained productive in educational, therapeutic and research terms. Perhaps a collaborative approach might be suitable, with students entering the project as co-researchers in the manner described by Reason and Rowan (1981). A totally collaborative design may not be appropriate, given the inevitable emergence of transference issues and students' level of knowledge about group work (and research) at the start of their training. However, an increasing degree of collaboration could be employed as the group and the research evolved; this could actively draw on the students' learning as their ability to observe and articulate their experiences in an art therapy group developed.

Changes in students' art practice were almost entirely positive. In the post-group interviews, all the students felt they had changed during their training, speaking repeatedly of increases in self-awareness, their ability to reflect, of being more in touch with their feelings, and able to face personal issues with a greater degree of honesty. Fourteen of the sixteen students felt their art work had changed. They consistently reported a greater freedom and spontaneity in their art and less concern with the finished project and, although they felt the underlying issues were the same, none the less the feeling was of becoming more honest and direct in their imagery. Nine students attributed these changes directly to their experiences in the group, the others attributing the changes to their experiences on clinical placement. The few who felt the changes in their art were either mixed or detrimental felt the changes in themselves were positive. Future research could explore whether the changes and developments in groups with art therapy students outlined here are repeated with other client populations. It would be interesting to see if artists encountered similar fears with regard to their imagery in art therapy groups, and if there were analogous changes in their art as a consequence of the experience.

Research which included quantitative and qualitative methodologies could present a balanced view of the processes and outcomes of art therapy groups with various client populations. I hope this work has demonstrated that quantitative data can provide useful information for practising clinicians. Further, that it is possible to stay in role as therapist and as researcher simultaneously. It is difficult and engenders strong feelings and complex dynamics but, if the research is actively brought into the therapeutic arena when necessary and appropriate, it can be an instructive experience for all concerned.

ACKNOWLEDGEMENTS

My grateful thanks are due to the students who took part in this part of my research, and to my supervisor, Dr Peter B. Smith.

NOTE

1 The reader is referred to Smith (1980), Bloch and Crouch (1985) and Bloch (1988) for comprehensive reviews of research on groups.

REFERENCES

Bloch, S. (1988) 'Research in Group Psychotherapy'. In: Aveline, M. and Dryden, W. (Eds) *Group Therapy in Britain*. Open University Press, Buckingham.

Bloch, S. and Crouch, E. (1985) *Therapeutic Factors in Group Psychotherapy*. Oxford Medical Publications, Oxford.

Borchers, K.K. (1985) 'Do Gains Made in Group Art Therapy Persist?' *American Journal of Art Therapy*. 23: 89–91.

Buoye-Allen, P. (1983) 'Group Art Therapy in Short-term Hospital Settings'. *American Journal of Art Therapy*. 22: 93–5.

Denny, J.M. (1975) 'Techniques for Individual and Group Art Therapy'. In: Ulman, E. and Dachninger, P. (Eds) *Art Therapy in Theory and Practice*. Schocken Books, New York.

Firth, J., Shapiro, D.A. and Parry, G. (1986) 'The Impact of Research on the Practice of Psychotherapy'. *British Journal of Psychotherapy*. 2: 168–79.

Gilroy, A.J. (1989) 'On Occasionally Being Able to Paint'. *Inscape*. Spring: 2–9.

Gilroy, A.J. (1992) 'Art Therapists and their Art. A Study of Occupational Choice and Career Development, from the Origins of an Interest in Art to Occasionally Being Able to Paint'. Unpublished D.Phil. thesis, University of Sussex.

Greenwood, H. and Layton, G. (1987) 'An Out-patient Art Therapy Group'. *Inscape*. Summer: 12–19.

Greenwood, H. and Layton, G. (1991) 'Taking the Piss'. *Inscape*. Winter: 7–14.

Henry, W.E. (1977) 'Personal and Social Identities of Psychotherapists'. In: Gurman, A.S. and Razin, A.M. (Eds) *Effective Psychotherapy*. Pergamon Press, New York.

Henry, W.E., Sims, J.H. and Spray, S.L. (1971) *The Fifth Profession: Becoming a Psychotherapist*. Jossey Bass, New York.

Lachman-Chapin, M. (1976) 'Training Art Therapists in Group Art Therapy'. In: *Creativity and the Art Therapist's Identity. Proceedings of the Seventh Annual Conference of the American Art Therapy Association*.

Lieberman, M.A., Yalom, I.D. and Miles, M.B. (1973) *Encounter Groups: First Facts*. Basic Books, New York.

Liebmann, M. (1981) 'The Many Purposes of Art Therapy'. *Inscape*. 5. 1: 26–8.

McNeilly, G. (1983) 'Directive and Non-directive Approaches in Art Therapy'. *The Arts in Psychotherapy*. 10: 211–19.

McNeilly, G. (1987) 'Further Contributions to Group-analytic Art Therapy'. *Inscape*. Summer: 8–11.

McNeilly, G. (1989) 'Group-analytic Art Groups'. In: Gilroy, A. and Dalley, T. (Eds) (1989) *Pictures at an Exhibition: Selected Essays on Art and Art Therapy*. Routledge, London.

Nowell Hall, P. (1987) 'Art Therapy: A Way of Healing the Split'. In: Dalley, T. *et al. Images of Art Therapy*. Tavistock/Routledge, London.

Racusin, G.R., Abramowitz, S.I. and Winter, W.D. (1981) 'Becoming a Therapist: Family Dynamics and Career Choice'. *Professional Psychology*. April: 271–9.

Reason, P. and Rowan, J. (Eds) (1981) *Human Inquiry: A Sourcebook of New Paradigm Research*. John Wiley, Chichester.

Shatin, L. and Kymissis, P. (1975) 'Transactional Group Image Therapy'. *American Journal of Art Therapy*. 15: 13–18.

Skaife, S. (1990) 'Self-determination in Group-analytic Art Therapy'. *Group Analysis*. 23: 237–44.

Smith, P.B. (1980) *Group Processes and Personal Change*. Harper & Row, London.
Strand, S. (1990) 'Counteracting Isolation: Group Art Therapy for People with Learning Difficulties'. *Group Analysis*. 23: 255–63.
Vogt, J.M. and Vogt, G.M. (1983) 'Group Art Therapy: An Eclectic Approach'. *American Journal of Art Therapy*. 22: 129–35.
Wadeson, H. (1980) *Art Psychotherapy*. John Wiley, Canada.
Waller, D. (1993) *Group Interactive Art Therapy*. Routledge, London.
Wolff, R.A. (1975) 'Therapeutic Experiences through Group Art Expression'. *American Journal of Art Therapy*. 14: 91–8.
Yalom, I.D. (1975) *The Theory and Practice of Group Psychotherapy*. Basic Books, New York.

Part II

Clinical work

Chapter 5

Starting out in music therapy process research

Sue Van Colle and Tim Williams

INTRODUCTION

In this chapter we describe the initial stages of a study to investigate the strategies used by a music therapist working with cerebral palsied children. Our aim is to describe how we worked together to develop a mutually satisfactory system of research. We hope that the reader will be able to identify with us in the early stages when the difficulties may seem overwhelming. New researchers may find gaps in their knowledge of terrifying proportions. They can be overcome but it requires persistence and the courage to admit to more experienced researchers that you do not know or do not understand something. A good supervisor will have the patience to explain and the wisdom to refrain from overly critical appraisal of the early efforts.

It will be helpful to describe our backgrounds and something of the contexts in which we worked together. Parts of the chapter have been written by Sue in the first person singular whilst others have been written by Tim. Where the first person plural is used the ideas are held jointly and either or both of us may have written the text. Our discussions have been shaped by our professional roles – Sue is music therapist/research student and Tim is clinical psychologist/research supervisor. The starting point for this research was a submission to the music faculty of a university for consideration as a PhD project. Sue's project was initially designed to address the following questions:

1 Do the children take more part in the music therapy sessions over time?
2 When do the child–therapist interactions take place?
3 When the music therapist focuses on a particular child, how can one know that the child is aware of this?

Before describing how the research is being done, we need to go back in time before the research project came to be formulated. We will try to describe how we came to work together, and the ways in which the supervisor and the student learn together about the project in hand.

There are assumptions about research built into this introduction. We consider research to be a means of finding out more information about a phenomenon. Furthermore we try to be good scientists in gathering and interpreting the observations we make. We have followed Reason and Rowan (1981) in viewing the basis of research as the systematic checkable inquiry. In some ways, however, we try to distance ourselves from the subject matter, so that we can understand more of it than when we are immersed in the actions of research. In this way we hope to develop conclusions that can be accepted by others, because if anyone attempted to repeat our work, they would find the same regularities or laws that we found. Research needs to be seen as a process by which ideas become better able to explain the phenomena in the real world, not as the search for the ultimate answer.

SUE'S STORY

The impetus for my research came when, as a newly qualified music therapist, I was working with a group of eight multiply and severely handicapped cerebral palsied children in the Special Care Unit of Cheyne Centre for Cerebral Palsy, London. The plight of these children appalled me. When on their own they appeared completely helpless. Left lying on a cushion the spastic quadriplegic children couldn't even change position. The athetoid children were relentlessly 'on the move'. None had expressive language, nor were they able to use other means of communication, such as Bliss charts. They were wounded and isolated prisoners inside their own bodies. During my initial work at Cheyne (which started as a clinical placement during training) my initial brief was to provide music therapy for the eight special care children as a group. I began running music therapy sessions with the help of a teacher and her classroom assistant.

We were all new to this venture. The children were held or sat in special chairs in a little gathering near the piano. I addressed each child in turn, vocally and with percussion, and worked spontaneously with his/her responses. This turned out to be a very lengthy procedure if only because each child was very slow to organise his/her responses. It was also a frustrating procedure. There was not enough time to address all the children, to follow through their individual responses and interactions or to facilitate group experience. If I used the piano with the aim of addressing the entire group it felt arbitrary and unfocused. It felt, too, as though I was simply providing yet another mode of sensory stimulation to which the children remained essentially passive. This feeling was enhanced by my not having a co-therapist who might have encouraged the children and helped with their motor responses. Despite the willingness of my helpers their input was mainly restricted to nursing children who were having epileptic attacks, or shaking bells in front of children's noses. The chaos of the children's pathology seemed to reflect itself in what I experienced as the chaos of my work. (This may be a point for later discussion.) I strongly felt that something else was needed if my presence – my musical presence – was to be helpful. I felt this particularly strongly, since the children's responses to my music were very strong. I wanted to organise the music in a way that would immediately address all the children and help them focus. I wanted them to know they were in a group and be able to be in this group without recourse to outside agencies or distractions. I wanted the music to do the work of providing a helpful environment.

I cannot remember precisely how I made a leap to a technique which I term the Basic Structure (which I shall describe in a minute). I remember two things about its birth. Firstly, it felt inspirational. Secondly, its essence was born out of the children being passive and socially isolated and needing constant assistance from able-bodied people if they were to make their mark on the environment. The children suffered with a massive handicap. I wanted to optimise the possibility for independent activity within a musical setting, and optimise the potential for every child music-ally at least to experience themselves as autonomous within a relationship.

The Basic Structure, then, was a musical artefact based on a classic Schenkerian Ursatz or ground plan: tonic, dominant (development) and back to tonic. That is to say, each week I pianistically extended to the group of children one vast quasi-composition – incorporating much impro-visation, conceiving it, and designing it as a structure of sounds into which the children were invited. They could know their way around it, I thought. It had distinctive and constantly repeated features. The classical Ursatz would, I conjectured, provide a subconsciously experienced balanced framework, a model of equilibrium that could be introjected. The design of the upper strata of the Basic Structure (that is, the melodies, passing modulations and harmonies) would contain consciously accessible infor-mation. It would be in some respects of teaching value, guiding the children in lieu, perhaps, of physical intervention by other people. At the same time the danger of projecting the therapist's own feelings onto the children was countered by reflecting and interpreting the child's actions within the improvisations.

The constituents of this Basic Structure were as follows:

1 Context music composed with the group's ethos in mind and incorporat-ing thematic references to the children;
2 A Hello Song, the melody of which was composed in a way that stressed the home note of the key in which it was written and was punctuated by assisted beating;
3 A development section which was completely open; and
4 A Context Reprise with Goodbye Song. In the Context Reprise I

reflected back to the children what they had done in the session whilst still using their own thematic material.

Assisted beating was the only time when helpers made any input to the session: they simply helped a child beat with its hand on a tambourine whilst I played the piano. In this way even the most handicapped could experience the physical sensation of generating rhythm and, secondly, experience the connection between the tonic note and strong downbeat which tended to occur simultaneously in the Hello Song. At times the melodic aspect of the tune took precedence over the rhythmic aspect. At such times it seemed that it was the affective quality of music which the children elicited in me rather than the driving will of the rhythm. Always the tonal logic of the melody provided a continuity of intention with which the children seemed satisfied.

It was an important feature of this Basic Structure way of working that the children contributed to the sound structures. Each child had a specially composed theme or leitmotif which was sounded or extemporised on by me – usually on the piano – and, indeed, sometimes modified and developed to fit a child's mood or activity. I tried to make the themes in some way match the children as they presented to me. I hoped they would hear themselves in it and therefore eventually respond to it. It was my way of presenting them with their musical identities. I later theorised that this had similarities to the mother–infant symbiosis where, after the language and ideas of D.W. Winnicott (1971), the child looks at the mother's face – here her musical face – and sees himself. What the mother looks like is related to what she sees in the baby. What the music therapist sounds like is similarly related to what she sees and hears in the child. The task of the therapist, of course, is like that of the mother. Clinical intervention is like that of the mother who not only supports her child but helps the child extend his range of expression and his experience of himself in the world. The children in my group at Cheyne were indeed like babies. They were helpless physically, and their mental ages did not correspond to their chronological ages. It occurred to me I might be a musical mother, hopefully the 'good-enough' musical mother in the sense that a 'good-enough mother' provides the nurturing environment which enables a child to explore the world and develop appropriately.

I wondered if perhaps I could say I was working in a Winnicottian way, since I made the music represent the holding, handling and object-presenting of the 'good-enough musical mother'. The Basic Structure is hypothesised as a means of indicating continuity of care, predictability and adaptability to the child's individual needs. Obviously the children contributed to the Basic Structure in other ways – by initiating musical material, by introducing in different ways their musical evolutions. This was reflected in changes, therefore, in the Basic Structure. To some extent I thought I could judge the development of the children by the degree of changes in the scope of the Basic Structure. There were other important features to the Basic Structure, which I should stress was conceived as an evolving and flexible artefact, one that accommodated the input of the children whilst, however, retaining certain fixed features, in particular the tonic–dominant–tonic sequence no matter if in real time the sequence was truncated or extended.

Two important features of the Basic Structure technique were emphasis on tonality and the emphasis on the children operating independently. Each was given a solo instrument – most often the chinese cymbals – which hung by his hand by a string and therefore pre-empted the need for a helper to be hovering by the child's side. It was to be the first time these children had experienced being in a group without being held or chivvied or cooed at.

TIM'S STORY

I am a clinical psychologist, who specialises in work with children with complex and severe difficulties. It has been my intention for a long time to find ways of understanding the processes of development. I feel that if normal development is understood, then it would illuminate the ways in which psychological development could go wrong, and enable effective therapies to be devised. Music therapy research interested me in the first place because I worked for several years in a hospital for children who could not communicate verbally. The hospital was visited by a music therapist who provided music therapy for many of the resident children. She and I shared a conviction that within music therapy sessions some of the most difficult children who were often autistic and lacking in social contact could forge relationships that were more normal than those they formed via speech. In discussing the way in which she worked it seemed to me that the development of the social interactions followed the same path that normal children followed in developing social relationships, at least as described by Trevarthen (Trevarthen 1987; Pavlicevic 1991). I managed to coax a psychology student into transcribing audiotapes of sessions of music therapy with particular children. We found, firstly, that the ability of the children to take turns was related to their general developmental level, although it was at a much lower level than might have been expected from the other skills that they possessed. Secondly, there did seem to be some improvements in the ability of autistic children to sustain dialogue with the therapist in a way that seemed similar to the increasing turn-taking complexity seen in the vocal interactions of normal babies (Williams *et al.* 1985).

DESIGNING THE PROJECT

Initially we needed to agree on what aspect of music therapy Sue wanted to study. Clearly she wanted to know what worked for her clients, but she felt that it would take too long to undertake an outcome study, and in addition she did not want to organise comparison groups with and without therapy. Sue also felt that she knew what did work for the children. She could describe to Tim aspects of the sessions that she felt were particularly important. It seemed to him, therefore, that what she was trying to do was to examine the *processes* of music therapy. This seemed a logical extension of Tim's previous research in music therapy. Our next joint task was then to describe a simple conceptual framework of what might be happening in music therapy. Figure 5.1 is a diagram of the elements of music therapy with an individual child. For groups, additional links between the children through the music, words and actions of the individuals are required. A diagram like this enables one to classify aspects of music therapy and provides a basis for thinking about the measures and analyses required to provide a test of the hypotheses advanced in the proposal.

Our problem was: how do you describe music therapy process in such a way as to make it meaningful for the theories of therapeutic process *and* for the practising music therapist so that the ideas, if successful, can be incorporated into music therapy? From the scientific standpoint there are really two ways of approaching this. Either start with a theoretical

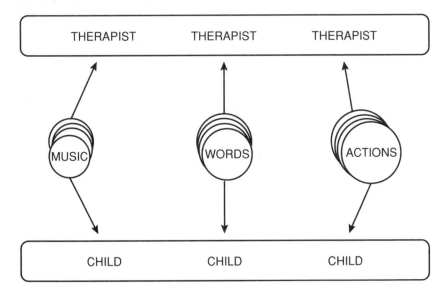

Figure 5.1 Basic system involving therapist, child and interaction variables of interest to the authors

perspective and find out if the predictions made by the theory are violated; or describe in as much detail as possible what is going on and see if it generates a theory or fits with a known theory. Sue came with a theoretical perspective, based largely on Winnicott; therefore the next stage of our discussions was a discussion of the ideas she had.

Starting with a theory

Winnicott (1971; and see Davis and Wallbridge 1983) was both a psychoanalyst and a paediatrician. In his work he relied heavily on the earlier work of Anna Freud and Melanie Klein. They tended to work with children who displayed psychological disorders rather than the grievous physical disorders that Sue was working with. They believed that the behaviour disorders of children were based on unconscious conflicts. Improvements occur through 'self-observation, self-awareness, and insight' (Wolff 1985), helped by the therapist's verbalisations. Therapy was aimed at mastering conflict and enabling maturation. There are discrepancies between the viewpoints of Melanie Klein and Anna Freud, although both believed that the therapist became a transference object. Anna Freud's contribution was to recognise that a therapist also acted as a teacher in fostering developmental change. Winnicott felt that much therapeutic change could be accomplished by enabling the child to develop mastery through a relationship with a significant other, usually the mother. The mother did not have to be seen as a paragon of virtues, but merely a 'good-enough mother'.

The phrase 'good-enough mother' implies that the mother and the child have a relationship which enables both psychological and physical growth. Using the term relationship implies that both partners make a contribution. It would not be enough to study only the reactions or response of the child to the behaviours of the therapist. We also assume that a relationship involves regularities in the patterns of interaction over time. Because the children with whom Sue was used to working were so handicapped, the changes we would be looking for would be small, which required the development of a system for classifying the observations of behaviour. Her initial list of behaviours contained 80 items, which Tim encouraged her to pare down to 40.

Pragmatic route

The pragmatic route transfers known techniques of measurement and analysis that have proved interesting in other areas such as psychotherapy process research. Our interests lie in the area of the relationship between the children and the therapist. In assessing the state of a relationship we would expect to take account of the psychological state of the participants and their mutual influences. Unfortunately most measures of psychological state used in psychotherapy research are verbally based, e.g. interpersonal process recall (Barker 1985) and are therefore inaccessible to our children. Therefore the focus has turned towards non-verbal measures of activities. The simplest, albeit most time-consuming, approach is to transcribe all the information contained on the videotapes. Essentially this is what ethologists do when studying behaviour. Once a stream of events has been identified, the regularities within that stream can be identified statistically, by such means as the computer program ELAG (Bakeman 1983). Although the ELAG program has not as far as we know been used to analyse the processes of music therapy, it has been used to demonstrate that the gaze avoidance normally thought of as characteristic of autistic children has probably been due to children with the Fragile-X chromosome disorder (Cohen *et al.* 1989). Autistic children show a lack of dependency or structure in their social interactions rather than gaze avoidance. Given our constraints we would anticipate analysing the effects of particular therapist musical behaviours on as many as possible of the observable behaviours of the children.

Greenberg (1991) describes an alternative: a 'paradigm shift in the world of psychotherapy research toward the study of sequentially patterned change episodes' (p. 3). He suggests that a process analytic approach will enable the lawful explanations of behaviour and experience. But this can only be accomplished if specific (possibly limited) therapeutic events are studied such as change episodes. This in its turn presupposes a classification system which will identify the critical episodes. Fortunately our experience suggests that certain events are likely to be particularly interesting, such as occasions in which a piece of music associated with a particular child is played.

Greenberg (1991) also suggests that process research should make explicit the implicit map of the experienced clinician, select and describe the task environment, make rational and empirical analyses of performance of tasks and compare actual and possible performances. This latter step enables the researcher to construct a model of the therapeutic process occurring in these episodes. The model should generate hypotheses about the task performance of the participants. These hypotheses can be tested both by incorporating successful strategies in controlled trials of treatment programmes but also in the therapeutic process itself by comparing successful and unsuccessful episodes.

Both of Greenberg's approaches rely on preconceived notions of therapy process, for instance, on concepts of critical episodes, or knowledge of what a successful intervention would look like. We would classify these as hypothesis-testing approaches.

We have attempted to consider how Greenberg's approaches outlined above could be used in our work. Although the 'improvisation' (Bruscia

1987, 1988) style of therapy was used, the sessions always began with a Hello Song and ended with a Goodbye Song. Such elements of structure enable the researcher to compare across sessions relatively easily, and can be construed as specific therapeutic episodes. We believed that children might learn to associate with particular musical themes which form part of the Basic Structure. In addition the use of tonal-harmonic music was considered desirable, since it is likely to be a musical form with which the children were familiar, and because there is a large research literature in this area providing both analytical techniques and theories of performance (e.g. Sloboda 1985, 1988; Krumhansl, 1990). In our study the Basic Structure was considered of particular interest, as we felt that it was a means of indicating to the child that the therapist was providing continuity of care, predictability and adaptability to the child's individual needs. We were also interested in the reactions of the children to the Hello and Goodbye Songs.

Krumhansl (1990) has evidence on the effect of deviations from the expected performance of a particular piece of music. For instance, she has shown that if a wrong tone is played in a melody, it will be noticed less if it is a tone from the same key, than if it is a tone from a different key. In the context of the Basic Structure we should observe markedly different reactions to tones of correct and incorrect keys. Similar considerations apply to aspects of metre and harmony. In practical terms this means that we should seek out errors of performance in the music therapy situation and observe the reactions of the children to them. Sloboda (1991) has ascertained the pieces of music which have the most emotional effect on people. Although the study is not without difficulties of interpretation due to the response rates, his respondents suggested that 'shivers down the spine' were generated most reliably by passages containing new or unexpected harmonies (i.e. a violation of expectancy).

We were then faced with the difficulty of measuring the response of the children to the events occurring in the therapy sessions. The measures used must be both valid (i.e. measure what you are interested in) and reliable (i.e. can be used by any trained person to give the same results). The subject population was profoundly handicapped children with disorders of motor control. Verbal interaction with the child following a session was likely to prove unhelpful. Nevertheless the nature and content of verbal or vocal interactions during a session might be a means of examining the child's internal state, just as ethologists use other observable behaviours. One problem with ethological methods of measuring behaviour is that it is often difficult to specify a sufficiently complete set of behaviours to cover all the activities of the child without resorting to a meaningless dustbin category. Behaviour categories must also be independent of one another (for discussion of these issues see Smith and Vollstedt 1985; Bakeman and Gottman 1986; Partridge and Barnitt 1986). However, an ethological approach does result in very rich data that can be used in many different ways to assess competing hypotheses (Martin and Bateson 1986; Slee 1987).

Alternatives to ethological methods with this subject population would require the use of rating scales or symptom counts by the researcher. Such methods are known to be very susceptible to rater bias and there is no simple way of ensuring that such biases do not occur, particularly where the subjects themselves cannot provide the answers. The resulting threats to validity might nullify the research entirely.

More fruitfully the account of the therapist is often a helpful way of examining the processes in the session. Good and Watts (1989) provide clear descriptions of several methods by which it is possible to analyse accounts of the processes involved in psychotherapeutic encounters. While much care needs to be taken over the interpretation of such accounts, if it is tied to the behavioural events that are recorded objectively, the method has reasonable explanatory power. A similar method is used by Pressing (1988) in understanding the processes involved in musical improvisation. Our use of this type of method is somewhat restricted, since we were not interested in understanding the decisions that the therapist made on a moment-by-moment level, but rather whether the therapist had made the 'right' decisions. Unfortunately this is not a straightforward issue since the therapist was also the researcher. We have attempted to separate out the observer from the process by videotaping the sessions for later analysis.

Summary of design of study

Two groups of four severely physically handicapped children would be observed for a large number of sessions (twenty-five) throughout the school year. All sessions would be recorded on videotape for subsequent micro analysis of behaviour, words and music. Sue was the therapist, video operator and transcriber. The aim was to detect the effects of the use of the Basic Structure on this population. We thought it would also be possible to analyse the tapes to investigate the nature of the developing relationship between therapist and clients. The use of two groups enables us to replicate the findings, although there may be difficulties with generalising the findings to other models of working in music therapy and to other populations.

PRACTICAL ISSUES

Getting the data

The first difficulty was finding a subject population with whom to work. Sue visited about ten schools, of which all but three were unsuitable as they had no spare rooms in which the music therapy could be carried out. Of the three schools one dropped out after a further term's negotiations because the staff group was changing so rapidly that no one could provide the authority necessary to agree to the research programme. In each of the two remaining schools only four children were available to take part in the music therapy sessions regularly. We also failed to take account of the fragile physical health of the children, and so did not anticipate that they might miss several sessions.

Data analysis

The data consists of videotapes of the sessions. Reference to Figure 5.1 will show that we intend to be able to describe the interrelationships of the therapist's actions, music and words with those of the children. In fact because of the rooms, the therapist is not visible, so only the music and the words of the therapist are available for analysis. The children's words, music and actions are, however, visible. Our intention was and remains to investigate all the interrelationships that we transcribe.

Transcription brings its own problems, however. One can imagine the benefits to be gained from detailed transcriptions of every music therapy session. The labour and time involved can be envisaged, even to the extent of being amused by the resulting piles of manuscript paper. The reality is rather different, and perhaps surprising. Transcribing takes longer than you imagined – perhaps one hour for every five or ten minutes of tape. Very often the same piece of videotape has to be viewed repeatedly in order to make an accurate record of the events. Problems with the transcription system appear, and the system has to be revised. Videotapes develop blurring through overuse. When it's going well, though, the process becomes mechanical, like mental elastoplast, according to Sue, although the reader can judge from Figure 5.2 the all-encompassing nature of this sticking plaster.

The most demoralising aspect is coming face to face with shortcomings in therapeutic technique. The pain of being a therapist–researcher is most acute. It becomes increasingly difficult to view the data objectively, and to notate it dispassionately. Sue found that much of her energies went into thinking about unhelpful therapeutic interventions instead of continuing to transcribe the tapes of her own clinical work. In retrospect it would have been easier to transcribe someone else's work. This might have been anticipated had there been earlier access to supervision.

Keeping going

One difficulty of doing research is that the researcher is usually enthusiastic about the work or ideas but it can be difficult to find others who are, so most people who do research find it necessary to have colleagues with

Figure 5.2 Example of tape transcription

Coding of transcription:

D	Daniel
E	Edward
B	Betty
F	Fred
T	Music Therapist

I	instrument
SI	Solo Instrument

o.o.s	out of sight

———	continuing event
———→	hand remains on tambourine or helper remains holding child's hand or arm
∧∧∧∧∧∧	repeated event

HR	head turns to the right, eyes in same direction
HL	head turns to the left, eyes in same direction
HD	head down towards self
HL	head moves at angle from due left
HSI	head and eyes towards Solo Instrument

E	eyes towards (EFI eyes towards Fred's instrument;
	ED eyes down towards self;
	ER eyes right;
	ET eyes towards therapist)

MWO	mouth wide-open

B	beat (as in drum) with hand
r/lp	uses palm of right/left hand
r/lf	uses fist of right/left hand
AB	assisted beating (helper assists child to beat)
ab	inaudible assisted beating

AR	assisted arm raising (scale 1–3 for height)

B.S.	Basic Structure

e	deviation from basic structure or repertoire composition due to technical mistake rather than conscious intention

▤	Benesh notation square for notating position of children from previous page of transcription

whom they can discuss their frustrations with supervisors, clients or non-significant results, or, worse still, meaningless results. Sue became increasingly concerned that she was losing touch with her music therapy skills, and so sought a colleague who could supervise the music therapy aspects of her work. From the point of view of a supervisor this could have seemed like a side issue, but it is often very lonely pursuing an idea for years at a time, with little tangible benefit to show for it.

A second difficulty for many students is the boredom that tends to strike about halfway through a period of study. Phillips and Pugh (1987) provide quotes from a several PhD students to illustrate the point. It is important to recognise that the boredom is a phase which will be replaced by a phase of pressure when the thesis neeeds to be finished as well as a rather more pleasurable feeling when the data begins to form patterns, results emerge and the adrenalin flows.

CONCLUSIONS

We hope you have been able to follow us this far. We have described only the design and the data collection phases of the study. Data analysis is just starting. Even this early in the research there are lessons we would like others to remember. Firstly, do not give up. Secondly, establish a partnership, based on mutual respect with your supervisor. Thirdly, stay on track, and do not get distracted into too many other sidelines. Make this part of your supervisor's job too. Fourthly, missing data does not spell the end of your project. Finally, supervisors are human too. Tim often says to students, both clinical and research, that there are many similarities between supervision and therapy. Our anxiety is that many people do not recognise them.

We are confident that this detailed observational approach to music therapy process will have significance for the advancement of our knowledge of how music therapy works. We feel that the results will illuminate the relationship between music therapists and their clients at a very basic level. We think that the work furthers ideas about tonality and its effects on the development of autonomy in children.

We have been working together for a while now. At first we found each other to be in rather different worlds of thinking and speech, but collaboration has brought us to a shared view. Our hesitant steps have brought us part way through a PhD project. Our horizons have expanded, yet at the same time our joint working is focusing ever more closely on the project.

ACKNOWLEDGEMENTS

We would like to thank the two schools who agreed to Sue working in their premises. We should also like to thank all our colleagues in the worlds of music therapy and Clinical Psychology for many helpful discussions. Tim owes a particular debt to Auriol Warwick and Janet Baker who worked with him at Smith Hospital on his first foray into the world of music therapy research.

REFERENCES

Bakeman, R. (1983) 'Computing Lag Sequential Statistics: The ELAG Program'. *Behavior Research Methods and Instrumentation.* 15: 530–5.
Bakeman, R. and Gottman, J.M. (1986) *Observing Interaction: An Introduction to Sequential Analysis.* Cambridge University Press, New York.
Barker, C. (1985) 'Interpersonal Process Recall in Clinical Training and Research'. In: Watts, F.N. (Ed.) *New Developments in Clinical Psychology.* British Psychological Society, Leicester.
Bruscia, K.E. (1987) *Improvisational Models of Music Therapy.* Charles C. Thomas, Springfield, IL.
Bruscia, K.E. (1988) 'A Survey of Treatment Procedures in Improvisational Music Therapy'. *Psychology of Music.* 16: 10–24.
Bunt, L. (1988) 'Music Therapy: An Introduction'. *Psychology of Music.* 16: 3–9.
Cohen, I.L., Vietze, P.M., Sudhalter, V., Jenkins, E.C. and Brown, W.T. (1989) 'Parent-child Dyadic Gaze Patterns in Fragile-X males and Non-Fragile-X Males with Autistic Disorders'. *J. Child Psychol. Psychiat.* 30: 845–56.
Cullen, J.M. (1972) 'Some Principles of Animal Communication'. In: Hinde, R.A. (Ed.) *Non-verbal Communication.* London University Press, London.
Davis, M. and Wallbridge, D. (1981) *Boundary and Space: An Introduction to the Work of D.W. Winnicott.* Penguin, Harmondsworth.
Elliot, R. (1991) 'Five Dimensions of Therapy Process'. *Psychotherapy Research.* 1: 92–104.
Good, D.A. and Watts, F.N. (1989) 'Qualitative Research'. In: Parry, G. and Watts, F.N. (Eds) *Behavioural and Mental Health Research: A Handbook of Skills and Methods.* Lawrence Erlbaum Associates, Hove.
Greenberg, L. (1991) 'Research on the Process of Change'. *Psychotherapy Research.* 1: 3–16.
Krumhansl, C.L. (1990) *Cognitive Foundations of Musical Pitch.* Oxford University Press, Oxford.
Martin, P. and Bateson, P. (1986) *Measuring Behaviour: An Introductory Guide.* Cambridge University Press, Cambridge.
Partridge, C. and Barnitt, R. (1986) *Research Guidelines: A Handbook for Therapists.* Heinemann Medical Books, London.
Pavlicevic, M. (1991) 'Music in Communication: Improvisation in Music Therapy'. Unpublished PhD thesis, University of Edinburgh.
Pavlicevic, M. and Trevarthen, C. (1989) 'A Musical Assessment of Psychiatric States in Adults'. *Psychopathology.* 22: 325–34.
Phillips, E.M. and Pugh, D.S. (1987) *How to Get a PhD.* Open University Press, Milton Keynes.
Pressing, J. (1988) 'Improvisation: Methods and Models'. In: Sloboda, J.A. (Ed.) *Generative Processes in Music: The Psychology of Performance, Improvisation and Composition.* Oxford University Press, Oxford.
Reason, P. and Rowan, J. (Eds) (1981) *Human Inquiry: A Sourcebook of New Paradigm Research.* John Wiley, Chichester.
Slee, P.T. (1987) *Child Observation Skills.* Croom Helm, Beckenham.

Sloboda, J.A. (1985) *The Musical Mind.* Oxford University Press, Oxford.

Sloboda, J.A. (Ed.) (1988) *Generative Processes in Music: The Psychology of Performance, Improvisation and Composition.* Oxford University Press, Oxford.

Sloboda, J.A. (1991) 'Music Structure and Emotional Response: Some Empirical Findings'. *Psychology of Music.* 19: 110–20.

Smith, P.K. and Vollstedt, R. (1985) 'On Defining Play'. *Child Development.* 56: 1042–50.

Trevarthen, C. (1987) 'Sharing Makes Sense: Intersubjectivity and the Making of an Infant's Meaning'. In: Steele, R. and Threadgold, T. (Eds) *Language Topics: Essays in Honor of Michael Halliday.* John Benjamin, Philadelphia.

Williams, T.I., Baker, J. and Warwick, A. (1985) 'Analysis of the Rhythmical Nature of Interactions between Autistic Children and a Music Therapist'. Unpublished MS available from TW.

Winnicott, D.W. (1971) *Playing and Reality.* Tavistock, London.

Wolff, S. (1985) 'Child Psychotherapy'. In: Bloch, S. (Ed.) *An Introduction to the Psychotherapies*, Oxford University Press, Oxford.

Chapter 6

Research in art therapy with people who have psychotic illnesses

Katherine Killick and Helen Greenwood

INTRODUCTION

This chapter explores two research processes which evolved in two different contexts. The art therapists concerned, Katherine Killick and Helen Greenwood, both developed interests in working with people diagnosed as having psychotic illnesses. Killick's research (Killick 1987) evolved from her experience of working with schizophrenic patients, who were often referred for individual assessment and treatment in acute psychotic states. Greenwood's research (Greenwood and Layton 1987, 1988) focused on a description of a community-based art therapy group set up for people with longterm psychotic illnesses. The editors of this book thought that there were similarities in both the processes and outcomes of our work with people experiencing psychotic illnesses, and suggested that this chapter be jointly written. This gave us, the authors, an opportunity to meet each other, to reflect upon our past work, and to arrive at new, common understandings in the present. The research process thus continued.

Both the research processes which we will describe in the chapter represent our attempts to understand and engage with psychosis within the context of medical-model psychiatry, and this is denoted by the use of the term 'illnesses' in the chapter title. We begin by exploring our motivation for research and illustrate how research grew directly out of our clinical practice in relation to our clinical contexts. After considering the outcome of our separate researches we conclude by attempting jointly to formulate aspects of a model of art therapy practice appropriate to the particular needs of psychotic patients.

The research processes explored in this chapter are inseparably intertwined with the therapeutic process. We have both come to believe that the therapist's way of thinking about clinical phenomena is an integral part of the therapeutic process. We also believe that the psychopathology, at work in psychosis, attacks the thinking of the therapist as well as that of the patient. Our experiences of this in our clinical work formed a common motivation for research, in that our attempts to clarify our thinking through research represented efforts to keep our thinking alive in relation to our patients.

Our separate literature reviews revealed that the quality of experience encountered in relationships with psychotic patients had been rigorously investigated in the field of psychoanalysis; this offered us significant theoretical models. We are assuming that the reader has a grasp of basic psychoanalytic concepts, but would refer the reader to Rycroft (1972) or Laplanche and Pontalis (1973) for clarification of the terminology used. Hanna Segal described the core issues encountered by the psychoanalyst working with psychotic processes, which, we think, are encountered in any psychotherapeutic work with psychotic patients, including art therapy. She writes:

> The psychotic tries to project into the analyst his terror, his badness, his confusion, his fragmentation, and having done this projection, he perceives the analyst as a terrifying figure from whom he may want to cut himself off immediately, hence the brittleness of the transference situation.
>
> [The patient's] experience of the transference is very concrete; so is his experience of the analyst's interpretation . . . he is apt to experience it as projective identification in reverse, that is, to feel that the analyst is now putting into him his own unwanted parts and driving him mad . . . when [the analyst] interprets an anxiety, the patient may feel that he is in fact attacking him, or if he interprets the patient's sexual feelings, the patient may experience it concretely as the analyst's sexual advances towards him or her.
>
> (Segal 1975, p. 95)

We agree that the therapist's awareness and understanding of psychotic anxieties and defences can make significant differences to the therapeutic relationship when these destructive processes predominate. At times the work of therapy can seem impossible. Psychotic processes attack those ego functions concerned with symbol formation, severely disturbing or destroying the capacity to think and to speak about experience. Accordingly the integrative aims of therapy, and the work of understanding which is crucial to these aims, form the object of attacks within the therapeutic relationship. Anxieties experienced in relation to integration are so severe that the therapeutic work itself is defended against. We found the work of W.R. Bion (1962, 1967) particularly helpful in understanding these issues.

We found that the patient may defend against experiencing the therapist as whole, and as separate, and the therapist has to find a way of keeping her experience of her wholeness and her separateness alive. Little's work on psychotic transference and countertransference (1981) investigates this. She writes:

[The analyst] allows the patient to enter his own inner world and become part of it. His whole psyche becomes liable to be subjected to sudden, unheralded inroads often of vast extent and long duration. He is taken possession of, his emotions are exploited. He has to be able to make all kinds of identifications with his patient, accepting a fusion with him which often involves the taking into himself of something really mad; yet at the same time he has to be able to remain whole and separate.

(Little 1981, p. 57)

We both found that working through these experiences in art therapy seemed to require us to engage in research as a way of renewing our capacity to think, and restoring a receptive state of mind in the clinical situation. This state of mind has been likened to the state of maternal reverie in the early mother–infant relationship by psychoanalytic writers, notably Bion and Winnicott. It is fundamental to Winnicott's concept of 'holding' (1971) and Bion's concept of 'containment' (1962). These concepts describe aspects of the maternal environment and of the analytic environment which foster the evolution of symbolising ego functions. These form part of every psychotherapeutic relationship and seem to be of crucial significance in work with psychotic patients and other patients disturbed at pre-symbolic levels of psychic functioning. The authors believe that in psychosis, a crucial aim of therapy is to facilitate the patient's internalisation of these containing functions through repeated exposure to their influence in the therapeutic relationship. The research processes described in this chapter explore different aspects of containment which the authors discovered as potentials within their art therapy settings through the 'making and matching' (Hill 1970) of clinical experience with reviews of the relevant literature.

MOTIVATION FOR RESEARCH

Motivation for our researches emerged from our experiences as clinicians working psychotherapeutically within medical-model psychiatry. We experienced a need to be able to describe the work we were doing to other colleagues and managers in the first instance. This was necessary in order to secure the future of this work, to secure appropriate referrals, and to establish a network of professional communications.

At Hill End Hospital, St Albans, Killick encountered considerable ambiguity in the attitudes of colleagues towards the purpose of schizophrenic patients' involvement in art therapy. She noted that patients with a medical diagnosis of schizophrenia were frequently referred for art therapy. (This art therapy setting is described in Case and Dalley 1992.) She also noted that the prevailing belief within the medical-model culture of the hospital appeared to be that psychotherapeutic work with psychotic patients was at best ineffective, and at worst 'dangerous', although the nature of the danger was not specified. She was puzzled by the fact that psychotic patients were referred to a setting in which psychotherapeutic work would take place, and concerned by repeated experiences of adverse changes in a patient's state being attributed to their involvement in art therapy.

When Killick began her work at Hill End in 1979, these patients were not selected for individual work by art therapy colleagues. She observed that they attended unstructured open sessions as long as they did not behave in ways which were described as 'ill' by these colleagues. This seemed to reflect the ambiguous nature of their referral to the department, and the anxiety which it generated in staff. At the same time, Killick noted that patients in acute psychotic states often seemed to engage particularly well with the setting as a whole. She began to work individually with these patients, with encouragement and support from the Consultant Psychotherapist, Dr Heiner Schuff, who had a particular interest in this client group (Schuff 1982). In the process of conducting this work, she became increasingly conscious of a need to be able to communicate effectively with medical staff, which was a strong motivation for her theoretical research.

The art therapy group described in Greenwood's research was set up in a small community-based unit called Stratford Road Day Centre in Birmingham. The focus of work in the Centre was an intensive psychotherapy programme and individual therapy for people with personality disorder and neurotic diagnoses. A depot injection clinic and lithium clinic were also held in the building, physically taking over the ground floor once a week but otherwise alienated from the main community. These clinics were attended by people with longterm psychotic disorders – schizophrenia and manic-depression. With the prospect of a new art therapy group session outside the core programme, referrals were made from the two clinics, primarily by Dr Layton, a psychiatrist, who later joined the group as co-therapist.

The therapists of this group became aware of the inadequacies of both the bio-medical model of psychiatry, on the one hand, and group psychotherapy and psychoanalytic models, on the other, in addressing the treatment needs of this client group. The group seemed to find a place of its own within the apparent polarities of these models. The therapists felt that the effectiveness of the art therapy group was demonstrated by the commitment of group members and the reduction in frequency of hospital admissions. They felt impressed by this in view of the severity of the illnesses of members, and the wish to describe what was happening was a strong motivation for the research they undertook.

We, the authors, both faced the task of understanding and describing experiences as art therapists engaging with psychotic processes in a way which could communicate effectively with other professionals. We found that the models for art therapy practice which were available to us at the beginning of our researches were inadequate for these purposes. There were few books on art therapy practice in print, and those that were did not address the particular issues encountered in work with psychotic patients which we described earlier. When psychotic processes predominate in the art therapy relationship, the symbolic order of experience is attacked. Accordingly the images produced in therapy with psychotic patients need to be thought about in different terms from those produced in therapy with patients for whom the symbolic order of experience is intact. This distinction is described in the context of the analytic relationship by the psychoanalyst Pankow (1981). In order to engage and maintain psychotic patients in art therapy, we found that we were using approaches which seemed original within the field of art therapy. The apparent absence of models of art therapy which could enable us to describe these approaches adequately to ourselves as well as to others often generated anxiety, and we both engaged in research in order to find adequate models.

A DESCRIPTIVE MODEL OF RESEARCH: FROM PRACTICE TO THEORY

The subject of Greenwood's research was an out-patient art therapy group for people with longterm psychotic illnesses. This was undertaken between 1984 and 1988 with her psychiatrist colleague, Dr Geoff Layton (Greenwood and Layton 1987, 1988). Greenwood and Layton's research was far removed from the model of an elegant, sophisticated research design set up to study outcome. The idea of the art therapy group grew out of anxieties about the adequacy of community treatment using a biomedical model of psychiatry. At the outset it was never envisaged as a research project. Greenwood and Layton were employed as clinicians, and became both the therapists and the researchers of the group. Their research follows a case study model, using a descriptive method of process research. They aimed to answer the question: 'what is going on?' There was no comparison to other studies. Hypotheses emerged out of the descriptive process but were not tested. Greenwood and Layton had set out to describe what happened in the art therapy group by a process of gathering information, giving a broad rather than a focused look. Their concern was with the meaning of changes rather than an assessment of outcome. They then moved from a broad descriptive process towards suggesting appropriate ways of working with people with a psychotic diagnosis.

To describe the group they firstly needed to review the relevant literature in order to find theoretical concepts and frameworks that fitted their experience. They began by considering the context of the group within the current shift of hospital to community care with historical and political reference.

Group members and their illnesses were described to establish a medical notion of psychosis. They explained how the group was set up, and the structure of the sessions, and then looked for meaning in the use of boundaries and spaces and the development of the group's use of the physical environment. Applying the psychological model of the ego psychologists they explored issues of compartmentalisation and integration in ego control over the environment (Hartmann 1958).

Different concepts were applied as they went along, thus modifying and changing their understanding. Theories of Hartmann (1958), Winnicott (1971), Kohut (1966), and Bion (1962) were useful to formulate a way of thinking about the nature of boundaries, spaces and structures in psychosis. They came to call their method of working a 'side-by-side' approach where the therapists participate in image-making and there is an emphasis on the equality of patient and therapist addressing something outside themselves, rather than on the relationship itself. Intensity of the transference is reduced, changing the difficult feelings that arise in treatment of formidable psychotic anxieties into a manageable stream so that the relationship is not destroyed by them.

When they arrived at Bion's concept of 'containment' this fitted and enriched their understanding in terms of working with group members, the group, their own anxieties, psychiatric services, and of the process of research itself. To explain the concept in terms of the patient/therapist relationship: intolerable feelings are projected into the therapist by the patient. The therapist struggles to digest this material, to come to some understanding of it, and once modified it can be given back to the patient in a form that is tolerable. According to Bion (1962, 1967), it is by the introjection of the ability to contain and transform projected material that we learn to 'think'.

It was as if the research process became necessary to contain, digest and understand material projected from the group into the therapists. Meeting together after sessions, and taking material to a psychotherapy supervision group was not always found to be an adequate container for the therapists, especially in dealing with countertransference issues (Greenwood and Layton 1987). Psychoanalytic concepts of group work learned in group psychotherapy training did not feel appropriate to them. The nature of addressing psychosis in the group necessitated new models of understanding and methods of working; this became the focus of the research process. When the therapists were finally able in some way to describe and understand what was happening in the group this was then fed back within the therapeutic relationship, not least by their peace of mind and ability to sustain their commitment to the group over several years. Members asked to read the paper 'An Out-patient Art Therapy Group' (1987) and despite reservations from its authors the effect was one of growth and understanding.

The first piece of research described the group in some detail from which methods of technique could be abstracted, such as:

- Side-by-side stance of therapist and patient.
- The need to relate to psychotic experience with respect.
- Importance of reliability and consistency of therapist and the physical environment to maintain 'containing' functions.
- The experience of therapy can be seen in terms of the relationship of the patient with the whole setting of therapy including the therapist and physical surroundings. Concrete aspects of the setting can assume a holding function.
- The need for a 'reticulum' of containers when working in the commmunity outside a hospital environment, i.e. a series of outer containers for unmanageable anxiety (see Greenwood and Layton 1987).

The first piece of research took three years to come to fruition, whereas the second followed in a matter of months (Greenwood and Layton 1988, 1991). In the process of struggling to describe the group the therapists had become aware of their use of the phrase 'taking the piss' to denote a type of humour which they saw as an adaptive mechanism at both social and mental levels. They played with this phrase and made associations with urination, satyrs and deflation. Their associations were explored in dictionaries and reference books, leading to a trail of meanings which began to enhance their understanding of the function of TTP. A literature search in 1987 of the past twenty years, cross referencing psychotherapy, humour and psychosis, revealed only one paper referring to humour in the treatment of psychotic patients in a group setting where Khan (1984) referred to a 'warm, good-natured kidding' which sounded similar to their experience. The therapists' researches were therefore able to move towards a hypothesis that a less serious approach may paradoxically be more appropriate when addressing more severe levels of pathology. They considered the implications of this especially with regard to the stance of therapist and patient – that in order to use irony in therapy we need to allow ourselves to be deflated by our patients. A hypothesis concerning the use of humour in art therapy groups for people with psychotic illnesses can now be clearly formulated and subjected to scientific testing in some future research.

As stated earlier, a review of the medical literature on humour in psychotherapy revealed little that illuminated the experience of phenomena referred to as 'taking the piss', but when TTP was matched with satire an understanding of the functions of this form of humour began to unfold:

Satire and TTP seem to us conceptually close. Satire is an art form. It is more than aggressive invective, it is playful and entertaining. When we described TTP in a clinical context we tried to show that this is not merely a cruel attack but a vehicle for transmutation of difficult feelings into humour and into play. This seems to share something with the social phenomenon of satirical art.

(Greenwood and Layton 1988, p. 79)

Training and personal experience had not equipped Greenwood and Layton to understand one particular member of the art therapy group either in terms of his psychosis, absence of open expression or his art. He had suffered many years of institutionalisation due to a schizophrenic illness, and detention under a prison section. He was a placid, taciturn man, uncommunicative to the extreme. His art had an absurd, seemingly cruel, style. When the humour of his work was finally enjoyed his stony face gave way to a sparkling wit and warmth belied by his usual appearance (Greenwood and Layton 1988). Unable to relate to the style of his art themselves they sought a model for his images in the art of Duchamp and Picabia. Through study of aspects of satire they began to understand his use of humour and his relationship to the world.

Greenwood and Layton saw that one of the principal objects in therapy was to learn to ride the tide of the unconscious better and achieve changes in self-mastery (Greenwood and Layton 1987). If potential madness is brought into consciousness it becomes accessible to ego control. Using Freud's model of unconscious energies against which the ego has to defend itself, they conceptualised therapy as an improvement and rearrangement of these defences in a direction of greater consciousness. Vaillant (1977) usefully describes a 'hierarchy' of defences where humour appears alongside sublimation, suppression, anticipation and altruism. He saw these as the highest defences associated with greater maturity and as being the most conscious, useful and adaptive. Humour was also described by Freud as the highest of defensive processes (Freud and Jung 1974). Hartmann (1958) described humour as an adaptation of the ego and as a 'detour' by which a path to the external world could be found. The holding and containing environment of the group facilitated a cohesive group where it was safe to explore the transitional world between our inner selves and the outside – the world of play, creativity and growth. The experience of being in the art therapy group led to the development of adaptive mental mechanisms.

In looking at the nature of the descriptive processes used by Greenwood and Layton in their research, their supervisor Dr Michael Radford (1983) introduced them to the 'making and matching' model of scientific method emphasised by modern philosophers of science such as Karl Popper, and applied to psychological understanding by a psychiatrist, Sir Dennis Hill (1970). He noted that we have to work on finding an internal model of experience to match with what we perceive. Models are learned, internalised and organised. If, when external experience occurs, it can be matched with an internal model, no further 'work' is required. This is an adaptive process. Existing models may be found or new ones created, but then the 'matching' needs to be forever scrutinised, modified and reviewed. This method of 'making and matching' becomes the essence of a research process. Hill usefully explores the relationship between the research methods of empirical science and those of psychoanalysis. The latter depends on the investigator using her- or himself, as psychic reality is brought into awareness through the relationship between patient and therapist. Hill writes, 'We can only know others {on the inside} by an act of identification, we can only know them {on the outside} by acts of perception' (Hill 1970, p. 614). The therapist thus becomes the research tool. Through different experiences of training, supervision and personal therapy, a therapist can become aware of how her or his own process is influencing her or his perception. The potential of using oneself as a research tool is limited by the extent of these experiences.

EXPLORING HYPOTHESES THROUGH THE LITERATURE

Killick's research was intertwined with the development of a way of working with individuals in acute psychotic states within an art therapy setting at Hill End Hospital, St Albans, which took place between 1979 and 1989. Academic research which enabled her to develop a clear theoretical framework for her clinical practice was essential to this process. She undertook this as part of her work towards an MA in art therapy between 1982 and 1987 (Killick 1987). Aspects of her therapeutic approach are described in two published articles (Killick 1991, 1993).

Her experiences with several patients led her to develop a hypothesis that the dimension of image-making, and activities associated with this dimension which are intrinsic to the art therapy setting, offers a medium for therapeutic intervention which is particularly appropriate to the therapeutic needs of patients in acute psychotic states. Her aim in the MA dissertation was to research a model of art-therapeutic approach to schizophrenic psychopathology which could be abstracted from her immediate clinical context and applied in other settings. At the same time she felt that the model which evolved needed to be one which would have meaning within a medical-model psychiatric setting, using a language which would be effective in this context. Reviewing the literature in the fields of cybernetics, family therapy and psychoanalysis enabled her to develop a model of schizophrenic psychopathology which emphasised the pathologically concrete thinking and relating characteristic of regressive ego organisation.

The work of several authors from different fields, notably Goldstein (Bolles and Goldstein 1938), a psychologist, Bateson (Bateson *et al.* 1956, Bateson 1978), an anthropologist working in the field of cybernetics; and Pankow (1981), a psychoanalyst, enabled Killick to differentiate between 'concrete' and the 'symbolising' elements in the thinking and behaviour of her patients. The distinction between that which, in Bion's (1967) terms, is contained, and that which contains – the content and the form of an utterance, an image, or other piece of behaviour, was central to the development of her hypothesis.

The work of Bolles and Goldstein (1938) and research into this subject by other psychologists and psychiatrists (Kasanin 1944) suggested that schizophrenic behaviour was 'pathologically concrete' and that 'abstract' or symbolic behaviour was avoided. The 'double bind' theory of schizophrenic behaviour proposed by Bateson *et al.* (1956) emphasised the role of pathologically concrete behaviour in avoiding experiences of relatedness. Various authors suggested, albeit in different theoretical languages, that the *form* of communication, which serves to define *relationship*, is distorted in pathologically regressed states of ego organisation such as schizophrenia.

The symbolising functions of the ego, which Pankow defines as 'body image' (1981), are attacked by the regressive processes at work in psychosis. It seems that the ego's capacity to use these functions in establishing relations between parts and wholes, and to process experiences of desire, content and meaning in relationship, is depleted. The concrete ways of thinking, experiencing and relating which result, disavow the fact of relationship itself. The only point of contention between different authors seemed to be whether this was due to organic, irreversible factors, or whether it was psychogenic, a defensive pattern emerging in relation to severe anxiety. Killick's experience led her to go along with the latter.

Killick found that writers from the object relations school of psychoanalysis such as Rosenfeld (1955) and Segal (1975) articulated her own experience: that the patient in an acute psychotic state tended to react to the therapist's attempts to establish relatedness with intensified symptoms. In exploring the theory of psychotherapeutic approaches, Killick followed the thinking of psychoanalysts Balint (1968), Little (1981) and Pankow (1981). These practitioners advocate an approach to patients which meets them at the level of their concreteness, thereby minimising persecutory anxieties, while exerting a challenge to the avoidance of symbolic behaviour and relationship, and at the same time offering new experiences of relationship which might exert a mutative effect on the pathology.

Thus, bringing literature and clinical experience together enabled Killick to propose that the concrete elements of image-making within the art therapy setting offered considerable potentials for work with this patient group. The art process itself offered potentials for a shift in the nature of the regression to a benign form. This could eventually result in restoration of symbolising functions and accordingly change in the level of ego function for the patient. These potentials – of the art process as an area of evolving the capacity to 'think the unthinkable' – and of the art therapy relationship as one which could foster the capacity to 'speak the unspeakable' could be realised if certain principles of approach were followed by the therapist (see Killick 1993).

In order to articulate the hypothesis Killick needed to develop a model of the art therapy relationship which emphasised these principles at work in the setting, and in the approach of the therapist, which she considered crucial to this therapeutic process. Her training had prepared her to attend to symbolic content and meaning within the image and the relationship, but both her experience and the literature suggested that a relationship within which images could have symbolic meaning does not exist between therapist and patient in acute psychotic states. Accordingly she proposed that the first aim of therapy must be to establish such a relationship (see Killick 1991). Using a cybernetic model, Killick identified three 'fields of communication' within the art therapy relationship. She described these as the 'intrapersonal', the 'intermediary' and the 'interpersonal'. These exist in relation to one another and exert continuous influence on each other.

She described the 'intrapersonal' as the interactive field established in the individual patient in relation to the potential for image-making. It is essentially exclusive of the therapist, and actively maintained as such by the therapist, who communicates the potentials of a space of this kind to the patient. Within this field, the patient can experience the uniqueness of his/her embodied relation with the art materials, and symbols can gradually evolve within this interaction which serve as healing agents. Killick proposed a model for a process of this shift to benign regression via image-making with reference to case material in which she observed processes of this kind occurring.

The 'intermediary' field is the realm of the 'transitional' phenomena described by Winnicott (1971). It is created by the concrete existence of art objects in the relationship, and is a field of play which enables the regressed patient to begin to develop symbolic activities in the relationship. By learning that the placing of objects in the setting is a symbolic activity which does not have concrete effects on self or other, the patient's capacity for play, and accordingly all kinds of transitional ways of experiencing and relating, can increase.

The 'interpersonal' field is that of one-to-one relations between therapist and patient, which in the art therapy setting include the images. The establishing of this field in the relationship forms the most confrontative of the therapist's interventions in that it works against the tendency to disavow relatedness. The folder containing the images or the absence of images, which form a concrete link between all three fields, is brought to a weekly session with a therapist who adopts a basically analytic attitude to the patient within the hour. Killick outlined some important potentials offered by the presence of the folder, and the images in the session, which enable the therapist to remain in analytic contact with the patient in states of severe regression.

Each field of communication includes containing (formal) and containable (content) elements. She advocated that the therapist working with patients in acute psychotic states suspend attention to content and meaning when speaking to the patient. The therapist focuses on those concrete transactions which establish boundary, pattern, structure and other formal, containing elements within the relationship until the 'interpersonal' field of communication is reliably established in the relationship. Her hypothesis was that containing elements, offered within the new experiences of the setting and communicated by the therapist in a non-persecutory way, would gradually be internalised by the patient and that this would result in a strengthening of symbolising ego functions. At the same time she proposed a particular role for the art process as a medium for 'regression in the service of ego'. She suggested that image-making may be used by patients in acute psychotic states in accordance with primitive defences and image-making may accordingly constitute a means of acting out the all-pervasive attack on reality (Killick 1993). She thought it essential that the therapist distinguish between the different meanings which image-making might hold for the patient. The approach a therapist might take towards image-making employed as part of a psychotic attack on reality will differ from the approach towards image-making which serves a creative process. At the same time she thought that the physicality of the experiences involved in image-making could serve containing purposes in themselves with patients in states of severe psychotic anxiety. Pankow (1981) and other practitioners emphasise the importance of physical containment for patients in severe states of ego fragmentation.

The therapist tries to understand what is taking place in the emotional reality of the transference and countertransference, and to refrain from interpretation until the patient indicates that s/he is able to maintain symbolising functions within the relationship. The realities of the therapeutic relationship, the setting, and the images offer experiences to the patient which foster the evolution of more symbolic relations to the image (Killick 1993). One and the same image can accrue many different levels of meaning within the therapeutic relationship over time.

Killick's academic research explored a way of thinking which could enable the therapist to attend consistently to the containing principles at work in each of the fields of communication which she defined. She felt that a consistent way of thinking would, in conjunction with empathy, contribute to the therapist's capacity for understanding. She was seeking a way of relating to the emotional reality of psychotic processes in her relationships with patients. The therapist's communication of containing principles can be experienced as extremely persecutory by psychotic patients. She felt it was important to try to understand what was going on for the patient. She felt that understanding, whether spoken or not, could avoid the potential escalation of defensive acting out, and facilitate a therapeutic environment within which the regenerative healing processes of the unconscious could come into play in the patient's art work. Thus, having developed a systematic way of thinking about the work in which she was engaged, Killick was able to arrive at a research hypothesis which could be tested empirically.

FORMULATING A MODEL

The processes of 'making and matching' described in our researches continued to expand beyond our immediate clinical contexts into a network of communicating ideas. Through publications, teaching and supervision we communicated, checked and modified our ideas. The process of 'matching' those aspects of our ideas and understandings which were common to both our researches led us to elucidate the common hypotheses outlined here.

There are significant differences in the nature, subject and method of our researches, and in some of our conclusions concerning art therapy practice. However, a clear hypothesis which is common to both, and which emerges strongly precisely because of the differences mentioned, is that experiences which can be described as containing (Bion) or holding (Winnicott) are crucial to useful psychotherapeutic work with psychotic patients, and that the art therapy setting offers specific potentials for facilitating experiences of this kind within the therapeutic relationship.

Our separate researches into different aspects of containment in the art therapy setting involved us both in an experience of shifting our focus in relation to clinical material from what might be described as the 'content' of material to its 'form'. In simple terms, what we mean by this is that what is being described or communicated by the psychotic patient is at times less important than how it is communicated. This was a new discovery for us, having been trained to take interest in content and meaning.

We both discovered that this shift of emphasis was leading us to value aspects of our work with patients which we had felt were rather banal. Therapists working with psychotic patients need to value and actively maintain an interest in particular aspects of approach which we believe many use intuitively but take for granted. Examples are the use of the folder in Killick's approach (1987) and the use of humour in Greenwood and Layton's (1988, 1991). Art therapists may find these aspects of practice hard to value because of a lack of concepts which accord them the status of treatment methods. It is precisely because they are taken for granted that they can be swamped by the onslaught of psychotic processes, which is why a model which emphasises them is necessary. Accordingly our researches represented efforts to discover models of clinical practice which would emphasise the value of these elements in the art therapy setting. Although we think that containing elements are of crucial mutative significance in therapeutic work with psychotic patients, we believe that they are significant to a greater or lesser degree in any therapeutic relationship at certain stages of the work.

On the basis of our researches, we believe that a model for effective art therapy practice with psychotic patients includes several specific elements of approach:

- The therapist aims to foster the evolution of a language for the patient, within the art process, of structures which initially mediate between concrete and symbolic ways of thinking, and which can serve increasingly symbolic purposes in the relationship.
- Clear, dynamically structured and maintained boundaries establish and maintain the fact of relationship between therapist and patient/group. These facilitate strengthening of psychological boundaries and the growth of intrapsychic structures. Negotiation of rules and boundaries offer significant points of therapeutic contact in the relationship.
- The therapist responds to formal aspects of the patient's relating, suspending references to content and meaning, until symbolising functions enable the patient to experience interpretation *as* interpretation. At times the focus may need to be entirely on the concrete aspects of the relationship, the art materials, and the physical environment.
- Projected material is contained within the relationship, in the art process and the countertransference, and held until the patient has developed sufficient ego strength to assimilate that which has been projected.
- Within the boundaries of the relationship, ego-strengthening opportunities for experimentation, exploration and creative play with the experiences offered are maximised.

When the therapeutic relationship is sufficiently established to enable the patient to contain experiences of loss, confrontation with the fact that a damaging process is at work in their lives can help patients with the work of changing their allegiance from the pleasure principle to the reality principle, fostering symbol formation and the capacity for thinking. Processes of integration, synthesis, reparation and creative growth are not straightforward. The evolution of adaptive mental mechanisms, such as humour, sublimation, anticipation and altruism, indicate increasing ego strength and, accordingly, can be valued as goals in therapy. The experience of being part of a group can support this process. This experience allows a supportive peer group and close friendships to develop.

Our researches began with a common belief that art therapy could be a useful and effective form of longterm psychotherapeutic work with psychotic patients. Our research methods necessitated our becoming 'research tools', and endeavouring to match our experiences with the literature in an attempt to understand the experience of psychosis while recognising that our personal experience and professional training, however well supported by personal therapy and supervision, would limit us in this line of enquiry. The degree to which therapists are familiar with those psychotic processes which are at work in themselves will determine the degree to which they can empathise with their patients.

REFERENCES

Balint, M. (1968) *The Basic Fault.* Tavistock, London.
Bateson, G. (1978) *Steps to an Ecology of Mind.* Granada, London.
Bateson, G., Jackson, D., Haley, J. and Weakland, J. (1956) 'Toward a Theory of Schizophrenia'. *Behavioral Science.* 1: 251–64.
Bion, W.R. (1962) *Learning From Experience.* Heinemann, London.
Bion, W.R. (1967) *Second Thoughts.* Karnac, London.
Bolles, M. and Goldstein, K. (1938) 'A Study of the Impairment of "Abstract Behavior" in Schizophrenic Patients'. *Psychiatric Quarterly.* 12: 42–65.
Case, C. and Dalley, T. (1992) *The Handbook of Art Therapy.* Routledge, London.
Freud, S. and Jung, C.G. (1974) In: Mcguire, W. (Ed.) *Letters.* Manheim, R. and Hull, R.C.F. (Trans.) Hogarth and Routledge and Kegan Paul, London.
Greenwood, H. and Layton, G. (1987) 'An Out-patient Art Therapy Group'. *Inscape.* Summer: 12–19.
Greenwood, H. and Layton, G. (1988) 'Taking the Piss'. *British Journal of Clinical and Social Psychiatry.* 6: 74–84.
Greenwood, H. and Layton, G. (1991) 'Taking the Piss'. *Inscape.* Winter: 7–14.
Hartmann, H. (1958) *Ego Psychology and the Problem of Adaptation.* D. Rappoport (Trans.) International Universities Press, New York.
Hill, D. (1970) 'On the Contributions of Psychoanalysis to Psychiatry: Mechanism and Meaning'. *British Journal of Psychiatry.* 117: 609–15.
Kasanin, J.S. (Ed.) (1944) *Language and Thought in Schizophrenia.* University of California Press.
Khan, M. (1984) 'Group Treatment Interventions in Schizophrenia'. *International Journal of Group Psychotherapy.* 43: 149–53.
Killick, K. (1987) 'Art Therapy and Schizophrenia: A New Approach'. Unpublished MA thesis, School of Art and Design, University of Hertfordshire.
Killick, K. (1991) 'The Practice of Art Therapy with Patients in Acute Psychotic States'. *Inscape.* Winter: 2–6.
Killick, K. (1993) 'Working with Psychotic Processes in Art Therapy'. *Psychoanalytic Psychotherapy.* 7: 25–38.
Kohut, H. (1966) 'Forms and Transformations of Narcissism'. *Journal of the American Psychoanalytic Association.* 14: 243–72.
Laplanche, J. and Pontalis, J.B. (1973) *The Language of Psycho-Analysis.* Hogarth Press, London.
Little, M. (1981) *Transference Neurosis and Transference Psychosis.* Jason Aronson, New York.
Pankow, G. (1981) 'Psychotherapy: A Psychoanalytic Approach. An Analytic Approach Employing the Concept of the Body Image'. In: Dongier, M. and Wittkower, E. (Eds) *Divergent Views in Psychiatry.* Harper and Row, New York.
Radford, M. (1983) 'Psychoanalysis and the Science of Problem-solving Man: An Appreciation of Popper's Philosophy and a Response to Will'. *British Journal of Medical Psychology.* 56: 9–26.
Rosenfeld, H. (1955) 'Notes on the Analysis of the Super-ego Conflict in an Acute

Schizophrenic Patient'. In: Klein, M, Heimann, P. and Money-Kyrle, R. (Eds) *New Directions in Psycho-Analysis*. Tavistock, London.

Rycroft, C. (1972) *A Critical Dictionary of Psychoanalysis*. Penguin, Harmondsworth.

Schuff, G.H. (1982) 'Dynamic Body Building'. Unpublished paper presented to Conference 'Art Therapy and Drama Therapy', Hertfordshire College of Art and Design 22–23 April 1982.

Segal, H. (1975) 'Psycho-analytic Approach to the Treatment of Schizophrenia'. In: Lader, M.H. (Ed.) *Studies of Schizophrenia. British Journal of Psychiatry Special Publications* No. 10.

Vaillant, G. (1977) *Adaptation to Life*. Little, Brown and Co, Boston and Toronto.

Winnicott, D.W. (1971) *Playing and Reality*. Tavistock, London.

Chapter 7

Making sense of marking space
Researching art therapy with people who have severe learning difficulties

Mair Rees

Many of the ideas outlined in this chapter have emerged from a research project I conducted single-handed over a period of some three years. The study's aim was to investigate clients' use of physical space and its potential symbolic significance. The people featured in this project were a group of women who have severe learning difficulties and whose home environment at the time of the study was a single-sex locked ward in a large mental handicap hospital. This research was partially stimulated by the work of Chance (Polsky and Chance 1979a, 1979b, 1980) and other researchers in the ethological field on the use of physical space in long-stay psychiatric hospitals.

I shall begin this chapter by taking a brief glance at some of the contemporary writing of art therapists who have worked with people who have severe degrees of learning difficulty. Subsequently, I shall trace the evolutionary path of my own research starting with the questions which perplexed me as a practising art therapist and earlier as an unqualified worker. I intend to explain some of the reasons why I chose to adopt this particular theoretical framework, which methodology was employed and, in conclusion, how I believe the process has enriched my understanding of clinical practice.

SETTING THE SCENE

In recent years art therapists working with people who have learning difficulties have found it useful to examine their relationship with clients in the light of various theories of ego development. Hughes (1986 ,1988), for example, has sought clarification of her work with this group of people in the writing of Winnicott (1971). A number of other art therapists (Wilson 1980; Hallam 1984; Spensly 1984) have placed their clinical experience within similar theoretical frameworks which relate emotional and psychological development to the development of a therapeutic relationship. It is easy for anyone who has knowledge of this client group to see why theories which have a strong developmental emphasis should be an attractive way of ordering understanding. Tipple makes some pertinent observations on the practice of art therapy with people who have severe learning difficulties: 'Establishing stable and positive relationships with these difficult and unattractive individuals is difficult. When artwork is possible, it appears that the client has merely repeated a series of simple motor movements with the crayon or marker and the resultant work may seem banal and indifferent' (Tipple 1992, p. 105).

Theories of ego development imbue the therapeutic process with a sense of direction and purpose; there is always the notion of progress, of working towards something. In the case of the art therapist a major goal would be the client's first tentative experiences of gestalt, i.e. perception of oneself as a separate, whole and boundaried entity. As art therapists we often make the implicit assumption that the client with severe learning difficulties has an impoverished sense of self: 'Her [Rose Hughes'] approach implies that the adult mentally handicapped person with severe disabilities does not have a capacity to recognise the otherness of the world, that they have a poor sense of self' (Tipple 1992, p. 108). I feel there is a real danger that art therapists (myself included) have unconsciously devalued people with severe learning difficulties by overstressing their inadequacy and incompletedness in our strivings for theoretical orderliness.

Even allowing for this potential bias, it is still undeniable that people's inherent disabilities have often been compounded by woefully inadequate parenting in grim institutional surroundings. Many of the women who are the subjects of this chapter have been institutionalised since early childhood. Cook conjures up a harrowing picture of the initial experience of a man with learning difficulties in a large institution in the 1960s, a time when the majority of people I worked with were already living in hospital.

> Walter was allocated a bed in a dormitory containing 69 other beds, all of which were occupied. . . . The time was 7.30 pm. All lights except the one in the glass booth at the end of the ward which was occupied by the staff were turned out. At 8.00pm the night staff arrived and the day staff went home. Walter was still awake in spite of the two pills and heard someone say 'We've got a new one, might be a bit of trouble. If he kicks up a fuss, give him the needle.' The man in the bed next to Walter was crying.
>
> (Cook 1980, p. 160)

One can only surmise what effect the lack of individual attention and warmth of human contact has had on many of these people. Many art therapists, myself included, have worked on the assumption that the individual is unlikely to have encountered (or in some cases to have been responsive to) 'good-enough' nurturing, certainly not to the level at which they may be presumed to have the rudiments of a coherent feeling of self. Without understanding of their physical or psychological boundaries, any individual must surely exist in a primordial quagmire of unlabelled emotion. The ability to make predictions about the world is impossible, as there is no order, consistency or continuity to one's experiences. If this is true, then how on earth do such people manage to survive at all in the world? Many clients I have worked with, and whom I have assumed to have a limited sense of self, actually manage to organise themselves quite well. They succeed in getting around the hospital, communicating their needs in various ways, and at the very least tolerating (and therefore presumably acknowledging) the presence of other people.

Killick has observed what seems to me to be a parallel phenomenon from her work with people labelled as suffering from psychoses (Killick 1991). There are some fundamental differences, of course, as Killick refers to individuals who have experienced a disintegration of ego function, whereas with some people with severe learning difficulties the likelihood seems to be that certain facets of ego integration have never been attained:

> Despite the fragmentation of ego function which destroys the psychotic patient's experience of his or her embodied self, the embodied person continues to exist and relate to the physical environment. To put it another way, even if the ego is absent, the patients 'soul' is still present, and to put it yet another way, the person is still there even if his or her sense of personhood is laid to waste. It is possible to experience relatedness with the person at some level which the defensive operations of the ego cannot destroy.
>
> (Killick 1991, p. 5)

As an art therapist, the sense I have come to make of this phenomenon is that some people manage to organise their intrapsychic world *despite* the absence of a clearly differentiated sense of self. In my opinion this 'make do and mend' strategy is one of the most fascinating and perplexing aspects of therapy. How do individual clients manage to bypass the experience of gestalt and with what do they replace it?

With the benefit of hindsight it seems clear to me that we all possess a powerful motivational urge to make sense of situations, often with very limited tools at our disposal. By ordering our experiences we ensure psychological continuity and our emotional survival. This seemingly simple homily was the long-awaited offspring of an arduous, complicated, frustrating, but infuriatingly absorbing labour. The process was euphemistically referred to as a research project!

The seeds of the inquiry were probably planted before I qualified as an art therapist. For a year following graduation I worked as a nursing assistant in a large hospital for people with learning difficulties. Mostly I was allocated to a ward which catered for young adults with profound and multiple disabilities, but on occasion I would be moved to other wards to make up staffing numbers. One such ward was a secure environment for women who had severe degrees of learning difficulty and also displayed 'challenging behaviour'. The large undifferentiated day room was bleak and forbidding. There was no carpet on the floor, walls were bare. There was minimum furniture, institutional armchairs placed in regimented lines, a television fixed high up on the wall so that no one could possibly reach it . In one corner was a dining area, five small circular tables with four chairs permanently bolted to each. Nothing else, nothing at all. A woman was screaming and banging her head against the window frame. Another was being dragged off her chair on to the floor by a fellow resident. Someone else was pacing up and down with her fingers in her ears whilst singing loudly. Mostly people were curled up tightly on chairs. Nobody was watching the television apart from a nurse who sat well apart from the residents, desperately, it seemed to me, trying to deny the grim reality of the situation. It certainly echoed Cook's description (1980).

My assessment of what I saw on that first day was deprivation, distress, chaos and mayhem. I was in fact quite wrong about the last two observations and the distress was at least partly my own. Later, as I worked more regularly on this ward, I came to realise that far from anarchy and disorder it represented a complex and organised social system. Certain individuals would only ever interact with certain other individuals. A number of people had a favourite chair which they would not tolerate anyone else acquiring. Some women seemed to stay in one place, others were constantly on the move, often taking well-rehearsed paths around the day room. One or two residents interacted almost exclusively with members of staff, ignoring or shunning other residents.

When, over a year later, I emerged from postgraduate art therapy training, I was offered a post as an art therapist in the same hospital. I received a number of referrals to work with individuals who were residents on this women's locked ward. Entering the same ward still filled me with some sense of trepidation, but I was increasingly of the opinion that there was more afoot than I was yet able to understand. My fears were that of a xenophobic: the culture of the ward was still quite alien to me; the language used (often non-verbal) was complex and unfamiliar; I was a tourist abroad without the services of a guide.

My reaction to this situation should have given me some important clues to my potential clients' greatest needs, but at the time I was too overwhelmed by my perception of the differences between us. I felt a strong urge to make sense of what I had seen, heard and felt. I needed to frame and organise my experiences.

At the time there was a conspicuous dearth of clinical writing on the application of art therapy with people who have severe learning difficulties and challenging behaviour. One notable exception was the then recently completed PhD thesis of Dubowski (1985). Dubowski had observed and catalogued the drawings and drawing behaviour of such clients in a systematic fashion, and I was interested to find that he had adopted the methodological framework of a specific school of zoologists in order to carry out his study. The discipline is referred to as ethology. It was a subject area familiar to me as I had already chosen it as a specialist topic at undergraduate level. It was this approach I eventually turned to in order to look more systematically at what was happening within this particular ward's social system and link it to certain spatial phenomena in the clients' art work.

Prior to commencing the research proper I had noted from conducting both group and individual art therapy sessions that a small number of clients I saw from various different wards within the hospital seemed to have a very similar approach to the way in which they used both the sessions and the art materials. These people were seemingly interested only in the use of thickly applied paint. Their primary objective appeared to be filling in sheets of paper. Some would confine themselves to overlaying onto one sheet per session, others would use several sheets in succession, responding to each page in a similar manner. Other aspects of mark-making such as colour and form clearly had little or no attraction for these individuals. Two such people were Chris and May.

Chris

Chris was a young man of 23 . He had a severe degree of learning difficulty and very challenging behaviour. The vast majority of Chris's time was spent engaged in what staff described as sweeping behaviour. This involved Chris spitting on the floor and subsequently brushing the saliva and accumulated debris with his hand. Chris performed this activity both inside the ward and outside in the small yard which enclosed the unit. Indoors, Chris would shuffle on his knees, moving furniture, and pushing people out of his way so that he could reach the extreme corners of the room. Although sweeping also took place in the centre of the room Chris concentrated his effort around the perimeters. Out of doors Chris would perform a similar sequence, sweeping small pieces of gravel along the edge of the fencing which surrounded the yard. Chris attended non-directive art therapy sessions for eighteen months. There were two qualified art therapists present in the once-weekly, hour-long sessions.

Chris's attention in the sessions was very spasmodic. Usually he would remain in the department for ten or fifteen minutes only. The only art material in which he expressed any real interest was paint. His paintings were executed in a couple of minutes at most, with two or three paintings being produced in most sessions. Sometimes when Chris had finished painting he would begin his sweeping routine on the floor of the department; on other occasions he might insist on sweeping in preference to painting. His paintings were at a pre-representational, controlled scribble stage of development. He would not actively select or change colour, but rather would use the pot nearest to him. After some time it occurred to me that the spatial organisation of his marks on the paper seemed to resemble the strategy employed in his sweeping. Despite the fact that much of the page had been covered in paint, special attention was awarded by Chris to the edges, and in particular the corners of the paper.

May

May was a 56-year-old woman with a severe learning difficulty; she was a member of a ward-based art therapy group for two years. In the sessions she would usually choose to sit in the extreme right-hand corner of the ward with her back to the wall, from where she could scrutinise the rest of the day room. She was constantly vigilant and would become alarmed by sudden noises or the approach of other residents. Her drawings during the early sessions were timid and reticent. Her response to pencil and crayons was fairly minimal; using these materials she would tap on the page, keeping to a small central area near the baseline. Only a small number of marks were produced in each hourly session. Usually May would discard the implements onto the floor after a while. May's introduction to paint, however, gradually brought about a change in her image-making process. Using short dabbing movements with the brush she gradually increased the area of the page she would cover, until eventually the majority of the surface would be filled. Other behaviours began to manifest themselves and developed in tandem with her painting. There was a rhythmic tapping of the brush on the paper, often accompanied by rocking and chanting. Later, she also began to paint the edges of the table, or the edges of an adjacent resident's paper. About this time May was also spitting on her fingers, daubing saliva along the edges of both the table and the painting in front of her. Ward staff had also noticed her daubing saliva around the edges of windows, mirrors and doors.

I spent quite some time thinking about my relationship with these people. Containment was clearly an important function of art therapy but it was difficult to make sense of some aspects of these clients' behaviour, in particular, why their considerable indifference to social contact was matched by an equal and opposite preoccupation with space and other physical aspects of the environment. Ethology provided me with some thought-provoking clues.

ETHOLOGICAL TECHNIQUE AND ITS APPLICATION TO HUMAN STUDY

Put simply, ethology is the study of behaviour within the subject's every-day environment. At one level, it evolved as a backlash from the increasing use of controlled laboratory studies as a means of investigating animal behaviour. Modern ethology did not really evolve as a discipline in its own right until the involvement of Konrad Lorenz in the 1950s (Lorenz 1950), and it was not until the 1970s that researchers began to see the possibilities of employing this framework as a means of researching human behaviour (e.g. Esser *et al.* 1970, Esser and Deutsch 1977).

Ethology is concerned with both the function of behaviour and the consequence or adaptive significance of that particular behaviour for that particular individual. Its methodology has many similarities with techniques employed in adjacent fields of study such as zoology and psychology. However, ethology places greater emphasis on detailed systematic observations of discreet units of behaviour. There is a basic principle that behaviour must be observed and described before any attempts at elaborate theorising are made. Often the entire behavioural repertoire of a given species will have been compiled by meticulous observation. Tinbergen (1950) outlined four basic questions which need to be asked of any specific behaviour:

1 Why does it happen now?
2 How does it help things?
3 How did it develop in the first place?
4 Has it changed over time?

Such questions serve to place the behaviour within a context. Ethological studies with people have largely been conducted in areas where it is difficult to employ the traditional tools of social research such as interviews or questionnaires. As with any other mode of study, there are advantages and disadvantages in using ethological techniques to investigate people's behaviour; often these issues represent both sides of the same coin.

One advantage is that the active participation of the subject is not required; an ethological approach asks nothing of subjects, only that they carry on with their everyday routine. This is a very important consideration if one is intending to study the behaviour of people who challenge services, or who are unable or unwilling to co-operate actively for other reasons. The negative aspect of this is the potential violation of people's right to privacy. This is a particularly valid criticism when working with people who are devalued, and who do not have any means of indicating their consent or otherwise. Another bonus of this type of observational approach is that there is no direct interference with the people studied or their behaviour. However, the presence of an observer in itself can be a major intrusion and may be a factor which significantly influences the results. Some researchers have tried to minimise this effect in questionable but ingenious ways, e.g. by ensuring that the observer wears dark glasses when collecting data to avoid eye contact with the subjects, or by constructing screens to hide behind.

Although reliance on direct observation minimises the ethologists' chances of embarking upon premature theorising, it is self-evident that the often copious amounts of data they collect must be organised in some way, in order to extract meaning. Whilst ethologists are very tentative in their formulation of hypotheses they may well focus on certain aspects of behaviour, and employ phenomena known as constructs. These represent a working compromise between direct observation and a fully-fledged hypothesis. Constructs form a flexible base for integrating and comparing different types and sources of information. They often clarify the 'how, where and when of behaviour', but further along the line hypotheses will be required to establish the 'why'.

Some of the clients I had encountered were considered by various other professionals to be exhibiting autistic tendencies. I had been impressed by the work of ethologists like the Tinbergens (1972) and the Hutts (1968) in this field, but felt that it did not address the issues arising in my clients' behaviour and art work. I began to take an interest in the writings of another group of ethologists, primarily Esser and his colleagues (1970, 1977), and Polsky and Chance (1979a, 1980), who had concerned themselves with investigating the behaviour of long-stay psychiatric patients within the restrictive environment of institutional hospital wards. I felt that this orientation was potentially useful in relation to my own quest for meaning, as it paid due regard to the exacerbating effects of the current social context on subjects' behaviour. These researchers had applied the ethological construct of territoriality to provide a theoretical framework for their investigations.

This construct of territoriality was originally employed to describe an animal's penchant for favouring and defending a particular niche. Early studies found that some bird species could be seen to select home grounds and defend them against intruders. This original concept has been extended throughout the animal kingdom and some aspects of territoriality have been looked at in human populations. Esser and Deutsch (1977) identified two aspects of territoriality in human society: firstly, private retreat – this is territoriality's original meaning, i.e. a private place; secondly, personal space – this is the area immediately surrounding an individual's body which he or she seeks to keep free from intrusion.

Esser and Deutsch also point out that in the course of social behaviour, all human interactions depend on the ability to share space reciprocally with others. This results in the formation of 'interactional territories', i.e. a spatial transformation of the participants' mutual engagement in the interaction. By entering into such a social contract, a person must forfeit part of an individual identity in order to create a new social identity. Obviously the degree of proximity involved will depend on a number of variables, such as the relationship between the interactors, the social context, and the sheer amount of space available. For example, when travelling on the tube people adopt strategies such as disappearing behind a newspaper, or listening to a Walkman with eyes closed, in order to alleviate the discomfort they experience from having been forced into inappropriate intimacy with total strangers.

Esser (in Esser and Deutsch, 1977) feels that some people with serious mental health problems (and this, in my view, applies equally well to people with severe learning difficulties and challenging behaviour) who have an impoverished sense of self may be unwilling or unable to compromise themselves further by operating within a mutual territory. Esser's ideas concerning psychiatric patients' spatial needs have resulted from extensive studies on a psychiatric ward of long-stay patients. He found that the patients exhibiting the lowest incidence of social interaction also displayed the greatest preference for particular areas on the ward. He has proposed that some people at certain times of their lives will have a reduced propensity for forming interactional territories. However, it is not only psychological difficulties *per se* which curtail the ability to establish spatiosocial relationships:

> The restricted environment of a hospital, compounds these difficulties in expressing transformations of their spatial needs. Research in closed environments has shown that inhabitants, be they mentally ill, prisoners or the crew of a submarine, exhibit territorial and dominance behaviour. Especially in total institutions, where inmates are forced to share few environmental resources we may view the emergence of such behaviours as adaptive.
>
> (Esser and Deutsch 1977, p. 128)

Subsequent studies have not always substantiated these findings. Polsky and Chance (1979a,b) found that patients who showed the highest incidence of social interaction also presented a preference for territoriality. Interestingly, their specific territorial preferences were usually for areas of the ward closest to the mainstream of activity. There seem to be additional factors operating here besides spatial ones; the more social patients appeared to choose the more prominent parts of the ward, with their attendant likelihood for interactions with others.

Having familiarised myself with the relevant literature my hunch was that clients who were preoccupied with spatial aspects in their image-making processes would also show a preoccupation with space and territory in their everyday lives. This consistency across situations might imply that these individuals were employing a specific strategy to organise their intrapsychic experiences. Consequently, there could well be clinical implications for how an art therapist might best adapt the therapeutic milieu to suit these individuals' needs.

THE STUDY

My research was carried out within a large traditional mental handicap hospital on the locked ward for twenty women with severe learning difficulties and challenging behaviour, as previously described. The study as a whole ran over a period of three years; the subjects were all twenty women who were then resident on the ward. For the first two years an open, non-directive art therapy group was held on the aforementioned ward. One purpose of the group was to establish if any of the women appeared to be attending primarily to spatial cues in the the execution of their art work. The final year of the study involved direct observation of the subjects' behaviour within the ward environment. A number of different observational measures were adopted; a detailed description of each is beyond the scope of this chapter. I shall therefore concentrate on one key type of observation made during the final year of the study.

Open art therapy group

As stated, for two years prior to the observation periods, a weekly open group was conducted on the ward in question. Two qualified art therapists were present in each session, and a non-directive (i.e. minimum intervention from the therapists) approach was adopted. All individuals present were encouraged to participate in this group if they so wished. There was a range of art materials available for use (paint, oil and wax crayons, felt pens) and participants were encouraged to select their own materials. Some individuals became regular members (n=5), some chose never to participate (n=3), and the remainder of subjects (n=12) participated occasionally and/or for brief intervals on their way to and from other departments. This section of the research was the one most open to subjectivity and bias of the researcher. Therefore, the analysis of drawings and drawing behaviour was completed prior to commencement of the observation and recording on the ward, to avoid retrospective evaluation. The ward group was in fact continued during the final year observation period for purely therapeutic reasons, although drawings from this time did not contribute to the data.

I analysed the clients' work by asking the following questions:

1 Which art medium if any does the client favour using?
2 What are the 'placement patterns' of the work produced? (see Kellog 1969)
3 Does the client actively select colours?

The hypothesis to be tested was whether some individuals attend primarily to spatial cues in their drawing. These people would be defined by the following features:

1 They exhibited a preference for paint, partially because it is a most effective agent for covering and filling in.
2 The placement patterns of their work were either attempts to fill the whole page, or to reinforce the corners and edges of the paper with paint.
3 They would not actively select colour, but usually employed the container nearest to them, changing colour only when the pot was empty, or if prompted.

Observation and recording on the ward

The reason for carrying out direct observations was to discover if any of the residents had a preference for a particular location within the ward's large communal day room. The results of these observations would hopefully give some indications of the individuals to whom the definition and maintenance of a particular physical space, i.e. territory, was an important activity.

Practical and ethical considerations dictated that there would be a number of restrictions imposed upon the observation and recording of these women's behaviour:

1 To respect people's right to privacy and, more specifically, right not to be included in this study, subjects were observed only when they were in the large communal living area, and not in any other part of the ward.
2 Observations were made only on weekdays when the ward routine was at its most regular and there were rarely outsiders present.
3 Observations were executed only at times when most subjects were likely to be present on the ward but not at times when it was likely to be overly intrusive, e.g. meal times or bath times.

Consequently observations were made within the following times:

```
After lunch....................................12.30–1.00 pm
Before tea.................................... 3.45–4.15 pm
Evening........................................ 7.00–7.30 pm
```

Thirty-seven observation sessions (i.e. 18.5 hours) were undertaken over a three-month period.

One major difficulty with the design of this study was that as the observations were being conducted by a single researcher (i.e. me!) it was not possible to establish inter-observer reliability, which usually eliminates bias. It was therefore crucial to keep the observational schedules and methods of recording as simple and as unambiguous as possible. Clearly it would seem most beneficial to record continuously throughout each observational period. However, as Parker points out, 'This is usually impossible, is always inefficient, and is probably not necessary anyway' (Parker 1975, p. 8).

Many of the studies previously carried out by ethological researchers on hospital wards (e.g. Esser *et al.* 1970) have employed time-sampling techniques to gather data. This procedure involves the recording of any given behaviour or behaviours at set intervals during the observation period, the proximity of sampling periods being partially influenced by the frequency of the behaviour being observed. Prior to commencing the observations proper I conducted a small pilot study in order to decide on the most appropriate interval between sampling periods, to practise my recording skills, and to familiarise the residents with the presence of an observer. An interval of five minutes between sampling was decided upon as the most appropriate, as it permitted adequate recording of change without unnecessary duplication of data. I compiled data sheets from floor plans of the ward, which were elaborated to include the position of chairs, tables and television (Figure 7.1). These were used to note each resident's exact position within the living room area at five minute intervals over the thirty-minute observation periods. I sat in the same position within the dining area for each observation period. At the given intervals I made a quick visual scan of the living area, and indicated the position of each individual by writing their initials on the data sheets. This is similar in design to the observational schedule developed by Polsky and Chance (1979a, 1980) and employed in a number of their studies.

RESULTS

Open art therapy group

Of the twenty subjects, examples of art work and general observations of art processes were made for seventeen individuals. The remaining three

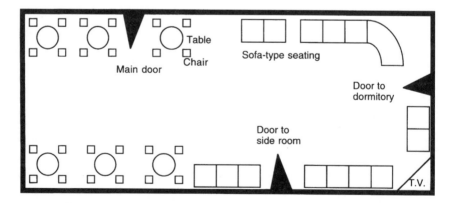

Figure 7.1 Floor plan of the ward

Table 7.1 Allocation of subjects to groups

	Spatial	Non-spatial	No result	Total
Territorial	4	5	0	9
Non-territorial	0	8	3	11

individuals were either unwilling, or unable (because of the severity of their disabilities) to join in with the sessions. Of these seventeen, four individuals were seen to attend primarily to spatial cues in their art work, i.e. a strong preference for the use of paint, and a preoccupation with filling in space, or reinforcing edges and/or corners of the page. Two other individuals displayed these tendencies to a lesser degree but, as this research was carried out single-handed, it was felt important to err on the side of caution in the interpretation of data; so these two subjects were not included.

Location observation

From completed data sheets subjects were allocated to a territorial group (T) or non-territorial group (NT), depending on their percentage occupancy of any given space. In reality this represents a continuum from the most to the least territorial subject. For the purposes of this study a criterion of 25 per cent occupancy of any given space was used to divide the subject population (after Esser *et al.* 1970).

There were roughly equal numbers of subjects in the territorial group (n=9) and the non-territorial group (n=11). Two subjects who were included in the non-territorial group did in fact favour more than one location and were almost equally likely to be found in either of their chosen places. Statistically no significant difference was found between these two groups for either chronological age or length of hospitalisation. The individuals had very diverse medical labels assigned to them, ranging from genetic aetiologies such as Down's Syndrome through to birth trauma and unknown causation. Two individuals from the territorial group and one from the non-territorial group were deemed by their medical notes to be 'autistic'.

All subjects who employed a spatial strategy in drawing (n=4) fell into the territorial group, although conversely, of course, not all subjects who were allocated to the territorial group exhibited a spatial preference in their drawing. Spatial preferences in drawing therefore seem to be a subset of a more general psychospatial strategy.

DISCUSSION

Art therapists and related practitioners will be familiar with the seemingly unpredictable, unboundaried behaviour of some clients who have severe learning difficulties. Moreover, they will doubtless have encountered clients like those in this study who are also preoccupied with some aspect of their environment or everyday routine. The individual's energies seem devoted to escaping the abyss of 'not being' by seeking to impose order and to establish some framework within which a form of reality and predictability can exist. This is also a viewpoint which Tustin (1974) has subscribed to, following her extensive psychotherapeutic work with children labelled as autistic. She feels that the individual finds the experience of incompleteness to be totally intolerable and will use any resources available to close the circle and complete the gestalt. People may use a range of devices to maintain or establish a sense of wholeness. For each individual this will be an adaptive strategy, doing the best they know how, sometimes in the face of appalling odds. I suggest that some of the participants in this study have attempted to solve this dilemma by employing a spatial strategy to provide some definition of self.

In the past, the concept of mental age has been employed to describe the levels of functioning of people with learning difficulties, although it is clear that no two people who have been ascribed the same mental age will function in exactly the same manner. For me, the most interesting thing about the concept of mental age is what it misses out, i.e. the personal strategies that people have developed to get by in the world. The concept of intelligence has been intrinsically linked with ideas about degrees of learning difficulty, but use of intelligence testing in this field is thankfully past its zenith. The results of such tests were, arguably, of very limited value at best, and at worst damaging and discriminatory. When employing the concept of intelligence, people are usually alluding to the notion of general intelligence or Spearman's 'g'. General intelligence describes an ability which is held to be both finite and unitary, and can be measured accurately by the application of intelligence tests, e.g. those popularised by Eysenck (1962).

In fact, many authorities are now quite critical of the concept of 'g' and there has been a shift towards viewing intelligence as a system or set of abilities. Some researchers go even further and have attempted to define, classify and describe various mental processes which contribute towards behaviour. As far back as 1938, Thurstone proposed the existence of a range of intellectual functions which could develop at various speeds, to various levels, and sometimes in apparent isolation from one another. In the mid-eighties Gardner (1984) compiled what he terms a 'theory of multiple intelligences', the central premises of which is that intelligence is not a single factor but a set of abilities. Gardner describes six such categories:

1 Personal
2 Spatial

3 Logical-mathematical
4 Body-kinesthetic
5 Musical
6 Linguistic

For each of these (with the exception of personal) Gardner cites cases when a particular ability may have been spared, or may be operating at a superior level. I found it helpful to consider Gardner's ideas concerning the categories of personal and spatial intelligences.

Personal intelligence

Gardner proposes two types of personal intelligence: firstly, intrapersonal intelligence, which refers to what individuals know about themselves and their feelings. '[Intrapersonal intelligence enables] access to one's feelings, one's range of emotions: the capacity to instantly effect discriminations between any of these feelings, and eventually to label them, to enmesh them in symbolic codes, to draw upon them as a means of understanding and guiding behaviour' (Gardner 1984, p. 239). Secondly, interpersonal intelligence refers to what the individual can perceive about other people: 'The core capacity here is the ability to motivate and make distinctions among other individuals, and in particular amongst their moods, temperaments, motivations and intentions' (Gardner 1984, p. 239).

Gardner says that symbolisation is at the heart of personal intelligence. Without access to culturally shared metaphors, individuals have only their own amorphous emotions with which to make sense of the world. It is through the development of the mother–child bond that personal intelligence flourishes. As the infant develops he or she will build up an understanding of the world by slowly associating different feelings with different experiences. Eventually the child establishes an internal representation of what it knows about itself. This is the basis of what Gardner refers to as a 'sense of person': 'The formation of self is a project and a process of the utmost importance. The manner of its execution will determine whether the individual can function effectively within the social context, in which he has chosen, or must choose to live' (Gardner 1984, p. 251).

Spatial intelligence

Like several of his other categories, Gardner feels that spatial intelligence is a collection of associated abilities which include the ability to perceive form, the ability to create a mental image, the ability to perceive an element and to recognise it again under different conditions. It is a function very much concerned with the ability to orient oneself in the physical world:

These spatial capacities can be drawn on in a number of different arenas. They are important for orienting oneself in various locales, ranging from rooms to oceans. They are invoked for the recognition of objects and scenes, both when they are encountered in their original surroundings and when some circumstances of the original presentation has been altered.

(Gardner 1984, p. 176)

Gardner does not cite examples of individuals whose use of personal intelligence is elevated or preserved but who have impaired function in other intelligence areas. Gardner argues that the evolution of personal intelligence relies fairly heavily on the uniform development of the other sets of abilities. Should there be curtailment or delay in a number of intelligence areas simultaneously, then it is likely that this will entail far-reaching effects on that individual's development of self and their adjustment to the social domain. It is my view that these difficulties have often been compounded by the fact that such individuals' opportunities for emotional development have been diminished rather than increased by the services which provide for them.

The irony is that despite being unable to rely on the facility of what Gardner terms personal intelligence, such individuals will still experience a profound and dire need to achieve gestalt in order to complete the circle, as Tustin describes (1974). Underlying this must be a powerful motivational urge to maintain internal consistency and control. I suggest that should it not be possible for an individual to gain a sense of self throughout maturation of personal intelligence, he or she may employ one or more of the other intelligences to provide some definition of self. I further suggest that the people who are the focus of this chapter draw primarily on their spatial intelligence to interpret and make sense of their experiences.

Herein lies a potential dilemma for the art therapist. Within the art therapy session, there will be ample opportunity to deal with the world in a spatial manner, both in terms of the use of materials and physical orientation within the room. But do these opportunities merely reinforce the client's use of spatial strategies, further removing the possibility of a socially acquired sense of self? In my experience the converse is true. Art therapy provides such individuals with the opportunity to function within a mode which is familiar and reassuring, and has profound personal significance. It can also act as a bridge between total reliance on delineation of space and territory as a means of achieving consistency, and the evolution of a symbolic function through the experience of a containing therapeutic relationship.

Following the completion of the research project referred to in this chapter, I began individual art therapy sessions with one of the women who had featured in the study and had been found to employ spatial strategies, both in her drawing behaviour and in her general behaviour on the ward, i.e. she had fallen into the territorial group. She had been referred for individual art therapy sessions because of her outbursts of aggressive behaviour. The account which follows attempts to capture a couple of the significant highlights, in therapeutic terms, of our work together and illustrates my understanding of what happened between us, informed by my research findings.

Trish

Trish is a thirty-four-year-old woman who has been institutionalised for most of her life. She has severe learning difficulties and a tendency towards explosive bouts of aggression. Trish has no language, either spoken or signed. She had been a member of an open art therapy group for three years. Trish always came readily to the sessions, working on her own at a small table. She preferred to use paint rather than any other medium; she did not actively select colour, neither did she change colour spontaneously, rather she would use the same pot of paint until it was empty. She often stood up to paint, using vigorous circular movements, or lines painted away from her body towards the edges of the page. In the early days her marks were concentrated around the edges of the page (see Figure 7.2), but as time progressed, she was filling in more and more space until the whole page was a solid block of colour (see Figure 7.3). About this time and in parallel with finishing data collection in the open art therapy group, it was decided as part of a multi-disciplinary review that Trish might benefit from individual art therapy sessions, and we began hourly sessions on a weekly basis.

Our relationship was on a rather inanimate level at first, with Trish using me as a tool to obtain things she was unable to get for herself. However, by the time the individual sessions had been running for a year or so there was a distinct qualitative change in our relationship. The following two incidents serve to exemplify this shift in position.

In one session, Trish had overlaid one sheet of paper so heavily with

Figure 7.2 Trish's early work

Figure 7.3 Trish's later work

paint that the edges of the paper began to disintegrate, leaving soggy lumps of pulp on the table. This was clearly causing Trish acute distress; I felt that the situation was becoming potentially explosive but instead of acting on my anxiety I waited to see what would happen. Suddenly, in a flurry of activity, Trish snatched up the offending fragments and thrust them into my hands, glaring intently at me as she did so. This action seemed to cast the relationship firmly into the arena of metaphor. Trish appeared to have experienced some degree of holding, having been able to use the therapist as a container, both literally and symbolically, for the anguish which her fragile affective boundaries seemed as yet unable to support. In another session some weeks later Trish inadvertently picked up two sheets of paper from a pile instead of one. When she returned to her seat there was great confusion over what she should do with the extra sheet. Again it seemed to me that Trish's ability to contain her emotions was declining, but she resolved this by putting one sheet of paper at her own place on the table, and the other directly in front of me. The sheet I had been 'given' over-lapped Trish's page. However, she was very careful to remain within the edges of her own paper when painting. In this example, I felt that Trish was tentatively exploring the boundaries of self and other, and gaining an understanding at some level that both she and the therapist were existing in mutual space as separate entities.

For Trish it seems that her intimacy with and reliance on the spatial aspects of her environment enabled her to respond on an affective level to the physicality of the art therapy session. For a long while she relied on the boundaries of the page to contain the feelings evoked within the therapeutic relationship. By the time Trish was testing the boundaries of the page to the point of disintegration, she was beginning to be able to find containment within the boundaries of the therapeutic relationship itself.

CONCLUSION

By relating to physical and spatial aspects of the environment some people who have learning difficulties may have discovered a personal and adaptive solution to the problems of maintaining some level of psychological and emotional integration. We as therapists should be respectful of such creativity and resilience. Such tribute to the tenacity and resourcefulness of the human spirit is for me sadly lacking in so many linear theories of psychological development. Further, I believe that art therapy may offer a unique opportunity for such people to continue expressing their sense of personhood through the employment of spatial strategies, whilst also facilitating the acquisition of integrated experiences of gestalt. Schaverien (1991) talks of the picture surface as an 'inner frame' which offers some insurance to both client and therapist against the potentially overpowering nature of unconscious processes. For these clients reinforcement of this inner frame is initially the only means available of re-affirming a sense of being. For the therapist the inner frame shields them from resonance with their own archaic sense of chaos and non-existence.

> The inner frame may be experienced as protecting the patient and the therapist from the overwhelming nature of the unconscious content of the picture. The picture which resonates with elements of the transference and countertransference relationship is a space set apart, within a space set apart.
>
> (Schaverien 1991, p. 66)

The process of researching is rife with perils and pitfalls ready to trap the unsuspecting. Single-handed researchers have particular difficulties to surmount, not least the lack of co-researchers to rejoice at the peaks and to overcome the troughs. The greatest problem for me was that I had simultaneously cast myself in the role of researcher and therapist. In such a union, the researcher facet may be compromised because one cannot guarantee the objectivity which is the hallmark of a rigorous observational study. The therapist's role is also undermined because he or she may intentionally transgress the boundaries of the therapeutic relationship in the name of research.

Research can also be a way in which therapists address countertransference issues. I can see that having the framework of a research programme helped me to cope with my feelings of disempowerment in relation to my perception of these clients' needs. Had I not had the containing framework of the research I very much doubt whether I would have been able to continue working under such grim conditions. In retrospect the dual role of therapist and researcher is a rather unholy alliance which raises almost as many questions as it resolves. However, there do seem to be some shared criteria which are important in the performance of both these roles. One such condition is the need for both the researcher and the therapist to avoid their own biases and to be open to new and unexpected outcomes.

> Discard your memory; discard the future tense of your desires; forget them both, what you knew and what you want, to leave space for a new idea. A thought, an idea unclaimed may be floating around the room searching for a home.
>
> (Bion 1980, p. 11)

ACKNOWLEDGEMENTS

Many thanks to Debbie Hyde for her support over the research period, and to Hilary Lomas for her help and suggestions for this chapter.

REFERENCES

Bion, W.R. (Ed.) (1980) *Bion In New York and São Paulo.* Clunie Press, Strath Tay, Perthshire.

Blurton Jones, N. (Ed.) (1972) *Ethological Studies of Child Behaviour.* Cambridge University Press, Cambridge.

Bowlby, J. (1975) *Attachment and Loss.* vol. 1. Penguin, Harmondsworth.

Cook, D. (1980) *Walter.* Penguin, Harmondsworth.

Dubowski, J. (1985) 'An Investigation of the Pre-representational Drawing Activity of Certain Severely Retarded Subjects within an Institution Using Ethological Techniques'. Unpublished PhD thesis, Hertfordshire College of Art & Design.

Esser, A.H. & Deutsch, R.D. (1977) 'Private and Interaction Territories on Psychiatric Wards'. In: McGuire, M.T. and Fairbanks, L.A. (Eds) *Ethological Psychiatry.* Grune & Stratton, New York.

Esser, A.H. *et al.* (1970) 'Territoriality of Patients on a Research Ward'. In: Proshansky, H., Ittelson, W.H. and Rivlin, L.G. (Eds) *Environmental Psychology: Man and his Physical Setting.* Holt, Rinehart and Winston, Inc., New York.

Eysenck, H.J. (1962) *Know Your Own IQ.* Penguin, Harmondsworth.

Gardner, H. (1984) *Frames of Mind.* William Heinemann, London.

Hallam, J. (1984) 'Regression and Ego Integration in Art Therapy with Mentally Handicapped People'. In: *Art Therapy as Psychotherapy in Relation to the Mentally Handicapped*, Conference Proceedings, Hertfordshire College of Art and Design.

Hughes, R. (1986) 'Destruction and Repair'. *Inscape.* Spring: 8–10.

Hughes, R. (1988) 'Transitional Phenomena and the Potential Space in Art Therapy with Mentally Handicapped People'. *Inscape.* Summer: 4–8.

Hutt, S.J. and Hutt, C. (1968) 'Stereotypy, Arousal & Autism'. *Human Development.* 11: 277–86.

Hutt, S.J. and Hutt, C. (1970) *Direct Observation and Measurement of Behavior.* C.C. Thomas, Springfield, IL.

Kellog, R. (1969) *Analysing Children's Art.* Mayfield, National Press Books.

Killick, K. (1991) 'The Practice of Art Therapy with Patients in Acute Psychotic States'. *Inscape.* Winter: 2–6.

Lorenz, K. (1950) 'The Comparative Method in Studying Innate Behavior Patterns'. *Symposium of the Society of Experimental Biology.* 4: 221–68.

Parker, C. (1975) 'Observing and Recording Primate Behavior'. Unpublished treatise, Psychology Department, San Diego University, CA.

Polsky, R.H. and Chance, M.R.A. (1979a) 'An Ethological Perspective on Social Behavior in Long-stay Hospitalized Psychiatric Patients'. *Journal of Nervous and Mental Disease.* 167: 658–67.

Polsky, R.H. and Chance, M.R.A. (1979b) 'An Ethological Analysis of Long-stay Hospitalized Psychiatric Patients'. *Journal of Nervous and Mental Disease.* 167: 669–74.

Polsky, R.H. and Chance, M.R.A. (1980) 'Social Interaction and the Use of Space on a Ward of Long-term Psychiatric Patients'. *Journal of Nervous and Mental Disease.* 168: 550–55.

Polsky, R.H. and McGuire, M.D. (1981) 'Social Ethology of Acute Psychiatric Patients'. *Journal of Nervous and Mental Disease.* 169: 28–35.

Schaverien, J. (1991) *The Revealing Image: Analytical Art Psychotherapy in Theory and Practice.* Routledge, London.

Selfe, F. (1977) *Nadia.* Academic Press, New York.

Spensly, S. (1984) 'Reflections on the Contribution of Art Therapy to Psychic

Development'. In: *Art Therapy as Psychotherapy in Relation to the Mentally Handicapped*, Conference Proceedings, Hertfordshire College of Art and Design.

Thurstone, L.L. (1938) *Primary Mental Abilities. Psychometric Monographs.* 1. University of Chicago Press, Chicago.

Tinbergen, E.A. and Tinbergen, N. (1972) 'Early Childhood Autism: An Ethological Approach'. *Advances in Ethology.* 10. Verlag Paul Parey, Berlin and Hamburg.

Tinbergen, N. (1950) *The Study of Instinct.* Oxford University Press, London.

Tipple, R. (1992) 'Art Therapy with People who have Severe Learning Difficulties'. In: Waller, D. and Gilroy, A. (Eds) *Art Therapy: A Handbook.* Open University Press, Buckingham.

Tustin, F. (1974) *Autism and Childhood Psychosis.* Hogarth, London.

Wilson, L. (1980) 'Theory and Practice of Art Therapy with the Mentally Retarded'. In: Ulman, E. and Levy, C. (Eds) *Art Therapy Viewpoints.* Schocken Books, New York.

Winnicott, D.W. (1971) *Playing and Reality.* Tavistock, London.

Chapter 8

Observing offenders

The use of simple rating scales to assess changes in activity during group music therapy

Sarah Hoskyns

INTRODUCTION

Music therapy with adult offenders has been documented and researched very little. Work that has been done, mainly on an individual basis with mentally ill offenders in forensic medical wards or psychiatric units of prisons (Nolan 1983; Cohen 1987; Thaut 1987; Santos and Loth 1993), has suggested that music therapy can make some contribution to changes in how the adult with a history of criminal offences perceives himself or herself and therefore adapts to their environment. This chapter presents some research with offenders in the community which involved the design of a sequence of simple rating scales. The rating scales were developed to assess changes in activity during a twelve-week period of group music therapy recorded on videotape.

The research I describe here is from the second of three projects in preparation for a doctoral thesis, entitled 'Group Music Therapy with Adult Offenders: An Investigation of Changes in Self-perception and Action'. The first project examines clients' own perspectives of music therapy (Hoskyns 1988). Group members collaborated with me in the design of a music therapy grid, based on Kelly's Personal Construct Theory (Kelly 1955). This second project centres on the viewpoint of the observer, assessing and rating music therapy on videotape. The final project presents my own viewpoint as therapist, describing case work and developing theory (Hoskyns 1990).

In this project, the questions that interested me were: do clients show observable changes in activity in group music therapy? Are any observed changes short-term (i.e. within one session) or are they sustained from early to late in the twelve-week period of music therapy? One might ask how these questions arose. I had worked for six years prior to this research as a music therapist running twelve-week groups for adult offenders in the community. The sessions were part of an intensive multi-disciplinary rehabilitation programme for recidivist offenders. During this period of work I initiated many new groups and observed their progress; I also discussed the role of this form of therapy with the group members. I formed the impression that early in the period of music therapy, group members' activity in the sessions often seemed to polarise either towards the extreme of dominant, intrusive, over-assertive musical playing or towards shy, tentative, very withdrawn contributions to the group. Self-reports by the clients in the first project demonstrated some similar extremes in their own perceptions of their activity (Hoskyns 1988, p. 35).

My experience as a clinician suggested that significant changes in people's playing activity did occur over the course of twelve weeks of music therapy and also within single sessions. As a researcher I wondered if group music therapy could stimulate change for clients who represented either ends of the 'dominant–withdrawn' dimension in their activity. That is, would the clients who 'acted out' be channelled by making a lot of musical 'noise' and discovering artistic boundaries for their chaotic play- ing? Would the withdrawn clients gain confidence, lose inhibitions and find appropriate instruments for quiet expression? I was interested in the flexibility of music therapy in the group context, and its potential to calm and to enliven within the same process. I needed to design a similarly flexible research tool which would incorporate change in both directions and not expect uniform changes from everyone.

The structure of the rest of the chapter is as follows: firstly, relevant literature and research are identified, some terms are defined, and the research context described. Then the format of the rating scales is outlined and the research design described. Finally the research methodology is given, two brief case illustrations provided, and some results presented, together with a discussion of the likely trends indicated.

BACKGROUND, LITERATURE AND RESEARCH

Surveys of literature indicate that there is no directly relevant experimental or descriptive research on music therapy with adult offenders in commu- nity rehabilitation. However, a number of studies in related fields have proved useful in the design of this project. Firstly, three clinical papers outlining cases in music therapy with serious offenders in the hospital and prison context made strong connections with my own observations (Wardle 1979; Nolan 1983; Cohen 1987). Nolan's case study of a mentally ill offender stresses the important role that non-verbal forms of therapy can play in treatment and assessment. He implies that the offending client may often have difficulties with fluency and expression in verbal language and thus is much more likely to be able to show rather than tell his thoughts and feelings (Nolan 1983, p. 44). The two other papers emphasise extremes of behaviour observed in offending clients. Wardle's two-part article on music therapy at a women's prison vividly describes the chaotic, aggres- sive, dominant playing of some clients and the valuable role of music therapy in channelling this into creative energy (Wardle 1979, p. 13). Wardle also makes a distinction between the polarities of introvert and extrovert and articulates how music therapy might address the needs of either group. (Wardle 1980, pp. 3–4). Cohen focuses on music therapy in a prison psychiatric unit with overcontrolled offenders. These clients had committed violent crimes but seemed passive, helpless and introverted in their usual behaviour. She describes music therapy as a particularly appropriate treatment for such clients in its ability simultaneously to challenge and maintain support. Cohen also advocates the development of musical rating scales for assessment of behaviour change (Cohen 1987, p. 220).

Secondly, two music therapy commentators in other clinical fields have drawn specific attention to the dual potential in music to move towards excitement and towards repose. Alvin (1975) had a particular interest in the direct physiological effects of music. She stressed that the initial impact of music is often physical and sensuous, perhaps because the alternations of tension and relaxation in music closely echo human physical patterns of activity and rest (Alvin 1975, p. 92). Standley's paper reviewing the use of music in medical treatment suggests that music is a potent therapeutic agent precisely because it can – unlike medication – both 'wake people up and put them to sleep' (Standley 1990). Both authors seem to give weight to the idea that the calming and enlivening effect of music in therapy could be worthy of further study.

With regard to assessment method in music therapy research three approaches are of interest. Kiesler's paper on experimental design in psychotherapy research emphasises the idea that clients will vary in the way they benefit from therapeutic intervention. The researcher will therefore need to identify the different ways in which individual clients change. Kiesler advocates the use of flexible models – multi-dimensional assessments which allow for such differentiated outcome (Kiesler 1971, pp. 40–45) . Bunt's research with young handicapped children analyses the effects of music therapy intervention on aspects of the children's development using video film which is sampled at fixed points in the period of treatment. Bunt developed a series of observational measures specific to children with developmental delay which were then used by observers to test aspects of music therapy outcome (Bunt 1985, pp. 128–133). The simplicity and clarity of the measures, with their high rate of inter-observer reliability, form a very useful model for the analysis of music therapy intervention on video. Finally, Gillingham, Griffiths and Care underline the importance of simple clear measures when analysing complex data on video. Their research on the social interaction of psychiatric patients also achieved high reliability on time-based measures such as 'time patient speaks' in observation of a fixed period of videotape (Gillingham et al. 1977, p. 187).

Thus the literature indicated the following issues: extremes of behaviour, either active or passive, can be anticipated from offending clients; music therapy can have a beneficial effect on such extremes of behaviour in its capacity to stimulate or to relax; uniformity of outcome in music therapy should not be anticipated; and the use of simple, clear measures spanning a variety of dimensions may be the most effective means to assess short periods of music therapy on videotape.

DEFINING AND DESCRIBING THE CONTEXT

The clients

The client group who have been the subjects and (in part) co-researchers in this study are adult recidivist offenders; that is, men and women over the age of 21 years whose repeated breach of the law in this country has resulted in court convictions and various forms of sentence (e.g. fines, imprisonment and probation service supervision). All have had backgrounds of a number of previous convictions (typical offences being shoplifting, theft, burglary, vehicle offences, deception, soliciting) and were at risk of going to prison for their convicted offences. Referrals came from the Magistrates' and Crown Courts, the 'sentence' in this case involving attendance for three months at a Day Training Centre (DTC), run by the Inner London Probation Service, as the condition of a two-year probation order. Clients signed a contract to attend the Centre during the assigned period. Everyone who took part in this research study opted to have weekly group music therapy as part of their rehabilitation programme. They attended the groups between 1985 and 1989.

The Day Training Centre programme: an alternative to prison

The Inner London Probation Service Day Training Centre (DTC) is situated in a residential area of south-east London and takes clients from all over inner London. At the time of this research the twelve-week programme at the DTC required clients to attend from 9.30 am–4.30 pm for four days per week and was divided into two main sections. The verbal morning groups emphasised self-responsibility, the encouragement of honesty in personal relationships, the frank discussion of offending patterns, and investigated attitudes to authority and how these linked with offending. The afternoon practicals (of which music therapy was an option) aimed to increase clients' self-esteem through creative activity, to increase their awareness of choices and interests open to them, and to provide a complementary non-verbal 'playground' where group members could experiment with different approaches, feelings and behaviours on which they had reflected in the morning sessions. The overall aim of this integrated programme was to offer responsibility back to the clients and to help them realise that they could make an active choice not to offend. The DTC's unpublished records in 1989 indicated that 70 per cent of those offenders who completed the programme remained out of trouble in the first year from their probation order being made. However, the adoption of therapeutic, as opposed to punitive, measures for petty criminals remains controversial (Mark 1986, p. 131) and any research which examines changes in clients' behaviour during such a rehabilitation programme provides valuable information from which to make an objective assessment of the benefits.

The music therapy group

Music therapy took place one afternoon per week (Friday) for one-and-a-quarter hours throughout the twelve-week programme. Though the sessions were optional, there was an expectation that each individual kept a regular commitment to the group, having chosen it. The groups were usually small, with between three and seven members, plus myself as therapist and a student assistant who periodically filmed the sessions for the research. A range of instruments were available for people to play – tuned and untuned percussion, ethnic instruments, drum kit, piano and guitars. The group would be encouraged to create its own music, usually improvised, often beginning from the styles and idioms known to group members. The primary focus of the group would be on the non-verbal playground mentioned in the previous section, and on helping the clients to play music that was directly expressive of the 'self'.

My clinical role was to observe, to maintain the boundaries of time and personal safety, to help the group members make music together, and to facilitate verbal discussion as appropriate. Although I did not demand that clients spoke about their musical experiences in the group, in practice discussion often occurred following the completion of an improvisation. I found that clients were able to: channel frustration through loud, intense sound-making; identify with particular harmonic and rhythmic patterns which could be played with and constructed into individual improvisations and into compositions; discover their musical voices; discover an affinity with a particular instrumental sound; be heard by other group members and discover the benefits of listening; acknowledge and identify with strong emotion expressed in music; make connections between life inside and outside the group, and see the possibilities of alternative, less destructive patterns.

The tight limits of the DTC's multi-disciplinary programme, and the clients' understandable mistrust of any sort of investigation of their thoughts and actions, immediately restricted my options for research. The Centre's staff team was happy with the undertaking of research as long as I was studying the natural course of music therapy at the Centre. Therefore there was no possibility of creating homogeneous groupings of clients for comparison, nor of comparing music therapy with other therapeutic inputs. The task was to study what happened with clients who would typically opt for music therapy and to follow the normal pattern of a twelve-week group. The clients themselves were often volatile and unreliable (attendance and lateness were always prevalent issues). It was important to give them as much autonomy as possible to gain co-operation. Above all, as a researcher I needed to be simple, straightforward and trustworthy, maintaining openness and always keeping people informed. Being over-ambitious could easily mean loss of trust and ultimately research subjects.

Rating scales, and video analysis

For the purposes of rating scale design and following the findings of Gillingham *et al.* (1977) and Bunt (1985), I needed to simplify radically such complex observations of change in music therapy. A pilot study, done by student observers at City University, London, tested whether observers could tell the difference between client behaviour at the beginning and end of a session, and asked them to identify the changes which enabled them to make this decision. The observers' judgements were 61 per cent accurate (suggesting that some change could be seen) and some simple observable constructs were generated. These were invaluable in evolving different dimensions for the rating scales. Constructs such as 'noisy–quiet', 'subordinate to others–more assertive with others', 'disruptive–co-operative', 'self-absorbed–eager to be involved' fitted very comfortably with my hunch about overactivity–passivity in the clients. These ideas, plus some of my own about instrumental choice and the continuity of playing, formed the backbone of the rating scales.

Five rating scales were designed, based on observers' and my own observations and comments. These cover the areas of loudness, continuity, resonance of instruments chosen, attention to group task and leadership. Each scale uses a simple five-point framework with a score of one being low and a score of five being high. With the aid of Guildhall music therapy students and staff, I went through many early drafts and trials with the scales in order to bring them up to an acceptable level of inter-observer reliability (finally 70–80 per cent reliable). For reasons of simplicity in this chapter, just two of the scales are demonstrated here in Table 8.1. The other scales appear in an appendix (see pp. 150–1). The scales chosen are No. 1, 'Loudness (music)' and No. 3, 'Resonance of instrument(s) chosen'.

Video, though potentially an intrusive and distorting influence on the groups, was much preferred by the clients to the presence in the room of observers noting down actions. All possible effort was made to familiarise

Table 8.1 Rating scales 1 and 3

Rating scale 1	
Loudness (music)	*Score*
No audible playing/singing	1
Soft playing, barely audible	2
Neither completely loud nor completely soft playing	3
Clearly audible playing at moderate volume	4
Plays loudly, exceeding general volume of group	5

Rating scale 3	
Resonance of instrument(s) chosen	*Score*
Has no instrument	1
Has instrument for making soft sounds	2
Has mixture of both sorts of instrument (soft-sounding and resonant)	3
Has one resonant instrument with potential to mask group	4
Has multiple resonant instruments with potential to mask group	5

the groups with the camera, allowing group members to film themselves before beginning the research filming and to play back extracts later in the day if desired. The drawbacks were that there was always the possibility that people would perform to camera: some clients refused to be filmed and thus had to be excluded from the research, although they remained in the group. However the benefits of using video seemed to outweigh its disadvantages, particularly because extracts could be replayed any number of times and rated for different measures.

Video provides very complex and lengthy data. The technique I chose to select from such rich material was that described earlier by Bunt (1985) and Gillingham *et al.* (1977) called 'time-sampling'. Time-sampling is a method widely used in research, particularly when studying behaviour in natural environments. In general terms, observers record certain aspects of a subject's behaviour (established in advance by the experimenter) after observing the subject for a fixed or randomly selected period of time (Plutchik 1983, p. 57). In this research, a fixed time interval was used – one minute per client – whatever the client's activity was at fixed points in the third and tenth weeks of the twelve-week group. The points were ten minutes after the beginning of the session, and fifteen minutes before the end. Members of the group were filmed in random order. The one-minute time slots were then edited, presented to observers in random sequence and rated according to the five rating scales.

Research design

The final research design of this part of my doctoral project was thus as follows. Twenty-two adult subjects with a history of offending were filmed on video in music therapy groups over a three-year period. This comprised twenty male clients and two females aged between 21 and 45 years who had committed a variety of offences, and myself. A student assistant filmed each subject according to the time-sampling plan. Data was thus collected early and late in sessions, and early and late in the treatment period. The video clips for the twenty-two clients plus one therapist were then randomised and rated by observers trained in the use of each rating scale. The scales were rated by at least two observers and an average score found.

The analysis of the group data for all the clients has yet to be completed and so for reasons of simplicity and clarity, the raw results for just two clients (plus myself as therapist) will be given here. The two clients chosen represent the two extremes of activity and passivity mentioned in the introduction. In order to make the results more vivid, brief case histories of the two clients – both male – are described before presentation of the numerical material.

CASE HISTORIES

Client B

Client B was aged 44 years. His convicted offences were four counts of shoplifting and he had received twenty-four previous convictions. B was absent from the Centre frequently through illness, but he managed to attend eight of the eleven sessions of music therapy available. On assessment, each client makes a written 'contract' of personal issues to be considered during the programme. Client B's contract was as follows: 'My life's a disaster. I've destroyed myself and my friends. Today was different. I met people who needed help and who could give help to me. I know this will be difficult, but it's something I must complete before it's too late.'

B often sat quietly in the group, watching others attentively and sometimes playing softly on small instruments. He said he particularly valued just feeling part of the group. Towards the end, when he had made a few bold experiments with the drum kit and had received some appreciation, he described his experience of music therapy as being 'like having my own little party'. Such social intimacy and acceptance seemed to be high prizes for him. His final asssessment at the Centre reported that B was beginning to combat his severe isolation and that his self-esteem seemed noticeably higher than on entry.

Client G

Client G was aged 32 years. His referred offence was burglary and he had thirteeen previous convictions for burglary and theft. His offending had been connected with abuse of amphetamines in earlier years. The social inquiry report emphasised the chronic invalidity and subsequent death of G's mother when he was 16-years-old as being crucial to the development of his pattern of offending. G had spent most of the last seven years prior to referral in custody. G's contract reads thus: 'Burglary – such a buzz. I'm not trusting in feelings to a certain extent. Get nervous.'

G found it very hard to commit himself to attendance at the DTC, and treated his three months like 'time-serving', missing as much as possible, without returning to court. He did commit himself to music therapy and education sessions, missing only two weeks in total. However both were once-weekly rather than daily workshops and there was much misused time in between. I felt G used music therapy well; he obviously felt comfortable with the non-verbal, relaxed format, though in early sessions he was intermittently disruptive and aggressive. He was concerned about his lack of motivation, feeling that being so long in prison had stripped him of any interests. Also, he was without sustained emotional relationships with partners or family as a result of constant imprisonment. G noticed himself how his mood had changed within two music therapy sessions. He was surprised at his involvement in music and at his co-operation with other people. Nevertheless his lack of involvement elsewhere in the programme severely affected his progress. He re-offended within three months of leaving the Centre.

Results

The scorings on the five scales for the two clients described above are shown in Tables 8.3 and 8.4, together with scores for myself as therapist in

Table 8.2 Complete scores for the five rating scales

Client B	
Early in session/early in treatment:	12.66 (out of 25)
Late in session:	12.5
Late in twelve weeks:	12.83
Client G	
Early in session/early in treatment:	18.66 (out of 25)
Late in session:	16.66
Late in twelve weeks:	15.0
Therapist SH	
Early in session/early in treatment:	18.16 (out of 25)
Late in session:	14.88
Late in twelve weeks:	18.33

Note 'Early in the early session' and 'early in treatment' are sampled at the same time and have the same score, so are shown together in this table.

Table 8.5. Complete scores for the five rating scales (possible total = 25) at the four time points – early in an early session, early in treatment, late in the early session and late in the treatment period – are calculated for each subject as shown in Table 8.2:

Discussion

Client B's results do not show many dramatic changes. His scores were generally towards the low end of the scales at each of the rating points, indicating some of his shy and reticent behaviour. The most prominent alteration was that B's playing became more continuous towards the end of the early session (score of 5). This is sustained towards the end of the twelve-week programme (4). It is as though he becomes more involved in the playing as music therapy progresses. His attentiveness to the group task early in the early session (3.5) is also higher than his general ratings although this is not sustained. As a whole the scores did not rise towards the end of the session and they rose only fractionally at the end of the twelve weeks. As therapist I remember some crucial moments when B's playing altered dramatically but these do not figure in a fixed-time sampling plan!

In contrast, Client G's scores seem to change noticeably from early to late in the early session, and from early to late in the twelve-week period. There is quite obvious 'quietening' of his activity, both in the course of a session and in the course of the programme. The complete added scores reflect this clearly in a reduction of 2 points from early to late in the session, and of three-and-two-thirds points from early to late in the programme. It is possible that he was an easier subject to rate than client

Table 8.3 Results for Client B

	Early in session	Late in session
Loudness (music/speech)	1.33	2
Continuity (music/speech)	2.5	5
Resonance of chosen instrument	2.33	2
Attention to group task	3.5	2.5
Leadership	2	1
	Early in twelve weeks	Late in twelve weeks
Loudness (music/speech)	1.33	1.33
Continuity (music/speech)	2.5	4
Resonance of chosen instrument	2.33	2
Attention to group task	3.5	2.5
Leadership	2	3

Table 8.4 Results for Client G

	Early in session	Late in session
Loudness (music/speech)	4.66	3.66
Continuity (music/speech)	4	4
Resonance of chosen instrument	2	2
Attention to group task	4	4
Leadership	4	3

	Early in twelve weeks	Late in twelve weeks
Loudness (music/speech)	4.66	2
Continuity (music/speech)	4	5
Resonance of chosen instrument	2	2
Attention to group task	4	4
Leadership	4	2

Table 8.5 Results for therapist SH

	Early in session	Late in session
Loudness (music/speech)	4	2.33
Continuity (music/speech)	4.5	3.5
Resonance of chosen instrument	2.66	2
Attention to group task	5	4
Leadership	4	3

	Early in twelve weeks	Late in twelve weeks
Loudness (music/speech)	4	3.33
Continuity (music/speech)	4.5	3.5
Resonance of chosen instrument	2.66	4
Attention to group task	5	4.5
Leadership	4	3

B. He was generally very active, and so changes were more noticeable to the observers.

I was very surprised at how high my own scores were on these scales. My favourite image of myself as therapist is one of a quiet facilitator. But what seems striking here is how active and dominant I appear to be from the complete added scores. I prove at least as assertive as my very active client, though perhaps this should be expected from a group leader. There is quite a large change from early to late in the early session (18.16 to 14.88) suggesting that my role became more passive as the session developed. It perhaps also shows a certain flexibility – an ability to move about the scales as the occasion demands, which is not indicated so clearly with either of the client subjects.

CONCLUSION

Obviously it is not possible to make definitive statements or striking predictions from these results. The research setting was, from an experimental viewpoint, uncontrolled, and one cannot establish whether the changes were caused by the process of music therapy or whether the clients would have changed anyway. However, to return to the original questions: do clients show observable changes in activity in music therapy? Are any such changes short-term (within one session), or are they sustained from early to late in the twelve weeks of music therapy? In looking at the two clients' results, it seems that one client, G, did show a number of observable changes which seemed to be held over the period of music therapy. The other quieter client, B, did not seem to make many noticeable changes in activity and kept a fairly consistent pattern to his observed behaviour. It is interesting that the second client stayed out of prison in the year following the DTC programme, whereas the active, more dominant client was reconvicted in the first three months away from the Centre.

What can these results tell us? Firstly, as a therapist the scales gave me a useful objective assessment of clients' activity–passivity, which was quite closely connected with my case observations. The results also gave me invaluable feedback about my own behaviour, which was more active than I had imagined but also quite variable. Working on the scales and acquiring these results suggests that beneficial outcome in the field of offending is a very complex procedure. Internal change is not necessarily indicated by external behaviours, though certain issues may be very clearly indicated in people's behaviour. For Client G it seems that music therapy was a very engaging process, and he made considerable short-term changes. However, I think he needed more longterm therapy and was just beginning to get involved as the programme ended. Perhaps the results indicate that he had good potential to use this sort of therapy. Client B's lack of change seems initially puzzling, but possibly suggests quite a stable and consistent reaction to the process of music therapy. It may have been more important for him to be accepted as he was, rather than make radical changes in his behaviour.

I would like to see the rating scales used elsewhere in a controlled context, where outcome could be studied in a more rigorous way than was possible in this study. Although current trends in music therapy research seem to be towards qualitative, detailed examination of the way music therapy works (Bruscia 1993), there is still a need for therapists to communicate and research the results of practice. External observers can check and often confirm our subjective hunches about client activity. They can also offer enlightening or sobering information about our own behaviour, which was perhaps the most striking discovery for me in this study.

ACKNOWLEDGEMENTS

To the Music Therapy Charity and the J. Paul Getty Charitable Trust for their generous funding of the Music Therapy Research Fellowship at City University, London. To clients and staff of the Inner London Day Training Centre for their involvement in this project.

APPENDIX

Table 8.6 Rating scales 1a, 2, 2a, 4, 5

Rating scale 1a Loudness (speech)	Score
No speech (or other vocal utterance e.g. laughing, crying, etc.)	1
Soft speech, barely audible	2
Neither completely audible nor completely inaudible speech (or vocal sounds)	3
Clearly audible speech at moderate volume	4
Talks loudly (may shout/laugh, etc.)	5

Rating scale 2 Continuity (music)	Score
No playing (or singing)	1
Very occasional playing/singing, many breaks	2
Neither completely continuous nor completely discontinuous playing	3
Playing tends to be continuous with some breaks	4
Continuous playing, no breaks	5

Rating scale 2a Continuity (speech)	Score
No speech (or other vocal utterance e.g. laughing, crying, etc.)	1
Very occasional speech, many breaks	2
Some continuity of speech combined with breaks in speech	3
Speech tends to be continuous, with natural breaks	4
Maintains continuous flow of speech (including e.g. interrupting others)	5

Rating scale 4 Attention to group task	Score
No apparent attention to observed group activity	1
Tends not to give attention (little evidence of awareness of others)	2
Seems to show an equal mixture of attending and not attending	3
Tends to give attention (including apparently passive attention e.g. listening, nodding, smiling)	4
Complete and sustained attention to observed group activity	5

Rating scale 5
Leadership   *Score*

Seems to have no involvement in observed group activity (Absorbed in own playing but completely isolated from the group also included here)	1
Tends to follow others or the music throughout	2
Seems to lead and follow	3
Tends to lead	4
Sustains leadership of task throughout the observed time	5

REFERENCES

Alvin, J. (1975) *Music Therapy*. Hutchinson, London.

Bruscia, K. (1993) 'A Framework for Qualitative Research in Music Therapy'. Paper given at the Seventh World Conference of Music Therapy. July, Vitoria, Spain.

Bunt, L.G.K. (1985) 'Music Therapy and the Child with a Handicap: Evaluation of the Effects of Intervention'. Unpublished PhD thesis, City University, London.

Cohen, J. (1987) 'Music Therapy with the Overcontrolled Offender: Theory and Practice. *The Arts in Psychotherapy*. 14: 215–21.

Gillingham, P., Griffiths, R. and Care, D. (1977) 'Direct Assessment of Social Behaviour from Videotape Recordings'. *British Journal of Social and Clinical Psychology*. 16: 181–7.

Hoskyns, S.L. (1988) 'Studying Music Therapy with Offenders: Research in Progress'. *Psychology of Music*. 16: 25–41.

Hoskyns, S.L. (1990) 'Foreword'. *Journal of British Music Therapy*. 4: 3–4.

Kelly, G.A. (1955) *The Psychology of Personal Constructs*. vols 1 and 2. Norton, New York.

Kiesler, D.J. (1971) 'Experimental Designs in Psychotherapy Research'. In: Bergin, A.E. and Garfield, S.L. (Eds) *Handbook of Psychotherapy and Behavior Change*. Wiley, New York.

Mark, P. (1986) 'Offending Behaviour or Better Adjusted Criminals?' *Probation Journal*. 33: 127–31.

Nolan, P. (1983) 'Insight Therapy: Guided Imagery and Music in a Forensic Psychiatric Setting'. *Music Therapy*. 3: 43–51.

Plutchik, R. (1983) *Foundations of Experimental Research*. Harper & Row, New York, 3rd edn.

Santos, K. and Loth, H. (1993) 'Music Therapy in Forensic Psychiatry'. Paper given at the Seventh World Conference of Music Therapy. July, Vitoria, Spain.

Standley, J. (1990) 'Music as a Therapeutic Intervention in Medical and Dental Treatment: Research and Clinical Applications'. Paper given at Ciba Foundation Seminar 'Advances in Music Therapy'. November, London.

Thaut, M. (1987) 'A New Challenge for Music Therapy: The Correctional Setting. *Music Therapy Perspectives*. 4: 44–50.

Wardle, M. (1979) 'Music Therapy in a Women's Prison. Part 1: The Old Prison'. *British Journal of Music Therapy*. 10: 11–14.

Wardle, M. (1980) 'Music Therapy in a Women's Prison. Part 2: The New Prison'. *British Journal of Music Therapy*. 11: 2–7.

Chapter 9

The sound-world of speech- and language-impaired children

The story of a current music therapy research project

Julie Sutton

This chapter will trace the development of a research idea from the original concept to a two-year project. There will also be some emphasis placed on the experience of reaching compromises when registering the work for an M.Phil. research degree. In this case the final study bears little relation to the initial idea and thus serves as a cautionary tale for those considering research. Research is by nature autobiographical, involving on-going processes of inquiry and discovery. I have therefore written this chapter in the form of an unfolding story. This is not only the way in which events occurred, but it also lays open my process of research, enabling the reader to react, form opinions and compare these to my own.

THE BACKGROUND

The motivation to ask questions and eventually to embark upon research came about when I was working with a number of children who seemed to follow similar pathways in their music therapy. These children had a diagnosis relating to a speech and language impairment (SLI) affecting both receptive and expressive areas. A two-year DHSS medical research award enabled me to work in a school for autistic and language-impaired children. I noticed that some of the children with what I will term speech and language impairment (SLI: see Bishop and Rosenbloom 1987; Bishop 1992) used their individual music therapy sessions in similar ways. Many were hesitant or unconfident and able to hold on to their music only for very short periods. They needed time to express frustration and rage with the instruments before vocalising, and most seemed confused by the patterns of sound that the music presented. It was also apparent that at certain points in their music therapy measurable progress was noticed in their speech and language by speech and language therapists. The children were all referred to me because, although they had sufficient speech sounds and vocabulary, they were no longer expressing themselves fully through speech. In one case a child had stopped speaking altogether and in spite of an adequate Paget–Gorman vocabulary was no longer communicating with a sign system.

The music therapy spanned between six and eighteen months, with an initial period of wild, angry attacks on the instruments during which none of the children vocalised. From my viewpoint their music was seemingly haphazard, with indiscriminate, shortlived outbursts utilising most or all of the instruments in the room. Gradually they began to build their music into phrases and later whole structures. In each case they also began to express themselves with their voices, with speech and signing returning to their world.

A TWO-YEAR PROJECT

In my next post I was able to base some clinical work in a school offering specialist provision for children with SLI from all over Northern Ireland. This enabled me to learn a great deal about both the language work of a speech and language therapist and also the range and complexity of the difficulties the children experienced. Up to this point my contact with speech and language therapists was confined to general discussion about a child's speech difficulties, along with some information about their language level; in this new job I was able to take part in the speech and language therapy department meetings as well as attend courses. It was a valuable period of information- and experience-gathering during which I clarified my research ideas. I had begun by reporting the ways in which three dyspraxic children had used their music therapy, noting the similarities where musical elements in the sessions echoed evolving speech and language. I observed that as the children explored and then constructed their music into increasingly larger forms, so they were able to formulate one-, two- or three-word utterances and later short sentences. Evidently the experience of spontaneously expressing themselves through the non-verbal medium of music had at least partially resulted in increased confidence to communicate through words. It was possible that other factors were also influencing the growth in speech. I decided to explore in more detail the ways in which SLI children constructed their music.

I began listening in detail to the music improvised during individual music therapy with these children. I coined the expression 'spontaneous musical responses' (SMR) (Sutton 1991), which described the instinctive ways in which the children played, vocalised or moved, reacting to, or with, our music. I now realise this was my first step towards research, for I had decided on the general area for examination. In a sense I was doing no more than asking questions about work with a particular client group – the type of inquiry inherent in our day-to-day work as therapists. To some extent, we all 'investigate' our clients. In another way I had moved beyond this inquiry, towards the research pathway. I was looking at something beyond my clinical reference points, because I wanted to clarify some thoughts I had about my work. With a speech and language therapist I wrote a combined case presentation covering six months' work with one boy (Cummings and Sutton 1990). We were amazed to discover how closely his speech and language development mirrored his changing SMR. At this point the consultant paediatrician suggested the research study.

I was now the music therapist and the researcher. Without previous research experience I enthusiastically set about planning the project. I decided to find a 'base line' – something that would acquaint me with a type of spontaneous interaction that occurred in children without SLI. I needed to discover an interaction close to both music therapy and speech and language present in the mainstream population, involving the sounds of two people responding to each other. This would also give me information I could compare to the SMR. The children taking part in such an interaction would form my control group, a starting point against which I compared the responses of my study group – the children with SLI.

I concentrated on a small number of infants up to and including 12-months-of-age and was supplied by friends and colleagues with audio-cassette tapes of babies vocalising with members of their families. This gave me an indication of the development of a mainstream group who could go on to acquire speech and language without difficulty. I could analyse and compare their sounds to those recorded during the individual music therapy of the SLI children.

I planned a clinical workload comprising a wide range of children with SLI. Apart from those at the specialist school I included children attending an early intervention unit (assessing up to the two-and-a-half-year age group), and children with severe learning difficulties including speech and language delay. At the time I thought that I would have a broad spread of children to observe, but in fact I had organised far too large a study group and case load (approximately fifty children). In retrospect I feel that this was due to my enthusiasm and my anxiety; if I saw as many as fifty children, this would surely give me enough evidence to confirm my hypothesis – that there would be parallels between the speech and language development and the development of the music therapy of the study group.

Despite these problems, by the end of the first year it was clear that the timing, placing and quality of the infant vocalising followed the same kind of development as the SMR of the study group. This tied in with the research of other music therapists, who would agree that the early sound and gestural interactions are indeed related to interactions within music therapy (Pavlicevic 1991).

I was now concerned with the nature of the sounds and movements stimulated by music and less with the interaction itself. I confined the area of inquiry to the quality and occurrence of SMR within individual music therapy sessions, comparing these to the pre-verbal mainstream infant responses. I felt that to consider the complexity of the interactions themselves would have expanded the project to a much broader brief, which would have taken more than my two-year funding allowed. At the same time, I acknowledged the central place of the growing therapeutic relationship and its influence on my observations.

I was meeting children at the 'single word level' (Derbyshire County Council 1982),[1] whose SMR were fragmented and often chaotic; it was difficult for them to organise or structure their sounds. Later in their music therapy these same children apparently discovered a sense of structure, for example, finishing or anticipating the end of a song or phrase, or developing an overall shape to their playing. At the same time, they began spontaneously to construct their first simple sentences. Clearly, function and structure in language and in music were related. This is an observation that is supported by other documented research, in particular that concerned with brain function.

The similarities between language and music have been observed and discussed for centuries, with literature covering this area found in publications as diverse as neurology, neuropsychology, musical psychology, developmental psychology, musical analysis, speech and language pathology, audiology and education. Over a hundred years ago it was discovered that certain types of speech/language problems were related to damage (lesions) in a specific area of the brain, frequently as the result of a stroke (Broca 1861; Wernicke 1874). These ideas have been modified and extended over the past fifty years, although the overall picture of speech processes located in identifiable areas of the brain has remained.

The effect of music upon the brain is less clearcut. Over twenty years ago much of the then current literature was gathered together in a book called *Music and the Brain* (Critchley and Henson 1977). In separate chapters, different aspects of the human response to music in physical terms are described, with one chapter in particular dealing with the possibility of areas of the brain linked with musical 'faculties' (Wertheim 1977). Wertheim implied that the areas of the brain apparently relating to our appreciation of music were in turn related to different aspects of musical awareness. Wertheim's suggestion is that the brain's processing of music may in fact be an entirely different function from that of speech. Paradoxically, he concludes his chapter with a discussion of the observed links between speech and music. The number of publications around this period shows that the brain debate had gathered momentum, with many scientists fascinated by the subject. This curiosity has continued to the present day and recently Erdonmez has described the relationship between different types of musical task and the ways in which the brain processes incoming information (Erdonmez 1993). The concept of one hemisphere of the brain being dominant for music and the other for language is still largely accepted today, although the picture is far more complex. In a study of a composer with severe dysphasia (the motor aspect of the loss of ability to use speech as the result of brain injury) Luria, Tsvetkova and Futer revealed that a loss of speech function does not necessarily occur with a loss of musical function (Luria *et al.* 1965). The debate continues although, as Storr observes, some conclusions may be reached during the next twenty years (Storr 1992, 1993).

One of the few examples of detailed examination of linked music and speech brain functions is a paper published in *Psychology of Music*, by Scheid and Eccles. This reviews the literature concerning the brain's left hemisphere (speech) as well as that of the right hemisphere (Scheid and Eccles 1975). It is observed that although stimulation to the right hemisphere motor area can activate the vocal muscles, it is not sufficient to produce meaningful language. What does this indicate? Initially, we have been led to expect that the two hemispheres of the brain are responsible for different functions, including those of speech/language as well as those of music. Scheid and Eccles reveal that, although in the majority of human subjects tested (65 per cent) the left hemisphere is larger than the right, there is in fact a complementary functioning by both hemispheres in the processing of linguistic and musical material. Furthermore, it is suggested that in evolutionary terms, this functional differentiation of the hemispheres occurred – out of necessity – at an early stage of evolution. We may well expect to see traces of this in the normal development of all young humans and it is likely that these links will also occur in the auditory world of unfolding speech and language acquisition.

In the light of the research I wondered if the children in my study needed to understand the rules governing music in the same way that they did for language? There were indications that pre-cognitive speech and language development and the spontaneous response to music could be related within their process in a way that differed from later, cognitive language growth. Some children reaching the syntax level of language (rules governing structure within sentences) did so after they reached awareness of musical components such as short ostinati or rhythm patterns – in a sense, a kind of musical syntax. Although many researchers had concerned themselves either with the structure of improvised or pre-composed music, or the structure of language, my observations were linking the two aspects in a new way, where the sound product of speech–language and music interactions is seen in parallel.

I was excited by the observations. It was possible that the SLI child had difficulty in processing patterns of sound in both music and speech, and I wondered what the implications might be for my view of music therapy.

As a researcher my hypothesis was being confirmed, but as a music therapist I was concerned with a developing client–therapist relationship and not SMR exclusively. From time to time I had to remind myself not to listen for the SMR I hoped to hear as a researcher. Could I unwittingly influence the research work within the music therapy sessions? The potential for tension between the clinician's and the researcher's role is present within art therapy and music therapy research. As clinicians we all inquire; as researchers we formalise and focus our questions. If we research our own work it is possible that we will prejudice both clinical and research findings, whether consciously or unconsciously. Perhaps part of travelling that research path is to accept the challenge of not allowing the one role to affect the other? Even if we have thought about it, few of us have written about this aspect of the research process, although Hoskyns has discussed the problem (Hoskyns 1987). I cannot be sure that my research role did not interfere with my music therapy role, although the fact that I was aware of this possibility was significant. Had the circumstances been different I would have preferred to observe another music therapist's work rather than my own, for in this way I may have been less likely directly to influence the music therapy sessions.

The funding for the project was extended to a second year and I eventually produced a full report of the clinical work along with my observations (Sutton 1991). The major part of the report was a series of case studies, detailing the development in music therapy of six children. I prepared a simple table indicating the main aspects of infant vocalisation during the first 12 months of life (compiled from the analysis of cassette recordings of babies and family members) and compared this with speech and language development literature as well as the unfolding SMR of the children in music therapy sessions. As stated earlier, I found that many of the children with SLI moved through stages in language development that were mirrored in their spontaneous responses in music therapy (or vice versa). It was as if they increased their general awareness of sound and sound patterns in relation to interacting with another. They were able to hold such interactions in memory, with an overall sense of the structure of the interaction. This was reflected both in music therapy (as indicated by changing SMR) and speech and language development. One case study I extended into a paper that I presented at a music therapy conference (Sutton 1993).

REGISTERING THE RESEARCH: DECISIONS AND COMPROMISES

Having completed this ambitious pilot study I decided to register as a part-time research student. I contacted psychology and music departments in local universities. At the University of Ulster I found supervisors in both departments I felt comfortable with and I eventually enrolled as a part-time M.Phil. student in humanities (music) with an additional psychology supervisor. I had been advised by fellow researchers that being joint-supervised was not always easy, yet I have found this a positive situation, with two complementary but differing, stimulating approaches.

However, during meetings with my supervisors it became obvious that I needed to alter radically my conception of the research. As the degree is one in research technique I was advised to confine myself to as small an area as possible. I should ask and develop ways of examining a specific question; it must be possible for another researcher to duplicate my work and come to the same conclusions. I had to clarify what was at the root of my thinking and evolve a methodology to test the idea. This was a time of conflict for me. Living in Northern Ireland I was some distance from specialist music therapy research supervisors and as a part-time student I did not have the financial resources for an external supervisor. I was also working four full clinical days each week, with my research hours tightly timetabled. My locally-based supervisors had not come across a music therapy researcher before and, although excellent academics, they too were inexperienced. My eventual decision – to separate the research from the clinical work – was therefore influenced by a combination of factors, of which inexperience, time, distance and finance were central.

I re-examined the two-year project and decided to concentrate on an aspect of how children with SLI perceived patterned sound. From the pilot study I speculated that they had difficulty in hearing, processing and assimilating groups of sounds that children with mainstream speech and language development did not. This formed the basis for my hypothesis: firstly, that children with SLI found difficulty in perceiving sound presented as pattern; this would be the case whether or not the sound was 'predictable' (that is, consisting of regularly occurring sound events) or 'unpredictable' (irregularly occurring sound events). Secondly, a mainstream or non-SLI group would find more difficulty with the unpredictable sound patterns and less difficulty with the predictable sound patterns.

The suggestion that it was the complexity and not the amount of sounds that caused the difficulty for the SLI child had been made by some Canadian psychologists (Sloan 1985; Phillips 1989; Trehub et al. 1990a, b). Work by Tallal (1980) and Trehub and Trainor (1992) had isolated rhythmic components of speech and presented these in sequences, beginning from short, simple patterns which became increasingly complex. The researchers discovered that it was not the actual length of the sound sequences but their complexity that proved to be the most challenging for the children with SLI/auditory processing disorder. This suggested to me that many secondary impairments (such as those described in terms of 'being disruptive', 'unable to focus attention' or 'difficult to motivate') observed in SLI children may stem from this basic processing problem occurring at a very early level along the receptive speech pathway. The implication that these children experienced a substantial difficulty in processing sound at an early stage along the auditory pathway was startling. In addition, studies of the auditory processing of infants of up to one year of age revealed that they were not only sensitive to pre-verbal musical aspects of speech, but that that their processing of speech sounds differed from that of adults. Trehub and Trainor state, '[the research] implies that infants' early processing of speech sounds differs from that of adults in having an acoustic or phonetic basis rather than being based on speech sound or phonemic categories' (Trehub and Trainor 1992, p. 394). Later in their paper they speculate, 'Perhaps music and speech are intimately connected in early life, with common perceptual processing mechanisms for musical features' (Trehub and Trainor 1992, p. 400).

This research seemed to fit with my observations. Not only were there some differences between the auditory processing of children with SLI and those from the mainstream population, but there were also fascinating developmental links between the processing of music and that of speech. Having chosen to concentrate on an aspect of how SLI children perceived patterned sound I decided to centre my study on rhythm – patterns of sound without pitch change. The pilot study had focused on the timing and placing of the SLI child's responses within music therapy sessions and rather than extend this study I chose to focus upon the central factor behind the responses, that is, the underlying auditory awareness of sound. Thus, in considering the child's perception of rhythm itself I could address the underlying auditory processing of both speech and of music. This took me firmly into the area of music psychology.

With the research focused upon finding ways of checking how rhythm was perceived, I reviewed a wide range of existing tests and measures relating to 'musical ability' in the broadest sense (Shuter-Dyson and Gabriel 1981). I developed a simple test incorporating two groups of short, simple rhythms that children were to copy. I presented each rhythm on a drum, after which the child would copy me using the same instrument. I recorded all the rhythms on high quality audiocassette tape for later analysis. In analysing how the children from the mainstream and SLI population perceived, processed, remembered and reproduced the rhythms I would have an indication of the types of difference between the auditory processing of the two groups.

The tests consisted of two sets of ten rhythms. The first ten rhythms comprised regularly occurring, predictable sound patterns, for instance:

 or

The second ten rhythms were far less predictable with irregularly occurring sound patterns:

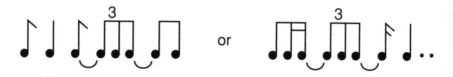

Both sets of rhythms became progressively more complex although still within a two- to four-crotchet beat range.

In the simple format of this test (presenting a rhythm to be heard, processed, memorised and repeated) I hoped to involve each child in a number of processes connected with the experience of receiving spoken language, without the use of the voice yet within the area of musical activity. The test rhythms relate to the supra-segmental aspects of speech; that is, the shortlived, individual sounds that comprise words, which in turn make up phrases and then sentences. Trehub and Trainor (1992) discovered that an underlying auditory processing – first seen in infants – is present both before and after verbal language acquisition and that this fundamental processing is at a pre-cognitive stage. It seems closer to music than to speech. Trehub and Trainor say, 'Theoretically, music and language could interact developmentally in several ways. From the beginning, they might be independent systems, such that once the input is identified as speech or music, processing would continue within the appropriate system. Alternatively, a single system for processing musical features might be operative until specialised music and speech processors emerge during the first year of life or beyond' (Trehub and Trainor 1992, p. 400). This Canadian research echoed my own observations some two years before, and in correspondence with Dr Trehub I was encouraged to continue my project.

I selected at random four primary schools in Belfast and took three groups of three children (one from each of Years One, Two and Three). I repeated the exercise with a comparative group of children with SLI. These had no learning difficulties apart from those directly related to speech and language (e.g. dyslexia). I expected the mainstream group to provide more accurate responses for the 'regular' rhythms. I speculated that the SLI children did not process sound patterns in the same way and I was hoping that they would provide inaccurate responses at an earlier stage than the mainstream group as well as responding to both sets of rhythms equally. Perhaps these children could not rely on pattern recognition in the way that the non-SLI children could?

CONCLUDING THE RESEARCH

At the time of writing I am analysing the 'copying' responses from both groups of children. Inevitably, the picture is more complex than I had imagined and I have included a consideration of the types of inaccurate response in my analysis, for there seem to be recurring features in the mistakes. The early indications are that my hypotheses are confirmed.

I am also discovering new areas and possibilities for future research work. It would be interesting to analyse the rhythmic responses of the SLI child within co-improvised music during music therapy sessions and to compare this with the responses acquired in the rhythm test. How would trained musicians respond to the rhythm test? How would the mainstream group react to improvising music with a trained music therapist? How could pitch patterns be added? Could pitch and rhythm patterns be looked at? How would any findings compare to the existing 'musical ability' tests and what could the discoveries tell us about these current tests? What are the implications for language learning?

This is a long way from my initial motivation. I believe that research is a combination of asking questions and making choices about how to look at those questions, and for a variety of reasons I have decided to focus my music therapy-inspired research within the field of music psychology. The decision was influenced by my non-therapist supervisors, geographical setting, financial and clinical restrictions as well as my research inexperience. As my research journey has unfolded the reader will have become aware of the potential influence of a diversity of factors upon their future research, whether positive or negative. What has happened to the music therapy process along my research path? In a sense, my current project is closer to the underlying auditory process that is contributing to what occurs in music therapy. This involves an interaction that is only part of the many-layered music therapy interaction. I believe that this registered research will inform some of the auditory aspects of our work, yet I readily acknowledge that it is limited in scope. Nevertheless, as I near the end of this work I know that those who feel the desire to try to answer questions about their work should continue. We may not always follow the pathways we originally plotted, but we will always unearth more tantalising questions in our journeys.

POSTSCRIPT

In writing this paper I have attempted to describe the unexpected development of a project with simplicity and clarity. It seems to me that there is a danger in research work of losing this simplicity, of taking refuge behind complex explanations of the obvious and of setting ourselves apart.

All we are doing is trying to shine a torch on a small area in order to illuminate our view of it.

Essentially, research work is not distanced from clinical work, for there are elements of inquiry fundamental to both. What is different is the commitment to spend time reading, inquiring, writing and cogitating, frequently at one's own expense. Research work is therefore personal, with much of the individual invested in it (this may partially explain the protecting response some feel when their work is under scrutiny). It is also a recent development in art therapy and music therapy and indicative of our growing confidence in our professional identity.

Undertaking research is a solitary business. It takes courage and gall to contemplate adding to a body of knowledge with an awareness that not everyone will agree with you. For me, my isolation was both personal and geographical; I had to redefine my clinical identity again and again in order to become accepted in the unknown Northern Irish setting, I was relying on my own resources and I had limited, periodic contact with others in my profession. At the same time, I had space to develop and to experiment.

There are also rewards for completing research. The more we think and talk about our work, the more we can offer it. My hope is that I will have helped encourage others to step on to the research path and to begin to travel.

NOTE

1 The scheme originally developed as part of a special school curriculum, including teacher and speech and language therapist input. Stages in language development are broken down (e.g. early vocabulary, simple sentences, grammar) and both assessment and learning activities are offered, following developmental pathways.

REFERENCES

Bishop, D.V.M. (1992) 'Autism, Asperger's Syndrome and Semantic-pragmatic Disorder: Where are the Boundaries?' *British Journal of Disorders of Communication.* 24: 107–21.

Bishop, D.V.M. and Rosenbloom, L. (1987) 'Classification of Childhood Language Disorders'. In: Yule, W. and Rutter, M. (Eds) *Language Development and Disorders. Clinics in Developmental Medicine.* Double Issue, Nos. 101–2. MacKeith Press, London.

Broca, P. (1861) (Communication with the Anthropological Society of Paris, 1861) Original source: 'Perte de la Parole, Ramollissement Chronique et Destruction Partielle du Lobe Antérieur Gauche du Cerveau'. *Bulletin of Social Anthropology* (Paris). 2: 235.

Critchley, M. and Henson, R.A. (Eds) (1977) *Music and the Brain.* Heinemann Medical, London.

Cummings, K. and Sutton, J.P. (1990) 'Case Study showing Parallel Development in Speech/language and Music Therapy in a Five-year-old Boy'. Unpublished paper given at Shared Creativity Conference, University of Ulster, Jordanstown.

Derbyshire County Council (1982) Derbyshire Language Scheme. County Educational Psychology Service.

Erdonmez, D. (1993) 'Music: A Mega-vitamin for the Brain'. In: Heal, M. and Wigram, T. (Eds) *Music Therapy in Health and Education*. Jessica Kingsley, London.

Hoskyns, S. (1987) 'Productive and Counter-productive Issues for Therapist and Researcher'. In: *Starting Research in Music Therapy. Proceedings of the Third Music Therapy Research Conference*. City University, London.

Luria, A.R., Tsvetkova, L.S. and Futer, D.S. (1965) 'Aphasia in a Composer'. *Journal of Neurological Science* 2: 288.

Pavlicevic, M. (1991) 'Music in Communication: Improvisation in Music Therapy'. Unpublished PhD thesis, University of Edinburgh.

Phillips, D.P. (1989) 'Neurobiology Relevant to Some Central Auditory Processing Disorders'. *Journal of Speech-Language Pathology and Audiobiology*. 13: 17–41.

Scheid, P. and Eccles, J.C. (1975) 'Music and Speech: Artistic Functions of the Human Brain'. *Psychology of Music* 3: 21–35.

Shuter-Dyson, R. and Gabriel, C. (1981) *The Psychology of Musical Ability*. Methuen, London.

Sloan, C. (1985) 'Auditory Processing Disorders: What are the Implications Regarding Treatment?'. *Human Communication* (Canada) 9: 117–26.

Storr, A. (1992) *Music and the Mind*. HarperCollins, London.

Storr, A. (1993) 'Foreword'. In: Heal, M. and Wigram, T. (Eds) *Music Therapy in Health and Education*. Jessica Kingsley, London.

Sutton, J.P. (1991) 'The Parallel Development in Speech and Language and Music in a Group of Children with Speech and Language Impairment'. DHSS Medical Research Award Report. DHSS, Stormont.

Sutton, J.P. (1993) ' "The Guitar Doesn't Know This Song'': An Investigation of Parallel Development in Speech/Language and Music Therapy'. In: Heal, M. and Wigram, T. (Eds) *Music Therapy in Health and Education*. Jessica Kingsley, London.

Tallal, P. (1980) 'Auditory Temporal Perception, Phonics and Reading Disabilities in Children'. *Brain and Language*. 9: 182–98.

Trehub, S., Thorpe, L.A. and Trainor, L.J. (1990a) 'Infants' Perception of *good* and *bad* melodies'. *Psychomusicology*. 9: 5–15.

Trehub, S., Thorpe, L.A. and Trainor, L.J. (1990b) 'Rules for Listening in Infancy'. In: Enns, J. (Ed.) *The Development of Attention: Research and Theory*. Elsevier, Amsterdam.

Trehub, S. and Trainor, L.J. (1992) 'A Comparison of Infants' and Adults' Sensitivity to Western Musical Structure'. *Journal of Experimental Psychology: Human Perception and Performance*. 18: 394–400.

Wernicke, C. (1874) Original source: '*Der Aphasische Symptomencomplex: Eine psychologische Studie auf Anatomische Basis*'. Cohn and Weigert, Breslau. (See also Eggert, G.H. (1977) *Music and the Brain*. Monton, The Hague.)

Wertheim, N. (1977) 'Is there an Anatomical Localisation for Musical Faculties?'. In: Critchley, M. and Henson, R.A. (Eds) *Music and the Brain*. Heinemann Medical, London.

Chapter 10

The effects of music therapy on a group of adults with profound learning difficulties

Amelia Oldfield and Malcolm Adams

INTRODUCTION

One of the major problems in working with adults with severe and profound learning difficulties is how to engage their attention and involve them in activities. This is clearly important, for example, in helping the development of skills. The studies on 'room management' as a way of organising 'activity periods' indicate that the way staff behaviour is structured and monitored can have a large influence on the level of participation by adults with profound learning difficulties (Porterfield and Blunden 1978; Cullen 1985). In reviewing these studies, Cullen (1985) points out that it is important to consider the choice of appropriate activities, and progression within these, if skills are to develop.

Music appears to be an effective means of motivating adults with profound learning difficulties and encouraging their involvement in activity. A survey carried out by a music therapist in one hospital found that staff in the hospital thought that music was particularly important for adults with a more profound learning difficulty. The staff were keen for the music therapists to spend as much time as possible with these clients (Odell 1979). Music encourages them to attempt movements or actions they otherwise find difficult. It may help them to relax or to increase their awareness of their environment. However, given that the range of responses by such people is extremely small these impressions need to be evaluated.

In music therapy, the therapist uses music creatively to establish an interaction with the client, providing a shared musical experience and activity leading to the pursuit of therapeutic goals determined by the client's problems (APMT 1986). In the study presented here, music therapy takes the form of the therapist singing or playing instruments, using both improvised and pre-composed music. The clients are thereby encouraged to sing, dance or play simple percussion or wind instruments. The aim is not primarily to entertain or teach people to play an instrument or a piece of music, but rather to use music towards the achievement of non-musical aims. These aims might include assisting with the development of communication, improvements in the control of movement, relaxation, encouraging social interaction and providing opportunities for expressing emotions.

There has been relatively little research in the field of music therapy, and the work that exists is very varied and approaches the problems from many different perspectives. These include monitoring psychophysiological responses in people receiving music therapy (Taylor 1973; Barger 1979; Scartelli 1984; Schuster 1985), investigating the musical preferences or abilities of people with learning difficulties (Lienhard 1976) and studying the effects of music on the learning process (Walmsley et al. 1981; Deutsch and Parks 1978; Jellison and Miller 1982).

The last two studies are particularly interesting since they indicate that music can be used to motivate adults with severe learning difficulties to do things which they otherwise find difficult. Deutsch and Parks (1978) found that music acted as a reward to increase the appropriate verbalisations of a boy with severe learning difficulties. Walmsley, Crighton and Droog (1981) demonstrated improved head control in three of their five subjects when music was used as a contingent reward. However, these studies do not investigate either the general effects of music therapy, or music therapy as an approach.

More closely related to the present investigation are studies by Walker (1972) and Carrington (1973). In the first, an experimental group, which had a daily thirty-minute music therapy session for twelve days, made better progress at acquiring a number of functional words than a control group that had daily talking sessions. In the second study, Carrington investigated the effects of music therapy on the attention span of eight hyperactive boys with severe learning difficulties. They received ten weekly music sessions, and observations were made in the classroom at the beginning and end of the study. No significant effects were found. Perhaps this is not surprising, since it seems unlikely for any progress achieved in ten sessions to generalise to the classroom. When evaluating relatively new forms of therapy, such as music therapy, it seems necessary to investigate first whether there are any effects on behaviour during therapy, and then to go on to study generalisation.

The study by Walker (1972) is one of the few in which the music sessions consisted of 'singing, rhythm and music creativity activities'. Therefore it is concerned with live, improvised music rather than recorded music, and is thus closer to evaluating music therapy as it is usually practised in the UK. However, the people studied were much more able than those in the present study who, with one exception, have no expressive language.

It is clear that there is very little research on the effectiveness of music therapy even though it appears to be a useful approach with people having severe learning difficulties. Further work is therefore needed. This study is concerned with adults with severe and profound learning difficulties, and aims to investigate the effectiveness of music therapy in helping to achieve a set of aims identified for each individual. Progress in music therapy was compared with the use of play directed at achieving the same individual aims.

METHOD

The study involved a group of twelve adults with profound learning difficulties resident in hospital. Four subjects were selected at random among them for intensive study, and randomly allocated to two groups. The other subjects were allocated at random to make up six subjects in each group. One group received a weekly, half-hourly music therapy session for six months, while the other group had half-hourly play sessions. These treatments were then reversed for a further six months. Both groups received twenty sessions of each treatment.

Music therapy sessions were led by the music therapist and she was usually assisted by one other member of staff. Play sessions were led by an experienced nursing assistant who knew the residents well. She had worked with each of the twelve experimental subjects for at least six months preceding the study, using the same play techniques. She was also assisted by at least one other member of staff. When an uneven number of additional staff was available they were divided between the groups, with the play group having an extra member of staff. This was so that any beneficial effects of music therapy that might be found could not be attributed to greater input of staff.

Subjects

At the time the experimental sessions started, the twelve adults with profound learning difficulties involved in the study had all been living in the hospital for at least three years, and most of them for over eight years. Nine subjects are severely physically handicapped in addition to their mental handicap. Eight of these are wheelchair-bound and one uses a walking frame. Most of the twelve are partially or wholly incontinent and nearly all of them need help to feed themselves. Only one of the subjects has any speech, although some understand a few spoken words and have learnt to use a few signs (e.g. 'drink' or 'biscuit') from the Makaton vocabulary. Their level of social interaction is extremely limited and in most cases involves interaction with staff rather than with other residents. All subjects except one had been in regular group music sessions for at least eight months in the three years preceding the study. For all

Table 10.1 Treatment characteristics: Comparison of music therapy and play

Music therapy	Play
Overall structure	
Therapist is clearly specified as group leader.	Leader and helpers have very similar, undifferentiated roles.
Definite plan for sessions with sequence of activities: greeting, theme and variations, group activity, goodbye.	Informal plan; open-ended with no fixed sequence.
Some whole group activity and some individual activity: taking turns, fairly brief interactions, repeating similar music with each person (though may use different instruments).	All activity on an individual basis. Usually each person is doing a different activity.
Music is being played most of the time and can be heard by all group members.	At any one time, two or three clients will be receiving attention whilst the rest receive none.
Clients arranged in a horseshoe with the therapist working in front of them or beside each person in turn.	Clients are not arranged around the room in relation to one another in any deliberate pattern.
Content	
Pre-composed music, both vocal and instrumental.	Painting. Rattling and selecting objects from a box.
Improvisation: Response to clients' behaviour and musical expression; development of musical dialogue.	Imaginary play with toy animals. Manipulating toys (e.g. Activity Centre). Feeling and scratching different textures. Building bricks.
Each individual has an instrument, e.g. drum, chime bar or cymbal. This may be changed during sessions.	
Staff behaviour	
Therapist: Leads session, decides activities and timing of these. Plays music. Gives appropriate instruments to clients. Responds to clients' music. Plays to whole group and works with individuals.	Leaders and helpers act in very similar ways. They make activities available to clients and encourage them to participate. They help clients to use play materials.
Helpers: Assist some clients. Encourage participation. May not be active much of the time.	They work closely with one individual for a time (at least five minutes), then move to another person.

subjects, the play activities which formed the other component of the study were similar to those experienced by them in their daily treatment.

Treatment

Since the aim of the study was to investigate the effectiveness of music therapy as it was usually conducted, no changes or simplifications were made to the usual procedures adopted. The play activities were also conducted in the way that was standard for the residents. In both cases, the form and content of activities were chosen on the basis that they were judged as being suitable by the staff and appropriate in assisting the achievement of individual objectives which had been identified. The characteristics of the two treatments and differences between them are shown in Table 10.1. Note that the study did not involve 'play therapy' as a formal and systematic treatment, but rather play activities of the kind often found with this group of clients and which, for example, form the content of room management 'activity periods' (Porterfield and Blunden 1978).

Although the music therapy sessions were very structured, this structure was used only as a framework. Much of every session was spent responding to, and improvising upon, the singing or playing of individual clients. As in any interactive therapeutic approach, the therapist adopted a framework and set of techniques (in this case musical) which could then be adapted to the material (activities) produced by the clients.

When the treatment was reversed, Group B received the same music therapy programme as had been used for Group A. Again, however, the precise content of the sessions would vary depending on the responses elicited from the residents, and the way in which the therapist could improvise upon and extend these.

Measures

Although all subjects in the study had profound learning difficulties they were extremely varied in their characteristics, interests and abilities. The aims of therapy differed widely among the subjects and progress was expected to be slow. Therefore, no single measure was appropriate to monitor progress in all cases. Measurement methods needed to be sensitive to small changes and tailored to each individual. The approach adopted, then, was to identify specific aims for each individual. For each aim, a behavioural index that could be derived from direct observation was specified.

For each subject, the aims of therapy were agreed in discussion between staff involved with the residents, including the authors. These aims were based on knowledge of the residents' difficulties and assessment of their abilities. The purpose of the study was to compare achievement of these aims during play activities and music therapy sessions and, therefore, it was necessary to observe subjects' behaviour during these sessions. It was clear from the nature of these aims that detailed and extensive observation was required. This meant that it would not be possible to observe all the twelve subjects every week. Rather than attempt to make only a few observations of each of the twelve subjects, it was decided that it would be more useful to observe, and monitor the progress of, a few subjects in detail. Thus, as indicated above, four subjects were selected at random for intensive study. The therapy aims and behavioural indices for these four subjects are shown in Table 10.2. The same aims and indices were used in relation to both music therapy and play so that a direct comparison could be made between the treatments.

The behaviour of these subjects was recorded on videotape. Each week, either a play session or a music therapy session was recorded. On each occasion, one experimental subject in the group was observed for fifteen minutes and then the other experimental subject was observed for a further fifteen minutes. The order in which the subjects were observed was randomised. Thus, by the end of the forty experimental sessions, each of the subjects had been recorded during ten play sessions and ten music therapy sessions.

The forty videotapes were analysed by the first author, who viewed them in random order. This was done to avoid bias arising from adopting different standards for earlier and later sessions. A time-sampling method with five-second interval was used to record the behaviour of both subject and staff using the categories shown in Table 10.2. A five-second interval was chosen because some of the behaviours were of very brief duration. It was necessary to record some staff behaviours because the aims for some individuals related to, for example, response to staff attention.

The second author analysed six of the tapes (three music and three play) chosen at random to investigate inter-observer agreement. Observation records were compared and each five-second interval classified as an agreement or disagreement. The overall agreement was over 80 per cent while the chance-corrected level of agreement (Cohen 1960) varied between 0.63 and 0.66. This was judged to be an acceptable level of agreement.

These observation records provided frequency and duration measures for both resident and staff behaviour in the sessions. These provided the data for the indices reflecting progress on the agreed therapy aims. Comparisons between play and music were evaluated for each individual separately using non-parametric statistics (Siegel 1956).

Table 10.2 Aims of therapy for the four experimental subjects and behavioural observations to assess progress

Subject	Aims	Behavioural index	Behaviours recorded
A	1 To increase the amount of time spent actively involved in any way.	Amount of time spent 'playing' or holding an object.	P: Scratch, tap, feel.
	2 To increase the amount of time holding or grasping objects.	Amount of time holding an object.	H: Closes hand around object.
	3 To increase number of positive responses to attempts to make contact with A.	Proportion of time spent 'playing' or holding an object when staff attention is given.	*Staff* A: Attention to client.
B	1 To reduce the time spent curled up in foetal position with head down on top of arms.	Amount of time head is held up independently without physical help from staff and one arm was stretched without help.	H: Head is held up unaided. R: Arm is held straight without help.
	2 To increase amount of time B closes his hand around objects and uses his hands and arms constructively.	Amount of time B closes his hand around object or moves hand towards an object.	P: Closes hand around object or uses arms or hands constructively.
	3 To increase B's awareness of the outside world, shown by e.g. looking at people or smiling.	Number of times B smiles. Proportion of time being active during staff attention.	D: Drops object. S: Smiles. *Staff* A: Attention to client.

	Aim	Measure	Codes
C	1 To increase amount of time spent playing with and using objects.	Amount of time holding an object or actively involved.	P: Holds an object, claps, scratches, or plays with an object.
	2 To encourage C to use objects without throwing them.	Number of times C throws an object.	T: Throws an object.
	3 To decrease C's screaming.	Number of screams.	S: Screams.
	4 To increase the amount of time spent interacting with staff.	Proportion of time receiving staff attention in which C is playing actively.	*Staff* A: Attention to client.
D	1 To increase the amount of time spent actively involved.	Amount of time using or holding an object.	H: Holds an object.
	2 To increase the number of different activities D would tolerate and take part in.	Number of different activities and amount of time involved in each one.	T: Plays tambourine. B: Plays with bricks + six other codes for specific musical instruments + 12 other codes for specific toys.
	3 To decrease the amount of time spent behaving in unacceptable ways such as screaming, spitting and swearing, and to increase amount of time spent in constructive conversations.	Number of 30-sec. intervals in which transcribed speech was classified as appropriate or inappropriate.	*Staff* A: Attention to client.

RESULTS

The main hypothesis to be investigated in the study was that, for each individual, the objectives which had been specified would be achieved to a greater extent in the music therapy sessions than in play sessions. It was further hypothesised that there would be progress over time in achieving these objectives during the block of music therapy sessions, but no progress during the block of play sessions.

Individual data

Performance on the achievement of specific objectives is shown for each individual separately in Tables 10.3–10.6. Scores are shown for each objective and the results of Mann–Whitney tests (Siegel 1956) comparing the level of scores in music therapy with those in play are also shown. In addition, the values of Kendall's rank correlation coefficient, indicating improvement across time within treatment conditions, are shown in cases where these values are significant.

For Subject A, the main hypothesis is supported. The amount of time holding objects and the amount of time playing with objects (including holding them) was greater during music therapy than in play sessions. In addition, a comparison based on the ratio of amount of time playing divided by amount of staff attention was also significant (U=9,P<0.02), with music therapy giving higher scores. However, there was no improvement over time during music therapy whereas there was improvement during play. Since the play sessions came first for this subject this last finding throws some doubt on the main result.

There was no difference between the amount of staff attention received during the two treatments.

With Subject B, the main hypothesis was supported for only one objective (relaxing arm) although there was also improvement over time during music therapy in both this and 'holding head up' unaided. There were no other significant differences for this subject.

For this subject, music therapy came first. Thus there was an improvement during music therapy and then lower overall scores subsequently during play sessions. This is in accordance with the initial hypotheses.

Subject C's results did not support the initial hypotheses. C spent more time playing actively during the play sessions than during music therapy. However, Subject C also received more staff attention in play than in music therapy. There were no differences in the other objectives and, indeed, the amount of screaming and throwing turned out to be very low during both treatment conditions.

For Subject D the only objective showing any difference between the

Table 10.3 Subject A: Observed behaviour during play and music therapy sessions[a]

Playing (including holding objects)

Play	0	10	8	10	11	55	x[b]	29	33	19
Music	23	x	24	77	23	20	43	74	24	34

$U^c=17$, $P<0.05$ $\tau=0.64$ ($P<0.05$) (for play)

Holding objects

Play	0	1	0	0	3	2	x	0	6	10
Music	15	x	0	61	17	8	37	16	0	10

$U=15.5$, $P<0.05$ $\tau=0.50$ ($P<0.05$) (for play)

Staff attention

Play	0	62	101	34	51	144	x	179	139	167
Music	25	x	22	79	68	119	65	73	107	128

$U=33$ n.s.

Notes:
[a] Subject A received play sessions before music therapy. Scores shown are the number of 5-sec. intervals in which the behaviour occurred in each session.
[b] x = absent from session.
[c] U is the Mann–Whitney statistic.

Table 10.4 Subject B: Observed behaviour during music therapy and play sessions[a]

Head held up unaided										
Music	30	21	11	50	52	x[b]	121	98	x	62
Play	33	67	x	39	30	56	28	45	x	x
U[c]=24.5 n.s. τ=0.57 (P<0.05) (for music)										
Arm relaxed (held straight without help)										
Music	35	63	53	66	100	x	140	108	x	129
Play	2	140	x	30	18	99	3	6	x	x
U=11.5, P<0.05 τ=0.79 (P<0.01) (for music)										
Playing (includes holding objects)										
Music	19	0	6	16	44	x	7	12	x	21
Play	5	21	x	26	14	6	1	0	x	x
U=21.5 n.s.										
Smiling										
Music	0	2	0	0	4	x	4	7	x	0
Play	3	2	x	3	0	2	8	1	x	x
U=23 n.s.										
Staff attention										
Music	19	76	68	127	101	x	60	104	x	32
Play	113	56	x	127	100	74	41	25	x	x
U=17.5 n.s.										

Notes:
[a] Subject B received music therapy before play sessions. Scores shown are the number of 5-sec. intervals in which the behaviour occurred in each session.
[b] x = absent from session.
[c] U is the Mann–Whitney statistic.

Table 10.5 Subject C: Observed behaviour during music therapy and play sessions[a]

Playing										
Music	3	61	7	35	39	17	29	17	49	30
Play	101	75	86	37	40	136	73	105	21	42
$U^b=13$, $P<0.02$										
Throwing										
Music	0	2	1	1	0	0	4	0	0	2
Play	1	2	2	1	5	2	0	0	7	4
$U=29.5$ n.s.										
Screaming										
Music	0	0	0	6	2	0	0	0	0	0
Play	0	0	0	0	0	0	0	0	5	2
$U=49.5$ n.s.										
Staff attention										
Music	13	52	25	44	46	30	37	28	54	53
Play	32	61	180	19	171	180	152	5	162	158
$U=23$, $P<0.05$										

Notes:
[a] Subject C received music therapy before play sessions. Scores are the number of 5-sec. intervals in which the behaviour occurred in each session.
[b] U is the Mann–Whitney statistic.

Table 10.6 Subject D: Observed behaviour during play and music therapy sessions[a]

Playing[b]										
Play	0	0	73	79	71	119	3	0	59	21
Music	74	61	46	0	19	95	40	39	43	78
U=43.5 n.s.										
Playing with objects other than main preference[b]										
Play	0	0	7	2	26	10	0	0	0	0
Music	6	4	1	0	9	51	8	15	6	31
U=25 (P<0.05)										
Staff attention[b]										
Play	50	4	65	70	6	96	29	23	47	28
Music	86	46	51	25	69	114	54	60	68	111
U=26 n.s.										
Number of activities undertaken in addition to main preference[c]										
Play	0	0	1	1	2	1	0	0	0	0
Music	3	1	1	0	1	4	2	2	2	3
U=16 (P<0.02)										
Appropriate verbal behaviour[d]										
Play	3	0	10	14	5	17	2	0	4	4
Music	9	4	11	0	5	10	15	1	4	7
U=42 n.s.										
Inappropriate verbal behaviour[d]										
Play	11	5	1	0	0	0	14	30	4	11
Music	0	3	2	9	4	0	2	1	7	0
U=36.5 n.s.										

Notes:
[a] Subject D received play sessions before music therapy.
[b] Scores shown are the number of 5-sec. intervals in which the behaviour occurred in each session.
[c] Score is number of additional activities in each session.
[d] Scores shown are the number of 30-sec. intervals in which verbal behaviour is classified as appropriate or inappropriate (swearing, screaming, etc.).

treatments was that D took part in a wider range of activities during music therapy and engaged in these for a longer time.

Overall then, three of the four individuals obtained higher scores during music therapy in achieving the specific objectives, although this was not true for all objectives. One subject obtained higher scores in play but this was associated with a greater input of staff attention in these sessions. When the ratio of play to amount of staff attention was compared for this subject the difference was not significant (U=49.5 n.s.).

DISCUSSION

This paper describes a small, evaluative study investigating the effects of music therapy on the progress of a group of adults with profound learning difficulties.

Clearly there are methodological limitations − mostly arising from practical constraints − which restrict the conclusions which may be drawn from the study. These include the small number of subjects, the fact that not all the subjects who were treated were studied in detail and that not all of the treatment sessions were videotaped and observed, and the lack of any assessment of treatment effect outside the treatment sessions. A further difficulty is that the single-subject design used was essentially a simple AB − baseline/treatment − design. However, this is probably inevitable when considering a treatment whose effects one would expect to be cumulative rather than immediate and with subjects for whom progress is likely to be extremely slow. Moreover, the design here is strengthened by including a BA sequence and by replicating both sequences across subjects.

Despite the shortcomings of the study it is clear that it has been possible to identify some positive effects of music therapy in subjects with profound and multiple handicaps. Conclusions that may be drawn will be examined using the validity concepts discussed by Cook and Campbell (1979).

The first question to be asked relates to statistical conclusion validity: has any change or difference been detected? Tables 10.3–10.6 show that, for all subjects, some differences in behaviour were shown between the treatments, and that for two subjects there were some changes over time in one treatment or the other. Most, but not all, of these differences or changes were in favour of music therapy.

A second question then arises, that of internal validity. Can the differences that have been found be attributed to treatment effects? Are there other plausible, alternative hypotheses that cannot be ruled out? For Subjects B, C and D it seems reasonable to conclude that the difference in behaviour can be attributed to the different treatments (although for Subject C this was in favour of play). Subject B received music therapy first and made progress in two aims during this: holding his head up unaided and keeping his arm relaxed without help. In one of these, his performance in the subsequent play sessions was at a significantly lower level. In neither aim did he continue to improve over the course of the play sessions. This data, then, supports the interpretation that the higher performance can be attributed to music therapy as compared with play rather than, say, general developmental progress. Subject D's behavioural repertoire was very restricted and one aim was to encourage him to play with a wider range of toys or instruments than the one he usually preferred. This was achieved more successfully in music therapy than in play sessions. Since there were no trends over time in either treatment (each lasting approximately six months), again maturation or adaptation to the treatment situation can be ruled out as alternative explanations.

For Subject A, the interpretation is more equivocal. Performance for two aims was at a higher overall level in music therapy as compared with play. However, the play sessions came first and there was a significant improvement over time during these. This improved level was then maintained during music therapy. For this subject, then, maturation or adaptation to prolonged treatment is a possible explanation for the difference found. Thus, for two of the four subjects it is possible to conclude that music therapy led to greater achievement of the identified individual aims.

Having attributed some difference in performance to the different treatments the third question concerns construct validity. What exactly are the differences between the treatments that have led to the effects found? What is the nature of these effects? From other accounts of music therapy (Nordoff and Robbins 1977; Alvin 1978; Boxhill 1985), it seems likely that the key factors are the use of music itself, the use of improvisation based on the individuals' own musical productions and the development of a relationship with the individuals in the group. In this study, these elements were all present and further research is required to identify their relative importance.

It is difficult on the basis of this study to say a great deal about the nature of the effects that music therapy can bring about. The measures used were different for each individual and were based on specific aims that were identified as appropriate for each person. There was some degree of overlap between the aims for different people, but no corresponding overlap in the ones that responded to music therapy. It seems that the response to music is very individual and that much more work is necessary before it would be possible to suggest which individuals will respond in particular ways to music therapy.

The fourth question to consider is that of external validity. To what extent can the results found be generalised across people, settings and trainers? Again, it is clear that a small-scale study such as this can give little information on these questions. However, it is worth noting that the four experimental subjects were chosen at random from the group and that the total group of subjects was amongst the most disabled group of people resident in the hospital. Thus, it seems reasonable to suppose that similar results might be found among other similarly disabled people elsewhere. A caveat to this conclusion, however, is the finding that treatment implementation (as indexed by the distribution of staff attention across group members) was uneven. This points to the difficulty of drawing conclusions about the effects of a group treatment when only a few members of the group are studied in detail. Further work is needed to clarify this and to examine the relative merits of group versus individual music therapy with people with such disabilities (Montague 1985).

This study did not examine whether the effects of music therapy generalised beyond the treatment setting. It is clear, however, for the two subjects receiving music therapy first that the effects found did not persist over time (Subjects B and D, Tables 10.4 and 10.6). It may be that with this group of people more intensive treatment than weekly sessions is required.

Although this is a small study carried out under various practical constraints, it has been able to identfy positive effects of music therapy with adults with profound learning difficulties. Further investigation of these effects and of how to maximise the impact of therapy is clearly required.

REFLECTIONS

This project has shown that music therapy was, to some extent, an effective means of treatment. Although this was the main focus, a number of observations were made which led us to ask some other important research questions.

One of these was how much the music therapist's work was influenced by the video camera. We looked at whether the presence of the camera influenced staff to spend more or less time with the subject being filmed, and found that staff in music therapy sessions were influenced to give more attention to the individuals as they were being filmed (Oldfield and Adams 1990). This was in spite of the fact that the music therapist did not know ahead of time whether or not she was going to be filmed or which individual would be filmed first, and despite the music therapist making a conscious effort not to let the camera interfere with her work. It appears, therefore, that there needs to be a greater independence between the investigator and the music therapist, or alternatively a research design that does not influence the therapist as much. Less intrusive observation methods might have helped, e.g. video cameras attached to walls and operated from another room, or using a one-way screen. If the music therapist had not been involved in the research project and had no idea what use was going to be made of the videotapes, she would probably have been less influenced by the camera. One could argue that it might be more useful for music therapists to design research projects for each other rather than investigate their own work. However, this would not have been satisfactory, for the authors' main question concerned the efficacy of one aspect of a particular therapist's approach. It was only by involving the music therapist in the research process that the question could be addressed adequately.

If the music therapist is involved in her own research, observations made during the project are likely to have practical implications for their work which will benefit the client. This project gave the music therapist the opportunity to study four people's progress in minute detail, making it possible to observe small reactions that can easily be missed. As a result, the music therapist modified her approach to the four subjects (who continued to receive music therapy after the research had ended). After observing videotapes of Subject A's independent finger movements on the snare drum, for example, the music therapist encouraged her to use finger movements on other similar instruments. From observing videotapes of music therapy sessions, the authors discovered that a relatively large proportion of the time was spent selecting and arranging appropriate music instruments. Subsequently, the music therapist did this before the sessions started. Neither of these developments would have occurred if the music therapist had not been involved in the research.

In some respects the results of this project are limited. Critics might conclude that this type of research only answers a few detailed questions and is, therefore, not worth the considerable amount of work such a project necessitates. The authors, however, believe that the advantages outweigh the limitations, and there is a great deal to be learnt from this type of study. This project enabled the music therapist, above all, to learn about research. It forced her not only to ask questions but to break them down and define them exactly. When analysing videotapes exact goals have to be determined, and the researcher must ask precisely what it is that is being aimed for and why. The research also awakened the music therapist's interest in other types of related research. None of this is easy, particularly since most music therapists have little previous knowledge of research. By undertaking such studies it is possible to define and understand one's work more precisely.

The main emphasis of this study was to look at the effectiveness of music therapy compared to play sessions; once this question had been answered, many others regarding the way the music therapist worked became of interest. For example, it was disappointing to find that there were no trends in the behaviours of the four subjects. It may be that in order to progress with people who have profound learning difficulties, daily rather than weekly sessions might be necessary. It would be of interest to initiate a project where daily sessions were compared to daily and/or weekly sessions.

It would seem that the best way to work with people who have profound learning difficulties would be to see each person individually. However, one could argue that for people with extremely short concentration spans, a number of shorter periods of attention spread over a group session might be more effective. Such clients may not have sufficient interpersonal skills to have an awareness of group dynamics, thus enabling the music therapist to work individually in the group without adversely affecting the group process.

It was encouraging to find that the results obtained from the on-going assessment procedure devised and used at the Ida Darwin Hospital were similar to the results obtained from the video analyses (Oldfield 1993). It would be interesting to evaluate the assessment procedure with other groups of clients and compare it with differing assessment procedures used by other music therapists. As there is no standardised music therapy assessment procedure in Great Britain, research into an efficient and practical procedure would be useful.

Perhaps the most important aspect of this type of study is that it forces the researcher to think about the effect of the music therapy on the client. As a result of the clients' progress (or lack of progress) other aspects may be analysed, such as the amount of attention staff were giving to the clients or the type of music and activities used. This is different from research which focuses primarily on the music and the activity of the music therapist. Although most aspects of music therapy warrant further investigation, research which focuses on the changes in the clients is bound to remain of paramount importance.

ACKNOWLEDGEMENTS

The authors would like to thank the residents and the staff at the Ida Darwin Hospital, Fulbourn, Cambridge, UK, for their help in this project.

This study was supported by grant No. 65 from the East Anglian Regional Health Authority Locally Organised Research Fund.

REFERENCES

Alvin, J. (1978) *Music for the Handicapped Child*. Oxford University Press, Oxford.
APMT (1986) *A Career in Music Therapy*. Association of Professional Music Therapists, London.
Barger, D.A. (1979) 'The Effects of Music and Verbal Suggestions on Heart Rate and Self-Reports'. *The Journal of Music Therapy*. XVI: 158–71.
Boxhill, E.H. (1985) *Music Therapy for the Developmentally Disabled*. Aspen Publications, Rockville, Maryland.
Carrington, F.M. (1973) 'The Effects of Music Therapy on the Attention Span of Hyperactive Mental Retardates'. *Dissertation Abstracts International*. 34: 3864.
Cohen, J. (1960) 'A Coefficient of Agreement for Nominal Scales'. *Educational and Psychological Measurement*. 20: 37–40.

Cook, T.D. and Campbell, D.T. (1979) *Quasi Experimentation: Design and Analysis Issues for Field Settings*. Rand McNally, Chicago.

Cullen, C. (1985) 'Working with Groups of Mentally Handicapped Adults'. In: Watts, F.N. (Ed.) *New Developments in Clinical Psychology*. British Psychological Society/John Wiley, Chichester.

Deutsch, M. and Parks, R.L. (1978) 'The Use of Contingent Music to Increase Appropriate Conversational Speech'. *Mental Retardation*. 16: 33–6.

Jellison, J.A. and Miller, N.I. (1982) 'Recall of Digit and Word Sequences by Musicians and Non-musicians as a Function of Spoken or Sung Input and Task'. *The Journal of Music Therapy*. XIX: 194–209.

Lienhard, M.E. (1976) 'Factors Relevant to the Rhythmic Perception of a Group of Mentally Retarded Children'. *The Journal of Music Therapy*. XIII: 58–65.

Montague, J. (1985) 'Letter'. *Association of Professional Music Therapists Newsletter*. 13.

Nordoff, P. and Robbins, C. (1977) *Creative Music Therapy: Individualized Treatment for the Handicapped Child*. John Day, New York.

Odell, H. (1979) 'Review of the Work of the Music Therapist at the Ida Darwin Hospital'. Unpublished MS.

Oldfield, A. (1993) 'A Study of the Way Music Therapists Analyse their Work'. *Journal of British Music Therapy*. 7:14–22.

Oldfield, A. and Adams, M. (1990) 'The Effects of Music Therapy on a Group of Profoundly Mentally Handicapped Adults'. *Journal of Mental Deficiency Research*. 34: 107–25.

Porterfield, J. and Blunden, R. (1978) 'Establishing an Activity Period and Individual Skill Training within a Day Setting for Profoundly Mentally Handicapped Adults'. *Journal of Practical Approaches to Developmental Handicap*. 2: 10–15.

Scartelli, J.P. (1984) 'The Effect of EMG Bio-feedback and Sedative Music, EMG Bio-feedback Only, and Sedative Music Only on Frontalis Muscle Relaxation Ability'. *The Journal of Music Therapy*. XXI: 67–8.

Schuster, B.L. (1985) 'The Effect of Music on Blood Pressure Fluctuations in Adult Hemodialysis Patients'. *The Journal of Music Therapy*. XXII: 146–53.

Siegel, S. (1956) *Non-parametric Statistics*. McGraw-Hill, New York.

Taylor, D.B. (1973) 'Subjects' Responses to Pre-categorised Stimulative and Sedative Music'. *The Journal of Music Therapy*. X: 86–94.

Walker, J.B. (1972) 'The Use of Music as an Aid in Developing Functional Speech in the Institutionalised Mentally Retarded'. *The Journal of Music Therapy*. IX: 1–12.

Walmsley, R.P., Crighton, L. and Droog, D. (1981) 'Music as a Feedback Mechanism for Teaching Head Control to Severely Handicapped Children: A Pilot Study'. *Developmental Medicine and Child Neurology*. 23: 739–46.

Part III

Context and culture

Chapter 11

Research and the particular
Epistemology in art and psychotherapy

John Henzell

INTRODUCTION

The word 'research' in English means the act of closely or carefully searching for or after a specified thing or person, an investigation directed to the discovery of some fact by careful study of a subject, or a course of critical or scientific enquiry (*Shorter Oxford English Dictionary* 1986). Yet as it is used in many institutions, both medical and academic, it seems infinitely more complicated, even to be surrounded by a certain mystique. It often sounds like an injunction, something we feel guilty and pained by when we respond to statements like 'why aren't you doing research?', or 'where's the proper research that supports this?' I shall argue that the answers to such questions might lie closer to hand and be more ordinary than we think, and while research may be both simpler and more complex than it appears at first sight, there need be nothing oppressive in it.

My first step will be to discuss science, another overburdened word, and show how, in spite of the privilege it enjoys in our culture, it is possible to be usefully scientific about many things not usually included within the popular idea of science.

Next I will discuss epistemology, the study of what can be known about different kinds of phenomena, the necessary preliminary to any actual research. Epistemology is, we might say, research into research. Furthermore, different epistemological frameworks can be run together in such a way that they create fresh understandings, rather in the manner that a good metaphor originates a meaning from several frames of reference.

I will then try to clarify how attempts to do research are often confused by extraneous political pressures as well as by misconceptions concerning people and things, facts and fictions, and art and science. Useful research stems from a clear understanding of what kinds of actual events, phenomena and activities we wish to investigate. Such clarity is particularly difficult in a clinical and therapeutic practice often dominated by institutional and professional orthodoxy. In addition, good research is not confined to science; it is just as much a feature of art and psychotherapy practice which moves beyond accepted routine.

This is followed by a discussion of art and the image. Art and images are not necessarily the same. The image is a distinctive way in which we experience things; it does not conform to any discursive ordering or grammar, it possesses its own order. Images, because they convey their sense *in* the matter that actually forms them, rather than *through* the conventional signs of a notation, cannot avoid the tendency to directly present their meaning as a *form*, rather than as a *content* to be deciphered via grammatical rules. The image also exists in an aesthetic dimension; it may become art. As such it moves beyond the personal, the pain or happiness of its creator, his or her psychodynamics, and becomes a cultural work which aspires to inform us about all our suffering and joys.

Finally, some of the implications of these matters for therapy are indicated. In order to practice psychological healing there must be a commerce with the body. Self-reflection, or *self-research*, the whole focus of psychotherapy, would be no more than an idle cerebral distraction if it did not engage our whole consciousness, our emotions, with all their vivid sense-perceptions, as well as our intelligence. The history of psychotherapy, as well as the later development of art therapy, demonstrates that this self-research inevitably involves images and the forms of understanding exemplified by art.

Throughout I will stress three essential features of research in art and psychotherapy. Firstly, that research arises from and then investigates the distinguishing marks or particular nature of the things or events that concern us. Secondly, in order to be coherent, research must be grounded in an adequate epistemology; that is, the forms of knowledge it seeks to establish must be derivable from the kinds of phenomena it examines. Thirdly, both art and psychotherapy are in themselves research – as with science, most so when they refuse to obey dogma and received opinion. In the case of psychotherapy, research is a collaboration between therapist and patient, perhaps we should think of it as a type of intersubjective inquiry. Some of these points are elaborated in a concluding section.

A reader who expects to find detailed discussions of specific examples of research related to local situations will be disappointed. Rather than do this I have treated the problem of research in our field philosophically rather than descriptively, and in the space available have often only been able to touch on issues that merit fuller exposition elsewhere. I have, as it were, dealt with the subject strategically rather than tactically. To my mind the field has often lacked this kind of treatment. I hope readers will form their own conclusions about this, and some of the things I say will help them shape their own explorations.

SCIENCE

'Science' (from the Latin *scientia* – knowledge) means no more than systematic investigation of a field in question. There are sciences concerning many matters of human interest, some of them quite ordinary and everyday, as well as the things with which science is supposed to deal in popular thought. This popular image of science is a kind of 'science fiction' without realising it. In fact, as well as physics, astronomy, or chemistry, we can be scientific about anything that is important to us; gardening, food, illness, social affairs, human feelings, art, all manner of things. Of course, the methodical investigation of these subjects is not necessarily included in the classical branches of science as academic disciplines; they possess their own labels. Our language by no means always privileges the 'scientific' investigation of some matter or other by designating it a 'science'. The study of the instances given above might be called horticulture, gastronomy, medicine, sociology, psychology or aesthetics. Yet there may be very different approaches within each avenue of inquiry; for example, food is of interest to gastronomes and nutritionists, cooks and farmers, and its production, retail and consumption must satisfy social need, as well as people's pockets, tastes, and religious or ethical scruples. Each area is the subject of different knowledge and much friendly, passionate and often angry argument. At given moments in history there are styles of knowledge and discourse which are favoured, as they widen their remit and push other views to the sidelines, or even try to prohibit them; conflict is engendered which creates in its wake the competing languages, idioms and practices which mark out a sphere of interest. The fields with which we are concerned here, art, psychotherapy and research, are no exception to this, indeed they are peculiarly the objects of heated debate because they so provocatively overlap each other.

There are at least two reasons why this should be so in any field which makes either explicit or implicit claims to be scientific. Firstly, the basic assumptions underlying scientific activity are not themselves scientific. The choice of phenomena we wish to investigate derives from metaphysical suppositions about the nature of the world, and our existence in it, that are more akin to belief than empirical knowledge. At the most profound level the sorting and testing of knowledge will take different forms if it derives from a worldview which is, for example, fundamentally materialist, on the one hand, or idealist, on the other. Within psychoanalysis, for example, think of the basic contrasts between the ways in which the Freudian and Jungian traditions have approached human experience. Similarly, inquiry into human action and emotion will be markedly different depending on whether or not those undertaking it assume the existence of an unconscious; for example, the dissimilarity, or indeed opposition, between psychodynamic and behavioural approaches in psychology. Secondly, science, like art, is not a disinterested or neutral activity. It takes place in the context of deep attachment and commitment to certain kinds of phenomena. As with its basic presumptions and beliefs, a science's interests are not themselves scientific; the motives that impel it are not pure. While the subject matter of a science possesses its own intrinsic interest it exists in a context determined in vital respects by complex cultural, political and psychological factors that may defy impartial examination. These factors constitute the prejudices which are the necessary starting points for any science and give rise to conflict and argument.

Wherever these interests, prejudices and disputes lead investigation, however, this destination imposes an unavoidable actuality on investigation and experiment. Neither science nor art can in the end function as wish-fulfilment, or play fast and loose with the world. This applies to method as well as meaning. Scientists can no more conjure experimental methods out of thin air than painters can personally invent colours, poets escape the possibilities and constraints of their mother tongue, or therapists substitute theoretical psyches for their patients' actual ones. Nor can any of these practices endorse a selective outcome in advance of their actual work. What proves them is their aptness and fitness, their ability to interact with events and experiences, anticipate consequences, be of use, and to provoke further argument and work. Whilst absolute empiricism may be impossible, contact with the phenomena that are actually involved in a field of research is an antidote to sterile theorising and argument in advance of relevant evidence, and helps to ground inquiry in experience. Although there are unfortunate exceptions – certain types of psychology and psychiatry, for example[1] – over time the general tendency is, as Mary Hesse (1980) has pointed out, for the methods and conclusions of science to be shaped through a kind of natural selection by its subject matter rather than by ideological preferences.

Given this last proviso, there is no reason why scientific procedures in their fundamental sense should not play a vital role in the aspects of art and psychotherapy we are concerned with here. The important things to understand are the ways in which the *particular* kinds of knowledge which our field affords us can be gathered and understood, rather than relying on standard procedures designed to illuminate categories of data often utterly different from those with which we find ourselves actually concerned in practice.

EPISTEMOLOGY

Epistemology is the theory of knowledge itself. It is an essential preliminary to research of whatever kind. Epistemology specifies what can be known about different sorts of phenomena, and the methods of investigation through which this knowledge can be acquired. It indicates the degree to which particular kinds of knowledge are genuine, how certain they are, and how we can distinguish knowledge from belief. Most importantly, epistemology possesses a negative as well as a positive capability; it helps us to see what sorts of things we could never know of a certain subject matter, or through a specific method of investigation. It is a prophylactic which helps bypass wasted effort and pointless conclusions.

The logical position of epistemology is midway between initial bias or suspicion, and later observation, reasoning and experiment (Harré 1972). Epistemology is an arbiter between the impulse leading to, and the act of, discovery. With hindsight we might see that the detailed practices involved in a form of inquiry are the last stage, or should be, in a logically sequential process. The epistemological phase in this is, as it were, to 'look before you leap'. Yet, just because we cannot easily examine our reasons for acting as we do in advance, our immediate experience of this sequence often occurs to us back to front.

The consequence is that we may only become aware of the claims to the truth of practice and investigation after the event. Regrettably, but perhaps inevitably, this is highly characteristic of research in the social and human sciences where so many interests impinge on fields that are already highly complex. With regard to one of the major players in the field with which this book is concerned, psychoanalysis, it has been said that its conclusions have been reached in advance of the evidence that would support them. For example, Freud's attempt in the *Project* (1895) to construct a 'psycho-physical monism' within the framework of the philosophical and neuro-logical precepts available to him in the late nineteenth century, first of all dismissed even within the psychoanalytic movement, has been praised in recent years as inspired conjecture (Pribram 1962; Solomon 1982). The value placed on conclusions arrived at in research may indeed wax and wane according to current knowledge and the climate of opinion.

Because our points of view are unavoidably partial, knowledge will always be acquired in this circuitous fashion. We do not have eyes in the back of our heads any more than we are capable of precognition. The overall estimation of what we come to know is in the end reached by a community of perceptions, criticism and thought; the criteria on which knowledge is based are essentially public rather than private. An awareness of epistemology gives us a measure of foresight at the outset of a line of inquiry, it minimises the risk of research being radically mistaken in principle. This is the least we can expect of it. It is possible, however, for it to play a far more constructive and daring role in research. It can accomplish this in a manner which parallels the creation of metaphor in poetry and the arts. By perceiving how phenomena of interest to us may be explicable in terms of two or more categories of knowledge, and by making models of this, different strands of understanding may be brought together in a new combination. If this novel explanation can be made to 'stick', it will not only have added to our knowledge, it will have created a new type of knowledge altogether. In the example touched on above, it was through his compounding together of neurology and consciousness within a single theory that Freud contradicted the tradition of Cartesian mind–body dualism and originated a new form of psychological knowledge.

It is also by means of epistemic understanding that we can see that knowledge is a *form* of knowing rather than a collection of facts. Categories of knowledge are *fictive* entities, a kind of scaffolding by means of which a version of the world can be constructed. Varieties of research make play with such versions of the 'real' and create further variants of these. While it makes sense to talk of true and false versions, and to argue about them, it is meaningless, though unfortunately extremely common, to reify such fictions into absolute truths – no matter how expedient these may be to us. In an important sense the fundamental work of research consists as much in inventing a truth as it does in discovering one, in 'making a world', as Nelson Goodman says (1978), as in tracing a pre-existent reality.

RESEARCH

Research assumes as many forms as there are things researched. There is no one kind of research, yet many people who wish to carry it out are persuaded to think as if there were, or at most that there are a limited number of research paradigms. When people involved in art and psychotherapy want to inquire further into their work, to question their own methods and purposes, to examine some consequences of their practice, or refine and develop it, this thought is often accompanied by a generalised idea of something called 'research' which possesses complex rules and requires a mysterious expertise. Connected to this is a closely related idea: in order really to count, the term research should on most occasions be chaperoned by the adjective 'empirical'. When such a person asks colleagues in related but perhaps more established professions for advice they are frequently told their research must be empirical if it is to be worthwhile. With a few variations this is the situation at present in our field, and is the historical context in which this book is being published. One should perhaps make a distinction here between what many therapists may be enjoined to do in institutional workplaces characterised by an overly medical ethos and what is in fact published. For example, Joy Schaverien's *The Revealing Image* shows how the straitjackets of orthodox empirical methodology and the refereed journal can be avoided.

An alternative version of the scenario I have just given would be more helpful, if by good fortune advice on research was sought from someone with a philosophical understanding of the issues involved, then those asking the question might themselves be asked detailed questions. For example: 'What actually happens in your work?' 'What do you want to find out?' 'Why do you want to find this out rather than something else?' 'What is the purpose of your research?' 'Are there other interests involved?' Questions like this locate inquiry in its home ground and provide the basis for various levels of research that really grasp the details of a practice. As a result research can be 'tailor-made' for our particular purposes. While this may be true in an ideal world it is equally true that our 'cloth has to be cut to suit our pocket'; no research at all is possible without the financial means to buy the time and resources it requires; and even if this is forthcoming it may be a hostage to others' institutional and political interests.

As a matter of common sense those undertaking research should bear in mind the general principles brought into play by prior epistemological understanding. These principles, however, always operate in the particular contexts of what is being researched. Indeed it is a purpose of epistemology to indicate the kinds of fit there may be between the data concerned and the kind of knowledge that is being sought. Hence the type of research under-taken must have an adequate relation to the type of phenomena being examined. To give a general example, research into the operation of 'insight' in psychotherapy must understand the relationship of fantasies and facts in a person's life; a catalogue of actual events cannot alone explain subjective experience, while the imagining which includes and fuses these events in endless combination explains it many times over. Research must be as aware as possible, therefore, of the degree to which certain phenomena (behaviour in the case of people) are under-determined or over-determined by factual information. It would very likely be fruitless, for instance, to claim that a single trauma by itself was a direct cause of someone's chronic depression, but fatuous to attribute such longterm distress just to fantasy or imagination.

Similarly, proof or verification depends upon the nature and complexity of our inquiry. If we question an instance of physical causality whose variables can in principle be limited, it is theoretically possible to devise an uncontaminated experimental situation and control its variables so as to regulate specific outcomes. This is the predictive quality that characterises natural science and we can here speak with relative certainty of proving the result of an experiment to be generally true. The situation is typically different in human affairs, however. Not only can we not speak of causes in the same way here, but rather of people's reasons or motives for acting as they do; nor can we control or decontaminate human dramas in a strictly experimental manner. If we try to do so we unwittingly become part of the action. To transpose the idea of 'proof' to this theatre is most often to speak of an outcome, a reading, or a verdict, as possessing a plausibility that outweighs competing interpretations. What counts in gauging an interpre-tation's strength in the intersubjective sphere nearly always consists of meaning yielded rather than facts confirmed.

There are standards and methods of validating personal or social meaning in and out of the conventional sciences. These procedures obtain in fields as diverse as law, history and art, as well as in psychiatry and psychotherapy. Law, of course, has its own use of the word 'proof'. In the case of literature one of the greatest novels ever written is actually called a work of research (*recherche*), *A la recherche du temps perdu*, by Marcel Proust (1913–27). In the case of the visual arts John Constable is reported to have written, 'Art is a science of which paintings are the experiments' (source unknown). Certainly the activity of painting at its most profound is an investigation into the mystery of visibility. As the ways of seeing that this research creates filter through a culture, they inform our view of the world and ourselves in it. Like science, the proof of art consists in persuading us of the possibilities of a new vision through distinctive forms of demonstration. These demonstrations refer to our experience of the world in different ways; such reference may be through cognition, sensation, emotion, or combinations of these. Like the remodelling of different referential schemes in metaphor, the reconceptions brought into being by research are an amalgam of phenomena hitherto kept apart. These heretical combinations shock received opinion and contradict dogma. For example, it was the originality of Freud to fuse mind and body together, most powerfully through the exemplar of sexuality, that created a scandal that would not lie down. This is why, as Ricoeur says, psychoanalysis is a 'mixed discourse' that cannot avoid both semantic and physical explanation at the same time (Ricoeur 1977/ 1981).

There are, of course, bigger and smaller types of research. Those that are big, the innovative stages of psychoanalysis, quantum physics, or to transpose the idea of research to inquiry in the arts, *A la recherche* or *Ulysses*, Cézanne or Surrealism, all involve large-scale shifts and radical realignments of conceptual and referential schemes, categories and paradigms. Those that are smaller work within, or on the surface of, these wider parameters. Nevertheless, whatever the scope of research, global or local, radical or refining, in practice it always displays an obsessive attention to particular phenomena, no matter how inconsequential these may appear to orthodox thought. This is a crucial part of its epistemic basis, whether this concerns the passage of time, sexual desire, human relationships, dreams and images, mountains or fossils, atoms and stars, or such supposedly ordinary things as lapses of memory, feeding babies, the play of light on water, or the experiences of the insane.

The fundamental questions about the phenomena we are concerned with here, which are so often overlooked, follow from the contexts in which they are placed, mostly medical and clinical settings. For the professions that exert the greatest influence here, medicine, psychology and management, for example, such epistemological issues seem to be long-ago settled.

For philosophical issues of this kind to be raised by small groups, not generally typical of the broad mass of health care professionals, might appear to be mere 'nit-picking', a luxury that can be done without. Yet, in whose interests is therapy provided? And who will stand to benefit most if therapeutic practices are more fully understood? In the first place it is unequivocally the patients whom therapy is meant to help, and whose suffering and unhappiness have for so long presented such an insoluble enigma to the investigations of medical psychiatry. Secondly, the import of a fuller comprehension of these *self* or *subject* therapies, whose primary objects are self-understanding and change, has a relevance which extends far beyond specifically clinical domains. This, I hope, is the prospective rather than reactive effect of a book like this.

ART AND THE IMAGE

We are often caught in a tension between ideas of art and concepts of the image, with all their respective riches and problems. On the one hand, art with its history, paradigms and achievements, of which the visual arts are one manifestation; and on the other, images as essential forms of our mental and communal life. Images and art are not synonymous with each other, but images are often essential features of art.

Epistemologically, the image does not conform to a linguistic code, it *shows* rather than *says*. Because images are non-discursive forms of symbolism they are not strung out in a definite temporal order which must be read from beginning to end. On the contrary, they can be moved across in a multitude of directions; there is no one place where our understanding of them must commence or terminate; several elements of an image may be apprehended simultaneously; and their relationship to time and space is radically different from that of writing or speaking. As opposed to a text which can only be read or heard through in its prescribed *sequence*, an image can be visited as a *place*; we apprehend it in space rather than through time. Furthermore, an image's meaning is not stored in a finite collection of signs. Whereas the meaning of a text is gathered up by a reading which progressively exhausts the limited number of words composing it, the perceptions involved in apprehending an image are potentially unlimited. While the individual words which make up a sentence, a paragraph, a poem or a book may yield a meaning which can be pondered in the mind, we do not increase our understanding of a text by looking at its words for longer – as if they were things. This is because the text and the image involve different referential schemes. Linguistic signs are deciphered by means of a code, possess a minimum of substance, and are relatively *transparent*; we see through them to what they signify. Images do not essentially function via a fixed code in the same way, except in the special and limited case of writing or notation. They are replete with substance and relatively *opaque*, that is, their meaning is embodied in their appearance. In this way we seem effortlessly to hear through speech and see through writing to a sense of what they indicate, while images present us with a more determined and obdurate surface.

Because of their 'thingliness' images *exemplify* labels, while labels *predicate* things. If I mark a surface with red I invoke 'red mark'. If I say or write 'red mark', I conjure up a virtual image of a red mark. The reciprocal relationship of images and labels indicates further properties possessed by each of them, and it is through their interplay that meaning is created. Nelson Goodman writes, of pictures and language, that:

> Pictures are no more immune than the rest of the world to the formative force of language even though they themselves, as symbols, also exert such a force upon the world, including language. Talking does not make the world or even pictures, but talking and pictures participate in making each other and the world as we know them.
>
> (Goodman 1981, pp. 88–9)

By and large predicates denote classes and sub-classes of things whilst images are inveterately particular. To say or write 'woman' denotes nothing detailed, only the general class of women; whilst immediately a drawing or painting of a woman is begun, a particular woman, whether imaginary or real, begins to be specified. No matter how many adjectives and other qualifiers we add to 'woman' we get no nearer her substance; instead we string out discursive branch systems of classes and sub-classes. 'A tall blonde woman' does not resemble any particular tall blonde woman in the slightest. The drawing or painting, on the other hand, would progressively add actual physical properties also possessed by a tall blonde woman; height, scale, colour, features and so on. Of course a description may contain properties literally possessed, and a depiction include labels. The subject of 'a tall blonde woman called Jane' literally possesses the label 'Jane', and the label 'Jane' may be attached to a portrait of Jane.

There are also discursive statements as well as images in which the referential function is lacking or suppressed. Imagine a drawing or a painting which refuses to depict, a writing which fails to comply with a notation, or an utterance which does not form words. The first two become scribble, doodle, or non-figurative art, the third babble or music; all three may express without denoting. By escaping obvious reference they may exemplify, through a deeper form of evocation, subtler states of affairs beyond literal apprehension.

I think it is fair to say that a great deal of inquiry into art and the image undertaken by psychiatrists and therapists misses many of these fundamental features. All too often non-discursive modes are made to conform to discursive ones as if no others existed, as in Freud's *rebus*. The wealth of symbolic and rhetorical play to be seen in human expression is reduced to a mere index of neurological disorder, or to a crude and vulgarised psycho-dynamics – where the world is seen in terms of therapy rather than as something to which therapy must apply. In either case expressions which are less than devoted to orthodox reference are thought, *ipso facto*, to be symptomatic of disease or a flight from reality.

There are exceptions and counter-moves within this broad scenario of the differences between language and images. Language can acquire a surface that denies easy passage or penetration, as in poetry, and the immediacy of textured and coloured surfaces can be obscured, as in *trompe-l'oeil*, photographs, or a mirror. But these gambits within a referential scheme 'tell' because we sense the way in which they work with or against the grain of such schemes.

Much as we may appreciate the functional requirements that differentiate presentational and discursive symbolisation, we must also be aware of their performative roles. Images and speech, as well as a vast range of other expressive modes, exist as practices impelled by the needs of communities and individuals. Theories of symbolisation, communication and expression are by necessity wise after the event. Symbols, communications and expressions are activities conducted between people; they are first and foremost *performances*. At an everyday level many forms of speech and images become quite incoherent if we abstract them from their context. In ordinary social intercourse speech acts are understood as directions, requests, entreaties, promises, confessions, commands, agreements and so on; images fulfil some of these but perform other functions too – diagrams, plans, maps, photographic images, posters, portraits, etc.

There are, furthermore, other and extraordinary levels of communication and expression that surpass commonplace usage. There are those that are cryptic, intended to be misunderstood, like irony, codes, propaganda, or rhyming slang. These typify an essential characteristic of symbolic inter-change – that the possibility of expressing the truth is founded on the capability of deception. Then there is the level of fantasy wherein expres-sion occurs within a person. Such intrapersonal communications are cap-able of all the nuances and shifts that figure in their public manifestations. By joining together the idea of lying with that of an individual's fantasising we encounter one epistemological basis for the Freudian unconscious and the repressive function. In addition there is a whole species of symbolic actions that are not apparently directed towards others in any immediate sense, which seem quite inconsequential in human affairs, and are com-monly known as dreams or doodles. Such little considered scraps of ordinary experience possess surprising theoretical interest (Freud 1900; Maclagan 1990).

Finally there are communications and expressions passionately directed to no one in particular, intended for unknown addressees whose only qualification is that they can comprehend the symbolic usage concerned.

At this point what had been expressions confined to the personal and private enter a public domain and become subject to different forms of understanding and standards of judgement; the contingencies of the individual and the local undergo a sublimation that makes them the property of a community. These are the cultural productions in which we find the criteria that distinguish art. While forms of art may be partially explained by biography and history, these may be necessary but are certainly not sufficient for our understanding of what a work of art means. This is because art transfigures ordinary experience.

Any research concerned with symbolisation and expression in therapy must concern itself with such epistemological considerations of human communication if it is to obtain a purchase on the events its practice involves.[2] This purchase holds both ways here; it should tell us something about art, that expression of human existence in all its vagaries and fancies, as well as about therapy with its more localised treatment of suffering and pathology. An obsessive psychodynamics cannot fully grasp the sense of an image, any more than it can adequately understand the meaning of human relationships, including, paradoxically, those that actually occur in therapy. This is because all the conversations, images, stories and gestures through which human relations are enacted evolve, no matter how incompletely, towards a style, an aesthetics, a transcendence of the merely contingent. We might say, as many have before us, that life aspires to art. If the task that psychotherapy offers the patient is to give meaning and shape to the mutilations and scattered fragments of their life, to help them recount this life in the form of a story or history (Ricoeur 1977/1981, p. 268), and as well to reshape it in an image, then therapy must be versed in literature as well as the case study, art as well as the 'disclosing' image, aesthetics as well as psychopathology. Nothing less than this will really do if both the practice and research of therapy are to help patients and stake a claim to truth.

PSYCHOTHERAPY

Within the general domain of therapeutics, psychotherapy is concerned with the psychological dimensions of suffering. The term 'therapy' can be understood in two senses; as the investigation and treatment of bodily ailments, or as the theory and practice of psychological healing. In this latter sense psychotherapy is dedicated to comprehending and affecting our sense of ourselves. Because of this psychotherapy tends towards understanding rather than explanation, interpretation rather than manipulation, and meanings rather than facts.

In a general sense it might seem wise to divide therapy into these two spheres of influence, the psychological and the physical. There are, however, dangers in doing this in a naive fashion; the soul can no more float above the body as an epiphenomenon than can a living body consist only in mechanisms and causal chains; an adequate epistemology of being cannot help but be essentially psychosomatic (Merleau-Ponty 1964). For all its advances, the history of modern medicine is littered with the consequences of misconceiving this issue. Nowhere are these more concentrated than in psychiatry and clinical psychology. For the last two hundred years psychiatrists have been signally unable to achieve the successes of their medical colleagues in other more predominantly somatic fields. Nor in the main has clinical or academic psychology produced more than weaker versions of the physical sciences from which they derive their paradigms. All this is the result of scientism rather than science.[3]

For both theory and practice to be coherent in a psychotherapy it must avoid rigid distinctions between mind and body and see how the two realms are essentially interconnected – just as a piece of paper cannot be crumpled on one side only. While the orientation of psychotherapy is towards the psychological side of being, towards a *semantic* rather than *factual* state of affairs, it will not proceed far if it cannot grasp the endless interplay between mind and body. Meaning must always assume a tangible form, exist by virtue of a sense-perceptible medium, and share in the fate of this material existence. The *prima materia* for the expression of meaning is the perceptible and perceptive human body with all its ingenious inventions and extensions. Indeed the origins of modern psychotherapy are rooted in an understanding of just such bodily semantics, in hysteria and sexuality.

It is because psyche, with its reasons and meanings, and soma, with its causes and matter, interpenetrate each other so deeply that psychotherapy possesses a distinctive notion, albeit often misunderstood, of how suffering may be cured. Whereas physical medicine treats an injury or pathological condition by acting on it causally – if possible it literally heals; psychotherapy contrariwise acts on pathology via its meaning or significance – it figuratively heals. But this figurative realisation must be far more than just cognitive if therapy is to change anything; it must have affective force. Mind and body meet in emotion and desire, and in so far as repression is instigated by our passions it must also be undone through them. Cure in psychotherapy is meant in a certain sense; that which cures is an intense form of self-reflection, or research into oneself, in which there is a fusion of thought, emotion and focused awareness. What is known as *working through* in psychotherapy is a metaphor which invokes the body through the muscular image of work; while thought is indispensable, much more is involved than a mere thinking through that avoids visceral feelings. It is the combination of incisive thought and gut reaction that makes an insight take hold of us. This amounts to a particular quality of consciousness, or attention, that grounds insight in the work of self-reflection. It is this quality that differentiates the subterranean realisations of unconscious pathology from the creations of a more critically attentive self; a heuristic self, that by allowing different and often contradictory fantasies to co-exist, encourages revision and instigates change. As Jung puts it, a practising analyst

> must believe implicitly in the significance and value of conscious realization, whereby hitherto unconscious parts of the personality are brought to light and subjected to conscious discrimination and criticism. It is a process that requires the patient to face his problems and that taxes his powers of conscious judgement and decision. It is nothing less than a direct challenge to his ethical sense, a call to arms that must be answered by the whole personality.
>
> (Jung 1931, pp. 146–7)

Such an understanding of consciousness leads to further consequences regarding modes of awareness. An open consciousness involves sensing as well as thinking, vision as well as cognition. Early developments in psychoanalysis, particularly Jungian depth psychology, led irresistibly to this conclusion. For the process of self-reflection to proceed as comprehensively as possible the essential function of the imagery implied in the word 'reflection' itself must be *seen*. Many of the practices of psychotherapy have invoked understandings of the psyche that antedate the Enlightenment. Of the human memory, for example, James Hillman says that in the Renaissance

> The human memory was conceived as an internal treasure-house or theater rather than as an alphabetical or chronological filing system. Whereas an encyclopedic filing system is a *method* by which *concepts* are *written*, available one page at a time, a theater is a *place* where *images* are *envisioned*, available all at once. In the art of memory events belong together in clusters or constellations because they partake of the same archetypal meaning or pattern, and not merely because these events all begin with the letter *A* or *B* or happened on the same day or in the same year. The organization of the mind was based on inherent meanings, not on arbitrary nominalistic labels.
>
> (Hillman 1975, pp. 91–2, emphasis in original)

This way of approaching psychotherapeutic practice led to an interest which extended significantly beyond the verbal reports or descriptions of internal fantasy imagery made by patients in therapy; it led to a hermeneutics of pictorial images themselves. Freud's 'talking cure' was implicitly extended to all the psychological imagery involved in a full understanding of language. As an explicit method it came about as a result of Jung's own practice during and after the First World War, and several decades later in the work of certain analysts (Baynes 1940; Milner 1950, 1969), and of the first art therapists, such as Segal, Hill, Adamson, Naumberg and Lyddiatt, whose backgrounds and interests often began outside psychotherapy, psychology or psychiatry (see Hill 1945; Dax 1953; Naumberg 1966; Lyddiatt 1971; Thomson 1989; Waller 1991). Parallel to this was a developing field of study initially known as 'art and psychopathology'. It stems first of all from psychoanalysis in its innovative phases, Surrealism, modernism in general, and those unconventional psychiatrists who in the early 1920s first wrote about what we now know as 'outsider art' (Morgenthaler 1921; Prinzhorn 1922).

These interests have been radical in their effects; they have taken issue with the view that the artistic works of psychiatric patients simply *project* their psychopathology in a diagnostic manner (rather in the manner of X-ray plates), or the more established and tendentious opinion that art and the imagination are nearer to pathology, less stable, and more primitive than our cognitive mental functions. Such prejudice is so widespread it is difficult to avoid; its philistinism ranges from the work of the influential nineteenth-century forensic psychiatrist Lombroso (1891), to the writing of Freud and Jung (for all Jung's sympathetic understanding of the image); it was obvious in the official aesthetics of Communism and Fascism, as well as playing a surreptitious role in the writings of many psychotherapists and art therapists whose understanding of images often derives from a reductive psychodynamics. (For treatments of the latter see Hillman 1975, 1979; Watkins 1981; Maclagan 1989.)

In its initial stages psychoanalysis attended to the patient's symptoms, their reflections in speech, and the transference. The developments I have referred to have transferred some of this interest to the patient's images. As our reception of images and pictures is more immediately sensual than our comprehension of language – the image conveying meaning via tangible forms rather than conventional signs – the balance of our understanding, both of therapy and our patients' predicaments, shifts towards aesthetic rather than exclusively logical judgement.

Because the meaning of a creative image arises so uniquely from its material composition we cannot in any simple fashion reach through or behind this for an unconscious or prior meaning. The 'manifest' does not give way so easily to the 'latent' here. Indeed there can be no question of an official hermeneutic dispensation being granted to psychoanalysis, or any other discipline, that adduces intellectual explanations of an image via the social or biographical contexts which surround its creation, no matter how much these circumstances may arouse our political or personal interests. The creation of an image is a work of the imagination, and that of a physical or pictorial image the work of an embodied imagination. It is always, particularly if it is a poetic image, a work without precedent. If in our research and practice we insist too much on the degree to which expression is disturbed by the psychological antecedents so powerfully demonstrated by psychoanalysis, we will miss what these demonstrations miss. The work of a therapist, because it feels an obligation to reduce this disturbance, to explore its origins, and expiate suffering, too often over-looks the felicity with which the patient makes his or her meaning felt. As Bachelard puts it:

> right away, the psychoanalyst will abandon ontological investigation of the image, to dig into the past of man. He sees and points out the poet's secret sufferings. He explains the flower by the fertilizer.
>
> (Bachelard 1958, p. xxvi)

CONCLUSION

The explorations of art and of psychotherapy share many features. This reminds us that art is too important to be merely a matter of dispassionate connoisseurship, and that the remit of psychotherapy runs well beyond the confines of therapeutic practice. It is when we encounter them off-limits, outside the gallery or clinic, that we become most aware of the human interest and value they share. Of course they are in important respects different activities, otherwise we would call them the same thing. We rightly think of psychotherapy as a relatively private and confidential affair, but it can and does function as a critique of culture, and its most indispensable documents and images, its case material can be of great public interest. Were this not so psychotherapy could hardly have developed as it has. Conversely, art is addressed to the public, but often deals with the most personal side of human life, and communicates intimately with each individual composing its audience. Indeed its appeal *is* to this individual, and rarely to some collective consciousness, no matter how many people see a picture, are in an audience, or read a text.

Perhaps their most striking similarities are the ways in which they dwell on consciousness, expression and human change. For in both we become more fully conscious by virtue of what we can actively imagine, and the degree to which this imagining might be shaped, embodied or conveyed to another. Furthermore, it is in the process of this incarnation that an existing consciousness is changed and a new one created. If we speak of research here, we can do so in two senses. We can conduct research *into* or *about* art and psychotherapy, and their common ground, as phenomena external to our research; or we can initiate research *from within* art and psychotherapy, accepting them as methods of research themselves.

First of all, research into and about art and psychotherapy, an inquiry that moves from the outside in. There are many questions that may be asked of art and of psychotherapy, sometimes separately and sometimes together. For example, what is creativity? What does it mean to people and does it help them in their lives? What is the value of art and are distinctive psychological processes involved in its practice and reception? How is artistic expression affected by the suffering or psychopathology of the artist? How does sexuality enter into the production and reception of art? How do art and therapy combine in a practice such as art therapy? Is psychotherapy effective and if so what is the nature of its efficacy? Does art, or the use of images, make it more effective? Is art therapeutic in itself? What therapeutic value lies in the aesthetic qualities of image-making? Is it possible for human beings to change psychologically? Can we be scientific about such issues? Can any of these questions be practically answered? And so on. If we wish to conduct such inquiries we must first ask what sort of questions they are that we wish to ask. Is the knowledge here an empirical and factual matter as in the physical sciences, is it an ethical or moral issue, or are the answers we seek essentially concerned with the aesthetics of living?

Depending on what we wish to discover our methods will vary accordingly; we need to think flexibly about the epistemological domains in which particular instances of research arise. It may, for the sake of argument, be important to establish the relative longterm costs of different psychiatric treatments of similar ailments, including art therapy and psychotherapy. Here, it seems, a classic comparative trial would be appropriate. If, however, we wanted to understand what exactly was being compared to what, a different kind of inquiry is called for altogether, involving qualitative discriminations between competing views of human meaning. In practice we often have no option but to attempt to answer such complex questions in a qualified and provisional fashion. If, though, the issues brought together in a research project are epistemologically too disparate, attempts at coherent examination of them may be impossible. The competing claims of, say, in-depth psychotherapy for a few, and brief counselling for many, given limited resources, cannot be adjudged logically or dispassionately. The solution will in all likelihood be politically rather than logically determined; that is, it will depend on which group is most articulate and possesses greater resources – 'he who pays the piper calls the tune'. Nevertheless, we have no option but to attempt to approach such issues rationally – this after all is what research is; and to realise that all research has its political side, and often comes about in order to change popular and established opinion in the interests of our emancipation.

If, however, we wish to engage in research from within the practices of art or psychotherapy, accepting that both are forms of knowledge in their own right, we might come to see that in essence our practice has been a form of research all the while. Perhaps this has not occurred to us, or no one knew enough about such things to tell us so. For neither art nor psychotherapy are, or, if they are practised to their fullest extent, logically could be, just applications of research that has taken place elsewhere. They stake their own distinctive claims to uncover what is hidden and create what has not yet been.

Science in the sense that it is popularly understood may be technically useful to our lives, but has nothing directly to tell us about living. It is art, both in its most elevated and popular forms, that teaches us how to fall in love, experience misfortune, traverse our emotions, and generally to engage in all the stuff of being human. Of course, it may also be true that we learn how to conceal ourselves through diluted versions of art, and of therapy, that restrict themselves to denial, sentimentality, and the fashionably 'right-on' techniques of ailment and cure. Even our most grievous psychological and psychosomatic maladies are imaginative constructions, though unconsciously created – a kind of upside-down 'active imagination'. It is just such ingenious self-deceptions as these that, in their different ways, art and psychotherapy attack.

One way in which art and psychotherapy may be sharply distinguished is in the relationship of their participants. Both may involve solitary work, but at some point the practice of psychotherapy always requires that patient and therapist be together. The communications between them must be made in the other's presence, even if these communications extend beyond conversation and, if they are pictures, for example, are made outside therapy. This is why the transference assumes such an importance in psychotherapy. The meaning of the patient's words or images, and the therapist's responses to them, take shape within their personal relationship. In the case of art, however, this relationship occurs entirely through the work. Artist and audience need have no knowledge of each other; both literally and figuratively the work survives the artist's personal life. But this divergence helps us see a convergence between the two activities. Both are vitally concerned with what can be said or in other ways expressed, with how meaning is formed. The criteria often used by psychotherapy here are just those that apply to art. The particular images, conversations, and accounts of therapy, which cannot be explained by any calculus, are validated by aesthetic judgements, this is their *episteme*. Cox and Theilgaard (1987) and Cox (1988), for instance, have forcefully drawn attention to these parallels between poetic images and therapy.

Whatever form research takes it must honour this *episteme* to be of value to us. This necessitates seeing that the phenomena involved in art and psychotherapy pertain to what can be understood between people as well as by individuals themselves; that such understanding is essentially a matter of meaning rather than fact; and that the changes, cures or effects that both art and psychotherapy try to bring about are in our perception and consciousness.

NOTES

1 Critiques of institutional psychology and psychiatry have become increasingly widespread since the 1950s. For example, Laing (1960), Goffman (1961), Szasz

(1961), Laing and Esterson (1964), Foucault (1973), Harré and Secord (1972), Hillman (1975), Smail (1984), and Barham (1984).

2 My case here derives from an extensive and well-enough known literature concerning different aspects of language, art and psychoanalysis, for example; Richards (1936), Wittgenstein (1953, 1966), Searle (1970), Wollheim (1970), Austin (1976), Ricoeur (1970, 1977/1981, 1978) and Goodman (1981).

3 Of this nineteenth-century imposition of scientific positivism upon psychiatry and its subjects, which substantially remains the origin of contemporary medical practice, Foucault says, referring to psychiatrists: 'they would increasingly confine themselves in positivism, the more they felt their practice slipping out of it' (Foucault 1967, p. 275); and of the patient: 'increasingly he would alienate himself in the physician, accepting entirely in advance all his prestige, submitting from the very first to a will he experienced as magic, and to a science he regarded as prescience and divination, this becoming the ideal and perfect correlative of those powers he projected upon the doctor' (Foucault 1967, pp. 275–6).

REFERENCES

Austin, J.L. (1976) In: Urmson, J.O. (Ed.) *How to Do Things with Words*. Oxford University Press, Oxford.

Bachelard, G. (1958) *The Poetics of Space*. Guiles, E. (Trans.) Beacon Press, Boston.

Barham, P. (1984) *Schizophrenia and Human Value: Chronic Schizophrenia, Science and Society*. Basil Blackwell, Oxford.

Baynes, H.G. (1940) *The Mythology of the Soul*. Routledge and Kegan Paul, London.

Cox, M. (1988) *Structuring the Therapeutic Process: Compromise with Chaos – The Therapist's Response to the Individual and the Group*. Jessica Kingsley, London.

Cox, M. and Theilgaard, A. (1987) *Mutative Metaphors in Psychotherapy: The Aeolian Mode*. Tavistock, London.

Dax, E. Cunningham (1953) *Experimental Studies in Psychiatric Art*. Faber, London.

Eco, U. (1977) *A Theory of Semiotics*. Macmillan, London.

Foucault, M. (1967) *Madness and Civilization: A History of Insanity in the Age of Reason*. Howard, R. (Trans.) Tavistock, London.

Foucault, M. (1973) *The Birth of the Clinic: An Archaeology of Medical Perception*. Sheridan, A.M. (Trans.) Tavistock, London.

Freud, S. (1895) *A Project for a Scientific Psychology*. SE 1. Hogarth, London, 1972.

Freud, S. (1900) *The Interpretation of Dreams*. SE 4. Hogarth, London, 1975.

Goffman, E. (1961) *Asylums: Essays on the Social Situation of Mental Patients and Other Inmates*. Doubleday, New York.

Goodman, N. (1978) *Ways of Worldmaking*. Hackett Publishing, Indianapolis.

Goodman, N. (1981) *Languages of Art: An Approach to a Theory of Symbols*. Harvester, Brighton.

Harré, R. (1972) *The Philosophies of Science: An Introductory Survey*. Oxford University Press, London.

Harré, R. and Secord, P.F. (1972) *The Explanation of Social Behaviour*. Basil Blackwell, Oxford.

Hesse, M. (1980) *Revolutions and Reconstructions in the Philosophy of Science.* Harvester, Brighton.

Hill, A. (1945) *Art Versus Illness.* George Allen and Unwin, London.

Hillman, J. (1975) *Re-visioning Psychology.* Harper Colophon Books, New York.

Hillman, J. (1979) 'Image-sense'. *Spring 1979.* Spring Publications, Dallas.

Jung, C.G. (1931) 'The Practical Use of Dream Analysis'. *The Practice of Psychotherapy. CW* 16. Bollingen, Princeton, 1954.

Laing, R.D. (1960) *The Divided Self.* Tavistock, London.

Laing, R.D. and Esterson, A. (1964) *Sanity, Madness, and the Family: Families of Schizophrenics.* Tavistock, London.

Lombroso, C. (1891) *The Man of Genius.* Walter Scott, London.

Lyddiatt, E.M. (1971) *Spontaneous Painting and Modelling.* Constable, London.

Maclagan, D. (1989) 'The Aesthetic Dimension in Art Therapy: Luxury of Necessity?'. *Inscape.* Spring.

Maclagan, D. (1990) 'Solitude and Communication: Beyond the Doodle'. *Raw Vision.* 3. Raw Vision, London.

Merleau-Ponty, M. (1964) In: Edie, J.M. (Ed.) *The Primacy of Perception: And Other Essays on Phenomenological Psychology, the Philosophy of Art, History and Politics.* Northwestern University Press, Evanston.

Milner, M. (1950) *On Not Being Able to Paint.* Heinemann, London.

Milner, M. (1969) *The Hands of the Living God.* Hogarth, London.

Morgenthaler, W. (1921) *Ein Geisteskranker als Künstler* (a study of the pictorial work of the artist and psychiatric patient Adolf Wölfli). Berne.

Naumberg, M. (1966) *Dynamically Oriented Art Therapy: Its Principles and Practices.* Gruyne & Stratton, New York.

Pribman, K. (1962) 'The Neuropsychology of Sigmund Freud'. In: Bachrac, A.J. (Ed.) *Experimental Foundations of Clinical Psychology.* Basic Books, New York.

Prinzhorn, H. (1922) *Bildnerei der Geisteskranken.* Berlin. English translation (1972) (Van Brokendorff, E. (Trans.) *The Artistry of the Mentally Ill,* Springer, Berlin & New York.

Proust, M. (1913–27) *A la recherche du temps perdu.* English translation (1983) Scott Moncrieff, C.K. and Kilmartin, K. (Trans.) *Remembrance of Things Past.* Penguin, Harmondsworth.

Richards, I.A. (1936) *The Philosophy of Rhetoric.* Oxford University Press, London.

Ricoeur, P. (1970) *Freud and Philosophy: An Essay on Interpretation.* Savage, D. (Trans.) Yale University Press, New Haven & London.

Ricoeur, P. (1977) 'The Question of Proof in Freud's Psychoanalytic Writings'. *Journal of the American Psychoanalytic Association.* 25: Reprinted (1981) in Thompson, J.B. (Ed. and Trans.) *Paul Ricoeur: Hermeneutics and the Human Sciences: Essays on Language, Action and Interpretation.* Cambridge University Press, Cambridge.

Ricoeur, P. (1978) P. Churn, R. (Trans.) *The Rule of Metaphor: Multi-disciplinary Studies of the Creation of Meaning in Language.* Routledge & Kegan Paul, London.

Schaverien, J. (1991) *The Revealing Image: Analytical Art Psychotherapy in Theory and Practice.* Routledge, London.

Searle, J. (1970) *Speech Acts: An Essay in the Philosophy of Language.* Cambridge University Press, Cambridge.

Smail, D. (1984) *Illusion and Reality: The Meaning of Anxiety.* Dent, London.

Solomon, R.C. (1982) 'Freud's Neurological Theory of Mind'. In: Wollheim, R.

and Hopkins, J. (Eds) *Philosophical Essays on Freud*. Cambridge University Press, Cambridge.

Szasz, T. (1961) *The Myth of Mental Illness: Foundations of a Theory of Personal Conduct*. Harper, New York.

Thomson, M. (1989) *On Art and Therapy: An Exploration*. Virago, London.

Waller, D. (1991) *Becoming a Profession: The History of Art Therapy in Britain 1940–82*. Routledge, London.

Watkins, M. (1981) 'Six Approaches to the Image in Art Therapy'. *Spring 1981*. Spring Publications, Dallas.

Wittgenstein, L. (1953) Anscombe, G.E.M. (Trans.) *Philosophical Investigations*. Basil Blackwell, Oxford.

Wittgenstein, L. (1966) In: Barrett, K. (Ed.) *Lectures and Conversations on Aesthetics, Psychology and Religious Belief*. Basil Blackwell, Oxford.

Wollheim, R. (1970) *Art and its Objects*. Penguin, Harmondsworth

Chapter 12

'The biter bit'

Subjective features of research in art and therapy

David Maclagan

'Research': the word brings up fantasies of clinical detachment, dusty scholarship and competitive ambition. Both institutionally and person-ally, it carries a certain clout, justifying status and promoting interests. It is sought after and jealously guarded; it is supported, but it can also be purloined. It is both a prize and a burden to the researcher; it may be hailed as a landmark in its field, but it may also be neglected and forgotten, or subject to misunderstanding, plagiarism or abuse. Above all, it carries with it the aura or halo of 'objectivity'; of detached, non-partisan description, demonstration, analysis or measurement that supports findings, or yields 'results'. By the same token, it is supposed to have aims and objectives that can be described in advance, methods that should be suited to those aims, and conclusions that can be reached.

It is a truism – or ought to be by now – that research in the domain of psychotherapy cannot simply import the methodologies appropriate to research in the physical sciences. Psychotherapy (and, arguably, also art) deals with an intersubjective realm, and it has to concern itself with precisely those features that have been filtered out of the conventional scientific method: feelings, fantasies and all the other phenomena tradi-tionally associated with 'inner' states of mind or the realm of the 'sub-jective'. To these familiar complications must be added a twist that almost any theory of unconscious motivation entails: that there is a hidden, and often antithetical, alternative to directed thought or manifest meaning. As I shall argue, this ties in with a powerful fantasy about research in general: that it will result in a drastic revision of accepted assumptions.

Indeed, far from being simply motivated by the desire for truth, I suggest that research in the field of psychoanalysis (and possibly in other fields) is likely to be informed by some of the very factors it purports to examine: namely transference phenomena, not just between the subject of the research and their clients or colleagues, but between the researcher and the material of their research. This complication is aggravated when a significant part of this material also includes painting or drawings; for here, besides psychological features, aesthetic factors also enter into the picture.[1] In different ways, aesthetic experience and its evaluation are also tarred with the brush of 'subjectivity' or arbitrary preference. This paper examines these issues in relation to a piece of my own research; but its implications are, I hope, much wider.

The subject of this research is itself a piece of research: the exceptional – and, as far as I know, unique – project embarked on by Dr Grace Pailthorpe, a middle-aged psychoanalyst in intimate collaboration with a young artist patient of hers called Reuben Mednikoff, to use art 'as a quicker way to the deeper layers of the unconscious than by the long drawn-out couch method'.[2] This unusual experiment, which was controversial even by contemporary standards, was begun in April 1935 and lasted until at least the 1950s. Not surprisingly, it seems to have evolved through a number of stages, both in its form and in its content. Much of the research material after 1940 is still inaccessible,[3] but a significant number of pictures and documents dating from its earliest phase (1935–40) have been in public circulation for several years, and these are what I have been working on.[4] Pailthorpe's research has one foot in the territory of psychoanalysis, since Mednikoff started off as her patient, and on account of the Kleinian idiom of her interpretations; but it has another foot in the domain of art, since both showed works closely related to their research in contemporary exhibitions of British Surrealist art.[5]

It is necessary to outline the nature of this research in order to throw into relief the kind of issues about research that I shall be addressing, even though I have written about it at greater length elsewhere (Maclagan 1992). Although Pailthorpe invited Mednikoff to be her collaborator from the very start, she began by treating him like a conventional patient; interpreting his drawings according to classic object relations theory, and analysing his fantasies in terms of his ambivalent aggressive and possessive feelings towards her as a symbolic mother-figure. However, they lived under the same roof and in other respects their relationship seems to have been much closer than an orthodox patient–therapist one: it soon becomes clear that Pailthorpe felt justified in acting out the role of mother for Mednikoff. Pailthorpe, who had in all probability never painted before, was also using drawings as an aid to 'self-analysis' (perhaps as a way of reflecting on her countertransferential feelings), and Mednikoff quickly started making comments on these; he must also have given her instruction and encouragement in painting (at which she soon became more than a match for him). In these various ways, while lip-service was paid to the theoretical constructs and interpretative strategies of psychoanalysis, Pailthorpe's research transgressed most of its conventional boundaries.[6]

As for the artistic aspect of the research, both were members, albeit somewhat incongruous ones, of the British Surrealist movement, and their work was certainly seen by some as quintessentially Surrealist in its spontaneous and 'unconscious' imagery.[7] Pailthorpe published a paper (1940), based on their research, in which she wrote in almost missionary terms of Surrealism ushering in a new form of morality based on a healthier relation to the unconscious.[8] Such a waft of moral improvement did not sit comfortably with the subversive and individualistic stance of early Surrealism, and it is no surprise that she and Mednikoff eventually parted company with Surrealism in 1940.

By that date the research had certainly got to a publishable stage; but Pailthorpe was so suspicious of its being misappropriated or abused (most of all by colleagues), that she refused to submit it to professional scrutiny and the result was that it, and subsequent work, ended up being effectively withheld from entering the public domain. There is thus a more than usual psychological loading to research into her work.

For all that, much of my own research on Pailthorpe's work has been of a straightforward historical character: reviewing the documents (including notes, photographs and paintings) and setting it against its contemporary background in both psychoanalytic and artistic terms. But more subjective factors have also entered into it. First, there are obvious gaps in the material available – most notably Pailthorpe's own notes on her side of the process – and these have had to be filled in speculatively, with guesswork that is inevitably coloured by my sense of the two personalities involved and my intuitions about what might 'really' have been going on. Then there is the fact that, as already mentioned, Pailthorpe regarded her research *at the time* as being of such a controversial nature that it had to be hedged about with all sorts of restrictions, many of which have persisted fifty years afterwards.[9] I know from my own experience that both the unorthodox content of her work and the tantalising circumstances of its survival can produce powerful reactions in the researcher, which could certainly be treated as a complex form of countertransference.

I have tried to suggest that there are three interacting levels at which research into this area of overlap between psychotherapy and art history involves factors that are 'subjective', in that they don't fit into traditional 'objective' modes of inquiry. First, there are the personal feelings of the researcher, which are bound to be stimulated, perhaps at an unconscious level, by the nature of the psychoanalytic material being dealt with. Then there is the question of how far the confidentiality that was originally established in the therapy should be respected now that the material has become of historical interest.[10] There is a weird feeling of eavesdropping in reading the notes on Pailthorpe's work, even though it was carried out with publication in view. Finally, there is the aura of subjectivity that clings to any translation between the aesthetic and psychological qualities of a work of art. In this paper I want to concentrate on two of these issues: that of confidentiality and countertransference, and that of the problematic relation between the aesthetic and the psychological and their evaluation.

COUNTERTRANSFERENCE AND THE QUESTION OF CONFIDENTIALITY

If countertransference is a part of therapy, it is also a part of any research on that therapy; and in both contexts it affects how confidentiality is viewed. At first sight, the domains of therapy and research appear to be quite separate. Therapy's primary concern is with the patient: with their treatment, or at least with an enhanced understanding of their condition, and with ensuring that this has as beneficial an outcome as possible. Research, on the other hand, is ultimately addressed to a public: while it may turn out incidentally to benefit patients, its immediate audience is specialists in the field and, in cases where wider cultural aspects of therapy may be involved, the educated reader. But this distinction is not as clearcut as we might like it to be. Many forms of therapy, particularly those less concentrated on problem-solving, could be thought of as a tacit enlargement or shifting of the patient's frame of reference, so that their experience is relocated and connected to that of others.[11] Much is made of the need to respect privacy; but this should not blind us to its burdens, which include unnecessary shame, guilt and torturing self-consciousness.

In this interplay between the private and the public aspects of therapy, 'confidentiality' is more flexible than is officially acknowledged: it becomes even more tricky to define within the culture of therapy itself – its supervision, its case histories, and even its scandals. Therapy serves patients, but patients also serve therapy: without them and the specific peculiarities of their experience therapy could never substantiate itself, let alone advance. Where a therapy is breaking new ground, there are powerful inducements for the therapist to report their findings, and this temptation to breach confidentiality is not confined to the therapist; it may also affect the patient. The history of psychoanalysis is studded with famous case studies. From Freud's 'Rat Man' and 'Wolf Man' (Gardiner 1972), through Jung's 'Miss Miller' (Shamdasani 1990), to the recent example of Joe Berke and Mary Barnes (Barnes and Berke 1973), the patient of a landmark case-study has acquired their own fame. Their status is an ambiguous one: they are partly a witness to the therapist's skill (though remarkably few of these cases seem to have been successful cures); but they are also a source of interest or insight in their own right. In some instances, for example that of Mary Barnes, they are transmuted into quasi-therapists, with their own idiosyncratic qualification.

These dramatic instances illustrate some of the more ordinary difficulties of writing about therapeutic work. Because much of the material being dealt with seems so obviously personal, it seems simple enough to protect its confidentiality by disguising names or other recognisable details, when bringing it into the public domain. But is it so easy to disentangle the personal from the clinical? Jung, in his usual no-nonsense manner, asserted that details of the patient's life history were of no relevance to the symbolic meaning of their pictures (Jung 1976, Part 2, p. 321). But in much psychotherapeutic work the detail and specifics – for example, the idiom of a dream or the vocabulary of a fantasy – while they may not be name-tagged, are still 'personal' in a significant sense, and cannot be erased without destroying the fabric of the material.

These problems are aggravated when what is being quoted is an entire picture or drawing: here it is almost impossible to edit, and there is also much more of the sense of immediate access to a person's inner world (even if this may be a fantasy on the viewer's part). In much of the pioneer work on the use of art in a therapeutic situation (e.g. Jung 1950, or Lyddiatt 1972), the patient's pictures are not just intrinsically valued as part of a healing process; they are also used as evidence for the construction and support of theory. Jung himself recognised that patients are, to some extent, collaborators in a form of research, whether they are aware of it or not (Jung 1963, p. 143); and re-visioning from a transpersonal perspective is, of course, a central feature of archetypal psychology.

Writing about therapeutic work also satisfies some quite strong counter-transferences. For example: the feeling that writing about this particularly interesting case is some kind of compensation for all the more tiresome ones, or that it is some kind of reward for all the difficulties I have encountered in working with this patient; or I may reckon that my professional needs should have priority over what may seem an over-zealous protection of their privacy. Professional codes of practice, and the ethical responsibilities that they can only formalise to a limited extent, are supposed to manage or contain a therapist's more egotistical or sadistic inclinations; but I doubt whether, if they were strictly adhered to, therapeutic culture as we know it would survive.

The historiography of therapy – that whole termite industry of re-readings of Freud, Jung or Klein and their case-histories – has its own counter-transference: all the more powerful for being safely second-hand. In just the same way as early psychoanalysis treated great artists and writers (Leonardo, Michelangelo, Dostoevsky, Joyce and Picasso) as if their works could be equated with dreams or symptom formations, and their life stories pathologised, so the founding figures of psychoanalysis have been hoist on their own petard and their lives, as well as their theories, subjected to analysis and criticism. Psychoanalysis has its own built-in penchant for homing in on the hidden or the repressed, and it cannot escape this in its own history: in addition, our culture has its own ways of inverting charisma, so that a great man's human failings eventually undermine his work, or even negate it.

It is against such a background that Pailthorpe and Mednikoff's joint research has to be looked at. From what I have already said about it, it must be obvious that it stretched even the comparatively relaxed boundaries of contemporary psychoanalysis, both in terms of its form (the intimacy of the collaboration) and of its content (including perinatal or even intra-uterine experience). There are two main issues I wish to focus on: one is what light the material produced during the research throws on the problem of the 'personal' and its disclosure; the other is the extent to which Pailthorpe's own countertransferences may have influenced the research and possibly distorted its findings. But with both of these my own feelings and opinions – call them countertransference if you like – must also enter the picture.

It is important to remember that the research, although it began as an orthodox analysis and continued to use analytic concepts, was not strictly confined within that framework. It seems that Mednikoff was flattered to be invited to be Pailthorpe's collaborator, and that while he played a 'subject' role within the sessions, he was quite capable of taking the initiative on other occasions. By the same token, he seems to have been quite happy to exhibit their work, and for samples of its therapeutic aspect to be published. Pailthorpe also gave illustrated lectures in the early years, though it is not clear whether Mednikoff participated. Part of this insouciance, of course, was due to Mednikoff's ambitions as an artist getting a good deal of incidental satisfaction from the research.

Even if he agreed to its publication, some analysts might baulk at the level of personal disclosure in Mednikoff's material (not to mention Pailthorpe's, which we will come to in a moment). But, bearing in mind the complications of confidentiality already mentioned, I would ask: how 'personal' *is* this material? The interpretations Pailthorpe supplied during the first couple of years (and which survive in Mednikoff's notes, corrected by her) are in what, even at that date, must have been an orthodox object relations idiom: there are envious attacks on savaged wombs, shrivelled breasts and penises, offerings of shit and so forth. Whilst this vocabulary was obviously underpinned by the history of actual childhood events, much of it refers to a realm of fantasy that by its nature cannot be identifiable in any literal sense. Like so many pantomimes of part-objects, it has a curiously impersonal aura to it. Although the ingredients are often strikingly concrete in their pictorial representation (Mednikoff seems almost to have taken a delight in detailed images of penises), the symbolic equations and translations between them (e.g. urine and milk, shit and food), and their dismemberment into parts standing metonymically for wholes (mother and father), give them a paradoxically abstract feel. Even the actual parents are reproduced as figures that are more symbolic than real.

But beyond this question of how personal 'unconscious' fantasy is,[12] there is also the issue of privacy in therapy, mentioned earlier. The word 'therapy' covers a wide spectrum of practices, not all of which are aimed at cure, in the sense of the relief of symptoms or the alleviation of suffering. Some forms of therapy (those with an archetypal perspective, for example) are more like a form of culture, or care, of the self (Hillman

1973, pp. 113–17). Even psychoanalysis has analogies with the Christian confessional (Foucault 1984, pp. 65–7). So there is a sense in which a patient in these kinds of therapy is subscribing – literally and metaphorically – to a cult; and this cult, while it is locally private, has a background that is more public. The therapist/confessor is the representative for a collective authority of some kind, to which the patient is tacitly being referred. For all its secular bias (in the case of psychoanalysis, at least), therapy is like a religion: it has its sacred texts (the canonical writings of Freud, and their almost Talmudic exegeses), its ritual observances (the fifty-minute hour), and its rule of abstinence (the substitution of transference for literal erotic relation). In therapy, as in religion, the boundary between personal and private salvation and membership of an invisible congregation is impossible to draw firmly.

So much for the patient; but in Pailthorpe's research it is the therapist who seems just as vulnerable to exposure through breaches of confidentiality. Her technique was controversial, even by contemporary standards. Early psychoanalytic practice ignored many of the restrictions and boundaries that have now become the suffocating norm: analysts socialised with their patients and often had more intimate relations with them than would be considered 'professional' today. The more sensational examples, such as Freud's or Klein's analyses of their own children, or Ferenczi's or Jung's involvement with female patients, are only the scandalous tip of a vast submerged iceberg of variations on mixing up the personal and the clinical, the private and the public, in therapy. Obviously, it is not just the patient, but the therapist who may be at risk when things get out of hand, especially when they do not yet have the protection of charisma.

Pailthorpe's work with Mednikoff went well beyond even the elastic therapeutic boundaries I have already mentioned, and perhaps, for all her no-nonsense radical attitudes, she felt that it might be seen as scandalous. It is not clear what kind of a contract the two of them were making when she proposed starting the joint research in April 1935. She was certainly alarmed by the speed with which he gave up his job as a commercial artist and precipitated their living under the same roof. While she had sexual experiences, rather late in life, they had been coloured by a curious mixture of naivety and scientific detachment. With Mednikoff she played the part of mother; and if she did not actually play that of wife,[13] she certainly invited exceptionally powerful transference feelings.

To give an idea of this, I want to refer to a mysterious incident that took place only a few months into the research. On the principle that 'everything reasonably possible' should be allowed the patient, Pailthorpe undertook an experiment to resolve Mednikoff's 'anal sadism'. She felt herself to be at sufficient physical risk to write a letter absolving him from any responsibility beforehand. The experiment took place, without the desired result (whatever that might have been), and Pailthorpe then showed Mednikoff the letter, whereupon he burst into a violent rage, which she defused by opening her arms and saying 'Come on then, kill me' in the 'sweetest tone of voice'. At the end of the letter, she wrote about their project in the most extravagant terms:

We are doing a piece of research work which is so amazing to us in its developement [sic] that we feel if we can bring it to a finish, and if it shall be in the smallest way understood, the results of our findings will metamorphose the whole of the pseudo-civilisation in which we live; and bring about such changes in society as will make our present-day immoral morality into a decent and clean morality.

There is a double countertransference here: one to the 'patient', and another to the research itself. Such overlapping is not uncommon: for example, students on placement or trainees with a case in process find that their needs as would-be therapists sometimes conflict with the patient's process, especially if this involves quitting therapy. I have experienced such dilemmas myself, when wanting to write about a patient's drawings from an artistic rather than a clinical point of view (Maclagan 1989b). Pailthorpe expressed anxiety to Mednikoff on several occasions that someone might seduce him away from his work with her.

But he was not simply the passive partner in this work. He probably helped her to shape its initial direction, and he contributed his artistic skills and an ability to handle symbolism that complemented hers. He almost certainly taught her to paint. There seems to have been a division of labour between them: he supplied the raw material and the artistic skill to elaborate it, while she used it as a basis for advancing new psychoanalytic theory. As with many other cases of pioneer therapeutic exploration, the patient is given the role of producing comparatively unorganised material, and the therapist takes on the function of intellectual understanding and integration, situating the unusual features of the patient's expressions within some more general framework, and 'making sense' of them.[14]

But Pailthorpe did not simply play the role of 'therapist' in the research: she made her own pictures, at first as a form of 'self-analysis', but soon as a part of the material to be worked on by both parties. Many of these pictures rehearse themes that seem to belong more to his inner world than to hers. It is impossible to tell from the outside whether this is the result of an unconscious resonance, or whether she was deliberately using her art work as a kind of mirroring – a way of responding by sharing her 'picture' of his inner world.

It is this aspect of her technique that is most debatable for art therapists. Conventionally, art work is produced by the patient, and is seen in the context of art psychotherapy as embodying transference phenomena (e.g. Schaverien 1991). If the therapist paints, this is seen as expressing aspects of the countertransference and is therefore not to be shared. In less formal situations, such as an open session in an art therapy studio, the therapist may paint, and allow their work to be seen, but not say much about it to patients. Only in exceptional circumstances is this convention broken. Reasons for so doing include: the modelling of free expression of fantasy, the acceptance of some transpersonal dimension, or a deliberate introduction of countertransference feelings. It is hard to know whether any or all of these applied in Pailthorpe's case. It seems plausible to suggest that some of her art work was an attempt to empathise creatively with him, and that some was a more conscious reflection to him of the infantile scripts his relation to her evoked. On a more superficial level, it looks as if she, with her freer and more humorous style, encouraged him to loosen up his rather meticulous technique – for example, by smudging or by using primary colours on wet paper.

There is the further possibility that both partners in the research were equally using painting as a means to explore the 'deeper layers of the unconscious', and that they may even have collaborated on some art works.[15] This would have been quite in line with Surrealist practice, as I shall show in the next section; but it could also be seen as a further dissolution of the distinction between therapist and patient.

Finally, there is the familiar problem of the extent to which Pailthorpe's theories might have influenced Mednikoff's imagery: if patients in Jungian analysis dream 'Jungian' dreams, then couldn't Mednikoff have produced Kleinian doodles to please the mother? Pailthorpe had claimed that 'traditional art (art that has become established and accepted)' was an attempt to 'please the parent' (Pailthorpe 1940, p. 1). It seems that she was talking about its conventional style; but if Surrealist art established its own tradition, then perhaps the same phenomenon could be observed? In later work with Mednikoff she wrote, of the use of painting and drawing, that they brought up unconscious material 'much more readily and with a far greater presentation of detail than by the classic method' (Pailthorpe 1941a, p. 305). Here, of course, it is impossible to disentangle the figurative biases of both psychoanalysis and early Surrealism, and this leads us to the second issue: that of the problematic relation between aesthetic and psychological qualities in an art work.

THE AESTHETIC AND THE PSYCHOLOGICAL

The psychological meaning of art works is deeply incorporated in their aesthetic qualities. Freud maintained that the aesthetic appeal was a kind of 'bribe' that distracted from the underlying (unconscious) meaning, or else made it more palatable (Freud, 1908); and Jung, in his own way, was also suspicious of what he called 'the aesthetic attitude' and its supposed irresponsibility (Jung 1976, pp. 365–7). But even in a therapeutic context the handling of an image, its *facture*, plays an important part in the entire spectrum of its expression, from the conveying of mood to the generation of 'unconscious' forms. There are two additional reasons why Pailthorpe's research raises the question of the interrelation between the aesthetic and the psychological: one is that she and Mednikoff exhibited some of the research material as (Surrealist) art; the other is that she believed that freedom of expression and aesthetic satisfaction went hand in hand. In different ways each of these in turn touches on the issue of how the value of these pictures as evidence of unconscious fantasy matches their value as works of art. We can try to answer this question from within the contemporary context of Surrealism, and adopt a more or less objective 'art-historical' perspective; or we can try to resituate it from the perspective of the present, where problems may be actual and controversial. I do not think that it is possible to take a detached position, and so I shall combine elements of both.

At first sight the Surrealists' original project, to discover the 'real functioning of thought' through the exercise of 'pure psychic automatism' (Breton 1962, p. 40) seems eminently compatible with both the aim of psychoanalysis, to retrace the tangled pathways that connect conscious and unconscious forms of thinking, and its preferred technique of 'free association'. However, the crucial difference between automatism and free association is that, while the first is an unstoppable stream, the second periodically stalls – and it is these failures of flow that signify a resistance to uncovering unconsciously charged material. There are also drastic differences between the objective of psychoanalysis, which could be said to be that of reaching an accommodation with both internal reality (instinctual demands) and external reality (natural and social limits), and that of Surrealism, which adopted a militantly individualistic and subversive stance. Breton and his associates were more interested in following, or even provoking, the ingenious and perverse connections illustrated in Freud's analysis of the 'dream work' than in engaging in any therapeutic work with the results (Maclagan 1992, pp. 36–7).

As part of their refusal of convention, the Surrealists asserted that the documentation of unconscious thought, whether in words or in images, was not to be subject to any kind of aesthetic judgement. Breton did insist that there should be a 'convulsive' side to beauty; but this only served to underline the need for there to be something shocking or disturbing about truly poetic imagery (Wright, 1990). While this might involve defying aesthetic convention, it paradoxically entails obeying certain artistic conventions of representation. To appreciate the strangeness of a typical compound Surrealist image (such as Lautréamont's 'chance encounter of a sewing-machine and an umbrella on a dissecting-table'), one must be able to recognise the individual ingredients. At the same time, it could be argued, Surrealist artists sought to reproduce dream or fantasy images with the same authority as had traditionally been given to external reality

(Mundy 1987). Both these factors meant that, if the content of much Surrealist art was extraordinary, its pictorial form was often quite academic.

There is an obvious paradox in unconscious imagery that is supposed to be spontaneous being represented with such painstaking fidelity; but Surrealism did develop other recipes for producing unconscious imagery more immediately. Max Ernst's *declacomanies* or his *frottages*, and André Masson's automatic drawings were ways of interrogating the actual materials of a picture (somewhat like certain divinatory procedures). However, the imagery that was conjured up still tended to hinge on what might be called a minimal figuration: figures, landscapes or body parts, of however rudimentary a kind. 'Automatic' techniques beg the question whether spontaneity and immediacy of execution are the guarantee of authentic 'unconscious' imagery. This issue has cropped up in the practice of art therapy, where it is often assumed that an improvised picture is more 'unconscious' than one that has been produced more carefully. The Surrealist example should make us wary of such quick and easy identifications.

How do the pictures made by Pailthorpe and Mednikoff fit into this context? First of all, it is clear that Mednikoff's early paintings are quite carefully worked up, and that this in no way prejudiced their alleged unconscious character. For Pailthorpe, 'freedom' clearly meant the absence of conscious interference or inhibition, rather than purely automatic execution. Furthermore, such spontaneity resulted in work that was *ipso facto* aesthetic:

> The unconscious is a master in its own form of art and its creations have qualities similar to those demanded of any form of art, whatever the media. It tells its story perfectly; with economy of language and with associations that convey the maximum effect.
>
> (Pailthorpe 1940, p. 6)

Later on in the same paper, she writes:

> Every unconscious creation is not a work of art, but where complete freedom has been possible the results are perfect in balance, design, colour, rhythm and possess a vitality that is not to be found anywhere else than in Surrealism.
>
> (p. 7)

This new art is, however, still in its infancy – in every sense – and the full effects of freedom in imagination have yet to be realised:

> fantasy or imagination bound by early infantile inhibitions and fears remains infantile in what it creates. In the process of becoming free, Surrealist paintings, drawings and sculpture will necessarily be infantile in content. This does not preclude its right to be called art. The infantile

fantasy, as it becomes freer and experiences more as a result of that freedom, will grow increasingly more adult in character and its creations will show it.

(p. 7)

This 'infantile content' is certainly displayed quite frankly in the work of both partners in the research. Mednikoff's drawings, in particular, parade an ingenious concatenation of body parts – breasts, anuses and penises – and their various secretions. There are also figures and faces, sometimes human, sometimes animal, one often packed inside another. They are, on the whole, quite specific and recognisable: if there is any multiplication of meaning, it is in the interpretations subsequently attached to them. These are, as mentioned earlier, couched in orthodox Kleinian terms. Klein's paper 'Infantile Anxiety Situations Reflected in a Work of Art and in the Creative Impulse' (Klein 1929) had been published only six years earlier, and many of the themes it rehearses – for example, the anxiety aroused by anal-sadistic attacks in phantasy directed at and coming from the parents – are to be found in Pailthorpe's readings of his drawings.

There is an interesting question here, as to whether this early imagery, which is 'regressive', not only in its infantile content, but in its somewhat literal representation of body parts, is perhaps more inviting to psycho-analytic interpretation than more 'mature' work, which may be less straight-forwardly representational, and less explicit. Looking at these pictures and their interpretations fifty years later, the fit between Mednikoff's linear style and particular detail and the equally specific unconscious scenarios that Pailthorpe read into them seems almost too good to be true, and one does wonder whether an element of self-consciousness hasn't crept in. There is often a grotesque, caricatural quality to them that matches the sadistic and persecutory idiom of the psychoanalytic interpretations. Further developments in the field of psychoanalytic aesthetics since Pailthorpe began her research focus more on the *facture* of a work than on its figurative components. Here features such as the blending of outlines or the bleeding of colours may be given an unconscious significance. Pailthorpe's work, in particular, seems amenable to this mode of interpre-tation – even more so in her later years – and I wonder how far this might have been under the influence of later artistic or psychoanalytic theories (see, for example, Milner 1950).

Given the collaborative, if not collusive, nature of the research, it is difficult to see Mednikoff's drawings simply as raw material or as 'uncon-scious' in any literal sense. This, too, has echoes in Surrealism, where the reproduction of 'Freudian' imagery by artists such as Dali is as much the conscious rehearsal of an iconography belonging to a mythological system (i.e. psychoanalysis) as a charting of previously undiscovered and uncon-scious imagery. This brings up again the tricky question of the complex relation between psychoanalytic theory and artistic practice, and the extent to which, past a certain historical point (Surrealism, for the sake of this argument), the 'evidence' of art can ever be wholly uncontaminated by the very theories that it is being used to support.

This problem is, however, not just one of overt historical influence: I would suggest that, particularly in relation to features of *facture*, a conceptual 'frame' effectively produces the phenomena it purports to describe or observe. The relation of image to interpretation is, in a sense, reversed: psychoanalytic or aesthetic theory is functioning, not just as a lens that brings certain subliminal features into focus, but as a way of creating them, by selecting and defining them. The process of interpretation, like an experimental intervention in fundamental particle physics, shapes its own data or creates its own 'facts': there is a sense in which the 'map' creates the 'territory' (Maclagan 1993). This phenomenon is much more evident once the realm of more or less representational imagery has been left. One can hold several alternative readings of a figurative image simultaneously, or in very quick succession; but with non-figurative imagery the distinctions between one reading and another are much harder to keep steady, and a kind of pictorial uncertainty principle operates.

Anton Ehrenzweig is one of the few writers on psychoanalytic aesthetics to have addressed this problem, with his concept of 'inarticulate' or 'Gestalt-free' form, and its subliminal functioning, beyond conscious awareness (Ehrenzweig 1963). He calls his model of unconscious form production a 'structural' (in other words, formal) one; yet it does also involve unconscious content in the orthodox psychoanalytic sense. But the questions raised by Pailthorpe's research still remain: is there a necessary relation between spontaneous form creation and unconscious significance?; and how do we evaluate the qualitative aspect of unconscious or 'depth–mind' imagery? To say, as she does, that what is truly 'free' is by the same token aesthetically satisfying, or that the authenticity of an unconsciously produced picture is to be judged by the absence of distortion in its story (Pailthorpe 1940, p. 3), is surely to take for granted what ought to be in question.

The psychological aesthetics of a picture are never, in fact, exclusively a matter of either its iconography or its handling, but stem from the interaction between them. The full evaluation of this complex texture of significance cannot really be the subject either of quantitative analysis or of value judgements according to conventional criteria: it calls for creative and exploratory description, that is at the same time a tacit interpretation. Such an account may have to use a net of analogical or metaphorical language in which to capture its 'facts'; and such a net is notoriously full of loopholes. The very qualities that are being conjured up – I am reminded here of Winnicott's description of the baby at once finding and creating the breast – have often been associated with inner worlds or subjective states: they are seen, not so much as phenomena, as the invisible lining to phenomena. As previously pointed out, this makes them peculiarly inaccessible to 'objective' research, which operates from the outside in.

These are, of course, exactly the same sort of problems that much research into psychotherapy must encounter, and similar criteria apply to assessing its accuracy. This is not a question of 'proof' in a scientific sense, but more of the kind of plausibility that is established in a court of law. To do an image justice (to turn this analogy into a metaphor) is to satisfy a cluster of requirements: it is to cover its principal features (rather than concentrate on minor details); to work out a fit or congruence between the figurative language being used and recognisable features of the work; to strike a note that is sympathetic to the work, rather than discordant or adversarial; and to expand or deepen our understanding of it.

CONCLUSION

Research into therapeutic technique and the measurement of its results can only be a limited part of research in the field of art therapy: both 'therapy' and 'art' are, as I have tried to suggest, creative forms of inquiry, which traffic in what Winnicott called the 'intermediate' area of experience, that is neither subjective nor objective but in between the two (Winnicott 1971, p. 113). Although I have frequently dealt here with the subjective elements in research in terms of transference phenomena, I do not feel that this term is really adequate to the subjective investments that research involves. Surely the spirit that inspires research at its best cannot be explained purely in terms of personal projections and agendas (they are more to do with its shadow aspect): it shares something of the passionate curiosity, as well as the pedantic obstinacy, of its subject matter. But above all, it is itself inspiring, breathing life into numb or anaesthetised areas, re-animating what has gone dead – if necessary, with shocks. Like therapy (or art), it deals in disclosures not just of the 'object' (the patient, the material), but of the subject (the therapist, the researcher) themselves.

I would like to end by citing a number of models for research in which the subjective element is valued instead of being disqualified. Pailthorpe and Mednikoff's own research, of course, is an early form of 'collaborative inquiry'. More recent work that I have found useful or encouraging includes the philosopher Michael Polanyi's theory of 'personal knowledge' (Polanyi and Prosch 1975, pp. 42–3); the novelist Christa Wolf's concept of 'subjective authenticity' (Wolf 1988, pp. 20–3); the idea of 're-visioning' put forward both by feminist researchers (Callaway 1981, p. 457) and by the archetypal psychologist James Hillman (Hillman 1975); and, finally, the model of intersubjective validity proposed by new paradigm research (Reason and Rowan 1981, pp. 132–4). As many of the other chapters in this book will – hopefully – show, the extent to which we are able to untie ourselves from the binding authority of 'scientific' objectivity will make a vital difference both to what we are able to know and to how we can share it with others.

NOTES

1 A number of recent publications deal with this overlap between the aesthetic and the psychological in art therapy, for example: Maclagan (1989a), McNiff (1992), Simon (1992).

2 Unless otherwise indicated, all references are to the collection of papers now lodged with the Tate Gallery Archives, consisting largely of Mednikoff's own notes on his sessions with Pailthorpe, these being corrected and commented on by her.

3 A selection from this material, together with relevant background information on Pailthorpe's life, is in the course of being prepared for publication by Dr David Rumney. I am extremely grateful to him for allowing me to read his work, and for advice on numerous factual details.

4 Exhibitions that have included some of this work have been held at Goldsmiths Gallery, London 1985; Birch and Conran, London, 1986, 1989; Canterbury College of Art, 1986; The Mayor Gallery, London 1986; and Leeds City Museum, 1986. James Birch and Paul Conran have both very kindly let me examine important material in their own private collections.

5 The most important of these was the famous International Surrealist Exhibition of 1936 held at Burlington House, London: it was in this show that André Breton remarked on the outstanding quality of Pailthorpe's work.

6 To be fair to Pailthorpe, many analysts of that period were more relaxed about boundaries than is now the case; and, of course, the founding fathers, Freud and Jung, were, in their different ways, notoriously cavalier.

7 It was in fact the experience of seeing Pailthorpe's work on exhibition that inspired Marion Milner to experiment with the 'doodle' drawings that were eventually incorporated into her *On Not Being Able To Paint* (Milner 1987, p. 11).

8 Although this paper was probably written in 1938, it was not published until 1940 – ironically at just the time that she had quit the Surrealist movement and was on her way to America.

9 For example, the 'Pailthorpe Papers' were obviously intended by her for eventual publication; yet they were left to friends rather than a colleague, and the process of gaining access to them involved something of a legal obstacle race (David Rumney, personal communication).

10 A recent example is the biography of the poet Anne Sexton, which draws explicitly on taped sessions made available with the consent of both Sexton's family and her therapist (Middlebrook 1991).

11 Particularly interesting work has been done on this by Andrew Samuels, subjecting both the 'personal' and the 'political' to mutual redefinition (Samuels 1993).

12 I leave to one side the question of whether it is 'fantasy' or 'phantasy' that is involved here; but I reckon that the rehearsal or re-presentation of what must soon have been a familiar vocabulary or 'unconscious' images in pictorial form cannot be called 'phantasy' without distorting the concept.

13 Mednikoff was recently divorced; but for psychological reasons might have

found it safer to relate to a Mother-figure, even in a sexual way. Conversely, Pailthorpe may have found being the initiator of a therapeutic sexual relationship easier than her previous somewhat exploited ones. This is, of course, impure speculation.

14 The case of Jung and Sabina Spielrein shown that this division of labour is sometimes reproduced after the event so as to cast the therapist as theoretician, when the patient may have performed this function (Carotenuto 1984).

15 The evidence for this is purely a matter of stylistic interpretation. Most pictures that were signed, were signed by Mednikoff; but there are some, dating from the early 1940s, that seem to carry both their artistic 'signatures'.

REFERENCES

Barnes, M. and Berke, J. (1973) *Mary Barnes: Two Accounts of a Journey Through Madness*, Penguin, Harmondsworth.

Breton, A. (1962) *Manifestes du Surréalisme*. J.-J. Pauvert, Paris.

Callaway, H. (1981) 'Women's Perspectives: Research as Re-vision'. In: Rowan, J. and Reason, P. (Eds) *Human Inquiry: A Sourcebook of New Paradigm Research*. John Wiley, Chichester.

Carotenuto, A. (1984) *A Secret Symmetry*. Routledge and Kegan Paul, London.

Ehrenzweig, A. (1963) *The Psychoanalysis of Artistic Vision and Hearing*. Sheldon, London.

Foucault, M. (1984) *The History of Sexuality*. Peregrine Books, Harmondsworth.

Freud, S. (1908) 'The Poet and Daydreaming'. *SE* 9. Hogarth, London.

Gardiner, M. (1972) *The Wolf Man and Sigmund Freud*. Hogarth, London.

Hillman, J. (1973) *Suicide and the Soul*. Harper, New York.

Hillman, J. (1975) *Re-visioning Psychology*. Harper, New York.

Jung, C.G. (1950) 'A Study in the Process of Individuation'. *CW* 9. Routledge and Kegan Paul, London.

Jung, C.G. (1963) *Memories, Dreams and Reflections*. Routledge and Kegan Paul, London.

Jung, C.G. (1976) *The Visions Seminars*. Spring Publications, Zurich.

Klein, M. (1929) 'Infantile Anxiety Situations Reflected in a Work of Art and in the Creative Impulse'. In: Mitchell, J. (Ed.) *The Selected Melanie Klein*, Penguin, Harmondsworth, 1986.

Lyddiatt, E.M. (1972) *Spontaneous Painting and Modelling*. Constable, London.

Maclagan, D. (1989a) 'The Aesthetic Dimension in Art Thearpy'. *Inscape*. Spring: 10–13.

Maclagan, D. (1989b) 'From Inside Out'. *Raw Vision* 1: 42–5.

Maclagan, D. (1992) 'Between Psychoanalysis and Surrealism: The Collaboration between Grace Pailthorpe and Reuben Mednikoff', *Free Associations*. 25: 33–50.

Maclagan, D. (1993) 'Inner and Outer Space: Mapping the Psyche'. *Cosmos* 9.

McNiff, S. (1992) *Art as Medicine*. Shambhala Publications, Inc., Boston.

Middlebrook, D.W. (1991) *Anne Sexton: A Biography*. Virago, London.

Milner, M. (1950) *On Not Being Able To Paint*. Hutchinson, London.

Milner, M. (1987) *The Suppressed Madness of Sane Men*. Tavistock, London.

Mundy, J. (1987) 'Surrealism and Painting: Describing the Imaginary'. *Art History*. 10: 492–508.

Pailthorpe, G.W. (1940) 'The Scientific Aspect of Surrealism'. *The London Bulletin*. No. 7.

Pailthorpe, G.W. (1941a) 'Deflection of Energy, as a Result of Birth Trauma, and its Bearing upon Character Formation'. *The Psychoanalytic Review*. 28: 305–26.

Pailthorpe, G.W. (1941b) 'Primary Processes of the Infantile Mind Demonstrated through the Analysis of a Prose-poem'. *International Journal of Psycho-Analysis*. 22: 1–16.

Polanyi, M. and Prosch, H. (1975) *Meaning*. Chicago University Press, Chicago.

Reason, P. and Rowan, J. (1981) 'On Making Sense'. In: Reason, P. and Rowan, J. (Eds) *Human Inquiry: A Sourcebook of New Paradigm Research*. John Wiley, Chichester.

Samuels, A. (1993) *The Political Psyche*. Routledge, London.

Shamdasani, S. (1990) 'A Woman Called Frank'. *Spring 1990*: 26–53.

Simon, R. (1992) *The Symbolism of Style*. Routledge, London.

Schaverien, J. (1991) *The Revealing Image: Analytical Art Psychotherapy in Theory and Practice*. Routledge, London.

Winnicott, D.W. (1971) *Playing and Reality*. Routledge, London.

Wolf, C. (1988) Pilkington, H. (Trans.) *The Fourth Dimension: Interviews*. Verso, London.

Wright, E. (1990) 'The Uncanny and Surrealism'. In: Collier, P. and Davies, J. (Eds) *Modernism and the European Unconscious*. Polity, Oxford/Cambridge.

Chapter 13

The development of art therapy in Bulgaria
Infiltrating the system

Diane Waller

INTRODUCTION

In this chapter I shall describe a project which was designed to introduce art therapy into the Bulgarian state health care system. The project gained 'official' status in 1986, as an element in the World Health Organisation's general psychiatric project 'Man and His Brain', based at the Medical Academy in Sofia. The project might better be perceived as a process, for the original aims have now been superseded and the context in which it began has dramatically changed. It was in itself a small-scale intervention in the functioning of an already existing system, accompanied by a close examination of the progress of the intervention itself and of the system. The method of 'action research' provided the framework for formulating, organising and ordering the various elements in the project and the material it generated.

As Cohen and Manion (1981) have pointed out, there are usually two stages in an action research project, namely the diagnostic stage in which problems are analysed and hypotheses developed, and a therapeutic stage in which these are tested by a piece of experimental work directed towards change (pp. 174–5). Action research is often used when some kind of organisational change is desired, and as a means of getting something done when going through normal channels would prove difficult or too time-consuming. Certainly, as far as the art therapy project was concerned, it was a way of infiltrating the system of health care in Bulgaria in a respectable and well-organised manner, and of contributing to a new pattern of psychosocial interventions. As the reader will note, my involvement in this project, at the time, was no accident but fitted into a long-standing interest and involvement with Bulgaria.

Some personal background

I first visited Bulgaria in 1967 as an art student interested in the ethnography of the Balkans and returned on several occasions to pursue my involvement in the traditional arts, music and dance of Macedonia and Bulgaria in particular. In 1972–3 a Leverhulme research scholarship in Bulgaria and Macedonia gave me the opportunity to explore the role of the arts in these rapidly industrialising societies.

At the same time, I was interested to know how the term 'art therapy' was understood (if at all) in these countries.To pursue this interest, I stayed at a hospital in a remote part of northern Bulgaria, learning much about the pioneering work in art therapy of Professor Alexander Marinov, the director. I followed up with frequent visits, some of which were arranged by the Bulgarian Committee for Culture and others by the British Council, and participated in a wide range of activities, including visits to the Union of Artists, art teacher training centres, folklore festivals, youth centres, industrial complexes, archaeological sites and co-operative farms. Thus I gained useful insight into areas of work as diverse as professional folk-dance and steel production, and experienced life in both new urban complexes and in villages, which was to prove valuable in subsequent years when engaged in research and training, and especially in the 'diagnostic' phase of the project described.

During an academic visit to Sofia in 1981, I was invited to run some informal 'courses' in art therapy, with the support of the chief of the department of psychiatry of the Medical Academy, Professor Ivan Temkov. These proved popular with the participants and attracted the attention of some of the more 'hard line' biologists, who became fascinated by the method. Sponsorship by the British Council enabled me to visit the major psychiatric hospitals in Bulgaria and to get to know the routines of the departments of psychiatry in Sofia. When in 1985 the Medical Academy became a World Health Organisation Co-Ordinating Centre, I was invited to join a team preparing proposals for introducing new psychosocial treatments into the Bulgarian health service. I was asked to draft up a proposal for an art therapy programme, which I gladly agreed to, and, with Professors Asen Jablensky and Toma Tomov and their team, prepared the submission for the art therapy project which is described in this chapter.

THE AIM OF THE PROJECT

This was to establish an art therapy provision in the Bulgarian national health service for the treatment and rehabilitation of psychiatric patients.

The objectives

These were:

1 To provide a training in art therapy, initially for clinical personnel and at a later date for a multi-disciplinary group, including artists;

2 To provide an art therapy service fitted to the Bulgarian national health service;
3 To research in a preliminary way the contribution of art therapy to the enhancement of visual creativity;
4 To produce a manual of art therapy theory and practice.

The context in which the project took place

It is important to point out here that the context in which the project started was a very different one from that in which it is likely to end, owing to the massive political changes of the late 1980s. In 1983 I observed the following in my notebook:

The major problems of establishing art therapy as we know it in Bulgaria are as follows. Firstly, there is no tradition of non-medical therapists. The profession which could, perhaps, take on psychotherapy, i.e. psychology, is new and still dominated by the Pavlovian (behaviourist) approach. Concepts from Freud and from psychoanalysis, or from humanistic psychology, are little known about, understood or appreciated. Secondly, it would be very difficult for psychologists and psychiatrists to obtain sufficient experience of using art for themselves to enable them to work effectively as art therapists, given that most of them have had little or no art education, even at school. Thirdly, there are very few people in Bulgaria who have trained in psychotherapy and who could act as supervisors. Yet the interest and enthusiasm is strong . . .

These statements, I believe, still largely hold true, yet the sociopolitical climate of today appears at least more welcoming towards psychodynamic psychotherapy than previously, and it is somewhat easier for interaction to take place between professionals with similar interests.

THE DIAGNOSTIC PHASE

Preparing the protocol: some issues which had to be addressed

To return to the beginning of the project and the mid-1980s context of Bulgaria, a working group to design the project was established in September 1986 in Sofia. The inclusion of art therapy in the programme had been taken very seriously, and warranted a high-powered Bulgarian presence, including the professor of psychiatry and the head of the WHO Centre. There were no artists included, though, because unlike the situation in Britain, there is no tradition of artists going to work in hospitals, so it would not have seemed logical. I did, however, suggest that the Director of the Artists' Union of Bulgaria be involved at a later stage and this idea was well received.

As a group, we had to bear in mind that art therapy as a process involving a relationship between the patient, therapist and the art objects was a new concept in Bulgarian hospitals. Art therapy (where it existed) was often conceived as a form of craft work, or involved patients painting in a studio either for their own satisfaction or with the encouragement of a psychiatrist who might use the art work subsequently for diagnostic purposes (e.g. Marinov 1972, 1975a, 1975b, 1983). Given that the trainees needed to be medical or paramedical personnel in order to be accepted by health and social services agencies, it was agreed by all that the training would have to be structured in a way which would at least sensitise them to materials and extend their visual awareness, and encourage them to have more confidence in their creative abilities. From previous research (Waller 1983; Waller and Boyadzhiev 1983; Waller and Gheorghieva 1990) I had come to the conclusion that there was a general lack of awareness of the visual arts among the young urban generation: a huge gap left by the decline of the traditional arts, with their associations of 'the past' and 'the village' had not been filled, even though many of the participants had expressed themselves interested in 'art in general'. It was recognised that the foundation art studies could not compensate for the trainees' lack of practical art background but, in addition to the reasons already mentioned above, may begin to create the link between the medical and the art world which was needed for the future.

As there had to be emphasis on practical art work in the training, the question of a suitable space to work in had to be addressed. If, as had been suggested, the training was to be held at each of the participating centres in order to draw the attention of other staff to the project, then each would need to provide appropriate working space, materials and so on. It seemed that this would not be a problem. The Institute of Hygiene in Sofia, the Radnevo Psychiatric Hospital near Stara Zagora and the Department of Psychiatry at Varna Hospital were the three venues selected for training.

ORGANISATION OF THE PROJECT

Bearing in mind its aims and objectives, and following the diagnostic phase of the research, the therapeutic stage of the project was conceived as developing in two parts: the preparatory stage followed by the working stage.

The preparatory stage

This was designed to last for four months and immediately follow the first intensive training course, which would give the trainees a modest but thorough theoretical and experiential introduction to art therapy. The

Bulgarian co-ordinators were to help the trainees identify and begin to organise art therapy sessions with one or two individual clients. This stage was to serve as a trial period for monitoring the progress of the co-ordination and supervision scheme developed for the project. Facilities for practice, patterns of recording sessions, assessing progress and discussing cases were to be established in each centre and staff prepared for the new intervention. Finally, all the groundwork for the evaluation of the subsequent working stage would be done, including selection of patients, preparation of instruments for data collection and measurement, training participants and the team to use the instruments, and planning the follow-up training for the participants.

The working stage

This stage was to last for one year, in which the trainees were to establish individual sessions and begin to work with an art therapy group on a regular basis. Team meetings were to be conducted regularly; supervision was to be carried out according to an agreed-upon scheme; two follow-up training seminars were to be organised. An evaluation would be run parallel to the above activities in the course of which baseline, mid-course and outcome data was to be recorded and analysed. At least one in-depth case study was to be prepared as an example of the way that art therapy was developing. Following this working stage, a manual was to be prepared, based on the experience of the project from beginning to end and containing case study examples.

TRAINING

There were three aspects to the training:

1 It was to take place in intensive blocks.
2 It was to be followed up through monthly contacts between the co-ordinators and the participants.
3 There was to be support for the co-ordinators from the consultant.

(My role was to design and deliver the training and monitor the progress of the trainees.) The objectives of the intensive training were to introduce the participants to theoretical issues, experiential methods and the clinical practice of art therapy. In order to facilitate fulfilment of the objectives, all three centres were to be involved and provide facilities for the courses, which were scheduled to happen every six months. The follow-up sessions, that is, regular contact between team members and the co-ordinators, were to start immediately after the introductory course, with the co-ordinators operating from Sofia and providing a focal point for the work being carried out in each centre.

In the case of the trainees, the work was to consist of:

- Selection of patients for individual work (not more than two); preparation of plans for group work;
- Using guidelines prepared by the consultant, recording of each session for personal use in order to share the experience with the team and the rest of the trainees;
- Meeting as a team in the centre at least once a week and preparing protocols of the meetings; formulating questions and ideas; sending protocols to the co-ordinators;
- Working out a mechanism for regularly informing the rest of the staff at the centre about the art therapy work, at least once a month;
- Storing art work in readiness for presentation to the consultant and co-ordinators;
- Initiating contacts with other professions in order to arouse their interest in art therapy;
- Writing at least one case study to be discussed with the team at each centre.

The co-ordinators' responsibility was to keep track of developments in all three centres and visit regularly; organise one meeting for all team members to replay videos, raise and discuss issues, draw up suggestions for subsequent training periods; compile a reading list and distribute reading material. The consultant's role was to provide support for the co-ordinators, keep track of the developments in the centres through regular correspondence and phone calls, receive and comment on audio-tapes and possibly videotapes of sessions. The director on the Bulgarian side was to be on hand to contact centres should there be any problems in trainees being allowed to carry out their work.

EVALUATION

The objectives of the evaluation were to monitor and to streamline the activities under the project in the course of one year and provide feedback on the progress of work. This was seen as essential in order to make use of the data and prepare a manual on art therapy at a later date. It was also anticipated that art therapy would be amenable to process research (i.e. the trainees would be able to engage in a collaborative process of evaluation with their clients) aimed at identifying the mechanisms of therapeutic change. An in-depth case study was felt to be the most appropriate method of focusing on the effects of art therapy on the patient. The study was to include discussion of the relationship between patient and therapist and the role of the art work, and the institutional issues arising from the art therapy sessions. This was incorporated into the research design.

The trainees had to choose patients from four broad categories (which actually reflected the main patient populations in the three centres): children with learning difficulties and/or physical handicaps; patients with depression and anxiety; patients with drinking problems; patients with functional psychosis. Details of the patients' age, sex, social background, length of illness, experience with institutional care and clinical diagnosis according to ICD–10 or DSM–3 had to be included. The patient was to be asked to provide a self-assessment, focusing on measuring change as perceived by the patient him/herself. The Personal Orientation Inventory was felt to be a useful instrument but a Semantic Differential technique was eventually devised. A patient's close contact (relative or selected friend) was to be interviewed (with the patient's permission) to record perceived changes in social behaviour and relating. Section 2 of the Disability Assessment Schedule developed by WHO was suggested as a suitable, easy-to-use instrument. The therapist was to provide an assessment every three months, using the instruments mentioned above.

This very complex structure, based as it was on action research methodology, required meticulous documentation at all stages by all the persons concerned. Over the period of the project described in this chapter, information was collected, shared, discussed, recorded in written, video or slide form, evaluated and acted upon (see Cohen and Manion 1981, p. 179).

WHAT HAPPENED

Here I will describe the way that the project took shape, who participated and what happened.

The trainees

Twelve people joined the course. Of these, seven were psychiatrists, two psychologists, two nursing sisters, and one a 'cultural therapist'. Eleven were seconded by their workplace, one had a personal interest and was admitted by the Bulgarian co-ordinator. Only two of the participants (both psychiatrists) had studied art, on their own, in any depth. Most had no art education at all; this meant that they literally did not know anything about the properties of colour, paint, etc. as art practice was only recently included in the Bulgarian school curriculum. Their art history studies had been of a classical nature and had not included study of modern movements. Most of them knew little about dynamic psychotherapy as opposed to behavioural, but they had plenty of experience in relating to patients with a wide range of emotional and psychiatric disturbances. Three had attended the informal art therapy workshops.

The space

In Sofia, the large conference room at the Institute of Hygiene was made available. Despite its daunting appearance of formal boardroom dignity, it was light and airy and the long table covered with green cloth was found to be composed of several metal-topped tables which could be moved around and were easy to wash. The sumptuous armchairs were placed carefully in an arc at the end of the room as a space where the theoretical discussions could take place. A washroom led off the conference room, giving easy access to water. Plastic sheeting took care of the carpet. This room turned out to be very suitable and thus was used for two of the three training blocks.

In Varna, a large room with formica tables near to the cloakrooms was a good base for the practical work. However, the somewhat spartan atmosphere of the hospital was not conducive to making a mess and proved inhibiting to art practice. The bleakness of the weather was echoed in the coldness of the room and, as I shall describe later, affected the workshops.

In Radnevo Hospital near Stara Zagora, there was a well-equipped department for creative activities, containing a variety of materials. However, due to the convenience of Sofia as a central location and the good facilities therein, and owing to staff changes at Radnevo, the third training block was held in Sofia.

Art materials and other equipment

'Traditional' art materials were very scarce and expensive, usually only available to students of the art academies. (Art materials were generally taken to mean oil paint and canvas.) Instead, scrap material, such as old boxes, magazines, string, wool, old toys and clothes were assembled and decorators' shops were located where useful oxides, tints, glues, large tubs of emulsion paints and brushes, etc. provided the basic source of colour. Texture was available in the form of sand and old wallpaper books and participants gathered several boxes of junk material. There was a range of felt-tipped pens, pencils, charcoal, coloured paper, wrapping paper and some tissue and shiny-textured papers which we brought from the UK. Clay was available in Sofia but not in Varna.

The process

The composition of the trainee group had led to a form of training being devised which included a much more in-depth art education than that of the UK (where art therapy students are normally art graduates). In common with the UK, trainees had to learn and understand the basic concepts of art therapy theory and practice, which is substantially underpinned by dynamic psychotherapy and developmental psychology. The intensive training periods thus included structured workshops on the use of and exploration of media. Over half the training period consisted of art practice sessions and experiential art therapy groups, followed by discussion. The remainder was a combination of basic psychotherapy theory and art therapy theory mainly taught in seminar style. Some formal lectures on specific aspects of art therapy (e.g. with anorexic patients) were presented to staff of the host hospitals and the trainees joined in.

The first training period

The notion of exposing oneself to a similar process to the one the patient would experience was absolutely new to the trainees, many of whom still thought that art therapy was a means of diagnosis of psychiatric problems, despite being advised right from the start that it was much more complex than that, and indeed that this aspect would be played down. We had anticipated that exposure to these intensive block programmes might well result in trainees being emotionally stirred up, and adequate support had to be provided afterwards.

My style of teaching and conducting groups (in which I used a group-interactive model) appeared to cause some unease among group members at first. The trainees were used to a very formal education system through-out school and university, to having lectures from the professors and to receiving instructions on what to do. The somewhat 'laid-back' and informal style, and my expectation that they would use their own resources as individuals and as a group, proved extremely disconcerting. They mistook the approach initially as a *laissez-faire* one, until they became more familiar with the model through experiencing the process themselves and through having seminars on group dynamics. They also appeared at first to find a relatively young female authority figure hard to take seriously.

After the first training period in September 1986, the co-ordinators met with the trainees and kept in touch by phone. The trainees were finding difficulty in establishing some art therapy practice. Often this appeared to be a result of their (reasonable) ambivalence about practising after such a short initial introduction as well as the obstruction and/or ambivalence of their own clinical teams. Therefore, on discussing this matter with trainees, consultant and co-ordinators, it was decided to slow the whole project down and not to make such heavy demands on the trainees. These demands had arisen from a desire on behalf of the working group to incorporate art therapy into the Bulgarian health service at the earliest opportunity, and were based on the enthusiasm and commitment of the Sofia team. But this ignored the fact that things usually moved very slowly in Bulgaria anyway, and that trainees (even psychiatrists!) could not perform art therapeutic miracles . . .

The co-ordinators found that, despite the stated co-operation in the project, many of the initial problems stemmed from lack of understanding and support from other staff in the centres, resulting in trainees being given inadequate time to practise art therapy. For example, one psychiatrist tried to arrange his timetable to see two individual patients in his role as 'art therapy trainee'. He found that his chief always called him to meetings at that time, so he either kept the patient waiting or the patient went away. The authority structure was such that he feared to stand his ground in case he put his job at risk. He was helped, through role play, to explain exactly what the project entailed and the serious nature of the art therapy process. The chief had thought art therapy was just a pastime and not a suitable indulgence for a psychiatrist. This attitude affected the trainee, who was already ambivalent.

Another problem, experienced acutely by the psychiatrists, and also the nurses, was change of role. Their patients found it strange that a doctor or nurse should ask them to use art materials, whereas previously they had been used to talking or being given medication. Being unfamiliar with the process themselves, the trainees could often not give a very good reason for engaging in image-making, and no art therapy was offered. There seemed to be much uncertainty among staff and the trainees themselves as to whether or not art therapy was (a) frivolous or (b) powerful, effective but also dangerous.

This role change to 'art therapist' was difficult to cope with not only because of the personal demands but because status as 'doctor' was seen as higher than 'art therapist' in the eyes of colleagues and probably of themselves: 'art therapy' had been used to describe very basic craft activity which could be supervised by poorly qualified staff. Patient expectations that once a drawing had been done the therapist would 'analyse' it also caused a problem. The trainees themselves felt that they should after all be able to do this and, if they could not, then the patient would lose faith in the process. These problems were experienced less acutely by trainees working with children, who found they could adapt to the art therapist role and 'play' with the children.

It is not surprising that the trainees became angry with the co-ordinators and with me because they were trying to meet too many conflicting expectations: theirs, the co-ordinators' and mine, the patients', their colleagues', their bosses'. To explore some of these issues, especially the ambivalence of the trainees and patients, role play was used during subsequent training blocks, and the experiential quota increased followed by intensive small group discussion to link experience with theory and clinical practice. This was found to be very helpful and illuminating.

The second training period

The second training period was punctured by difficult events. The journey from Sofia had been appalling, due to plane cancellations and bad weather. The hospital, in which the co-ordinators and I were staying, was far from the centre of town, where the participants were staying. None of this had been known beforehand, meaning that the timetable had to be re-done at the last minute. On the second morning, none of the non-Varna participants turned up, having been thrown out of their hotel to make room for some Greek (Western) visitors who could pay in much-needed foreign currency. They had, as a result, been wandering around Varna looking for non-existent accommodation. After much protest by myself on behalf of the group – for being a visiting 'foreigner' and representative of WHO I could get away with it – they were reinstated. They expressed their feelings about this by a violent group painting in which they destroyed the Greeks and the manager of the hotel. My feelings around this were of acute discomfort and shame about being identified with the 'West'. While acknowledging the need for 'valuta' in the disintegrating Bulgarian economy, I could not accept the value system which underpinned it. This did not seem like socialism as I understood it. The week proceeded in a tense and somewhat fraught manner.

In the final workshop in Varna, the group spontaneously made a large portrait of a woman with a Bulgarian headband, necklace, earrings and passport. She was going off to New York and had a purse full of dollars, a gun to protect herself, some smart clothes and boots. She wore bracelets, which someone commented looked like 'handcuffs'. She had an English cheque book, a letter of introduction and various other useful things which were made out of scrap material and put into a large bag. It was clear from the various comments of the group that this was me. I found this whole workshop very moving, and was close to tears, having strong counter-transference reactions: the group's ambivalence towards me – as an outsider who wasn't really an outsider, and as someone who could fly off with a bag full of dollars while they had to remain – was graphically expressed in this image. It was as if the picture had got inside me: I desperately wanted to stay. Yet I also more desperately wanted to escape from Varna and go back to Sofia. The whole week had been characterised by anger, envy, sadness and fear that the work would be in vain. The economic recession was affecting the country severely; there were shortages and people were depressed and felt betrayed. The art therapy workshops gave trainees a chance to express their despair in a way which was quite overwhelming. It affected me very strongly then, and for months after I got back to England I experienced not knowing where I belonged, together with a crushing sense of loss. I have heard many immigrants to Britain say the same thing: 'I have lived here for so long that I no longer belong at home. But I do not belong here either.' (See Waller 1993 for further discussion of this and other workshops in the project.)

The 'follow-up' period between April and September took place as planned, with the reverberations of the Sofia–Varna relationship continuing to be felt. Several of the participants began to establish themselves securely in their role as art therapist, but unfortunately others were struggling and one dropped out. The Bulgarian economy was in an increasingly poor state, with standard, popular foodstuffs (such as yoghurt, garlic and cucumbers) being unobtainable in Sofia.

The third training period

The third training period was held again in Sofia in blistering hot September weather. The focus was on family relationships, ideal and impossible families, families in crisis, and group interaction. There was substantial 'reparation' of the quarrels in Varna. I was able to draw on material from the two 'unofficial' art therapy courses which I had conducted in Sofia in 1981 and 1982, in which the problem of honestly expressing feelings about one's fellow group members and the leader, and one's family, had been discussed. Bulgaria is a very close-knit society where to speak ill of one's family is regarded as shameful. The family network is strong and extended, providing a major support system in all aspects of life. To suggest that one has negative feelings about a relation could literally be damaging. Likewise, disturbing the hierarchy could be dangerous and alienating. In Bulgaria strong social networks existed: people went to school together, remained at college together, lived in the same town all their lives. Families were often acquainted for generations. So the risks involved in direct expression of negative feeling, even in a therapy session, seemed enormous.

Understanding this important feature of Bulgarian life, complicated as it was by the bureaucratic system which prevailed, was essential for anyone trying to work within a psychodynamic model.

By the end of this block, the participants had 'gelled' into an active group, with individuals exhibiting varying degrees of commitment. Some were engaging in all elements of the project, including the research. It was clear that others had found the training personally valuable but the difficulties of 'role change' too drastic. One trainee had become a 'chief' himself, and was struggling with his art therapy practice, albeit without the problem of an immediate boss but with patient and staff expectation an even bigger problem. Some optimism had returned, even though the economy was in a worse state than before. One of the most ambivalent and sceptical trainees had succeeded in setting up an art therapy service in her place of work. She had benefited from the workshops and had seen at first hand how powerful the process could be. She continues to work successfully at the time of writing.

The co-ordinators were meticulous in carrying out their role. They were supported by the medical team in Sofia and as far as possible by myself, through letters and phone calls. The long distances between Sofia–Stara Zagora–Varna and London made it imperative that the trainees should meet at least weekly in their own districts, and that staff at their centres should be sympathetic to the project. The training group found many resources among themselves, and the regular meetings in the centres proved vital to the survival of the group's developing ethos.

The co-ordinators and I all felt an enormous responsibility, but the complications of acquiring a visa and official permission to visit Bulgaria meant that frequent or spontaneous visits were impossible.

More work clearly had to be done on informing staff in participating centres of the function of art therapy, so that they ceased regarding it as pastime or diversion and, in any case, non-serious. (These are problems still faced by our profession in Britain today, after nearly fifty years, and twelve of those as a recognised NHS profession.)

Evaluation and preparation of the manual

This part of the project is not yet complete. The co-ordinators were due to visit the UK on two occasions to spend some time as guests of hospitals with large art therapy departments and of the Art Psychotherapy Unit of Goldsmiths' College. Unfortunately at this point (1988) the Bulgarian economy went further into recession and a period of political and social upheaval began, making the continuation of the project well nigh impossible. All the data remains, together with recordings of our experiences, and many of the trainees retain a desire to continue. Time will tell if and how the project will develop.

DISCUSSION

Looking back, it is clear that the aims and objectives of the project were far too ambitious. There was a problem in setting it up, in that its progress had to be seen to be 'measured' (and seen to be 'successful') in order for art therapy to gain a foothold in the system. It has to be remembered that this was a psychiatric system dominated by Pavlovian or behavioural methodology, which had shown itself hostile to psychoanalytic concepts, but which, on the other hand, was beginning to open out as a result of WHO projects and more movement of professionals between Bulgaria and the rest of the world. To ask the trainees and the then still inexperienced co-ordinators to undertake the tasks described was asking far too much, but there was a kind of determined optimism in the team which was somewhat deaf to the cautionary words of its consultant.

The trainees themselves were in an unusual and perhaps anxiety-provoking position. They were not art graduates seeking a professional role, as in the UK. They already had other professions. So why, then, did this group want to train in art therapy? This is a question needing careful research, as it not only applies to Bulgaria but to most other European countries without the historical link of art education with developmental psychology. Writing specifically about Bulgaria, Gheorghieva (in Waller and Gheorghieva 1990, p. 32) pointed out that by being selected by their institutions, the trainees were themselves representative of the psychiatric system. They could have been selected for a variety of reasons – for example, being the closest person to the chief; a 'devoted carrier of the biological approach'; a person who could be sure never to carry out the work; a low- or high-status person, or someone who had a deep interest and commitment to art therapy. In fact, all these persons were present in the group. The important thing was that the group actually consisted of people through which the system was ready to accept the changes that the project would bring.

Gheorghieva felt that there were only two really motivated people in the group, one who had been sent by his institution (a child guidance clinic) and the other who had been admitted by herself. The former was highly committed personally, yet despite his institution 'sending' him his attempts to work with patients in art therapy were constantly frustrated, suggesting much ambivalence about the inclusion of art therapy in the treatment programme (Waller and Gheorghieva 1990, p. 32).

The question of trainees being 'sent', or chosen by an institution to participate in a project at that particular time in Bulgaria's political history is an important one to address though difficult to have done openly before 1990. I do not feel, though, that the picture was as bleak as Gheorghieva painted it because on interviewing the trainees before the first course it seems that some had read about art therapy, seen films of patients painting, and had thought that it offered a radically different treatment from the 'traditional' models of psychiatric care on offer. Some had, clearly, been 'sent' by their hospital and were unsure why they were there. Others were eager to participate in a project with a Western flavour. I did not become fully aware of these very mixed reasons for attending until after the third training workshop. Perhaps it is just as well that I assumed from the start that all the trainees were keen to be there because they were interested in the subject!

One of the important issues to emerge from the project was that, because of the length of time between each training period and the newness of the work, the trainees needed much more input on institutional dynamics especially because they were working within a rigid system and because they were ambivalent themselves about changing role.

About half the group managed to establish some art therapy practice on a regular basis and were able to bring case studies to the training blocks and to the co-ordinators. Only one did not succeed in doing any art therapy, but she was a very active participant in the course, especially the experiential workshops and used the experience for herself.

As far as the evaluation is concerned, this posed many problems and it was far too ambitious a demand for these beginning therapists. However, much of the trainees' case material prepared for the evaluation exists but has yet to be organised and incorporated into the proposed manual for Bulgarian art therapy practice. Work was to have started on the manual during a visit of the co-ordinators to England in 1988. Unfortunately the visit could not take place for economic reasons and the rescheduled date proved impossible because of political events in Bulgaria at the end of the 1980s. Among other things, these events caused the break-up of major institutions, including the Medical Academy in Sofia.

Some current reflections

Perhaps the most important issue to emerge from this experience is that of the complexity of transferring psychotherapeutic concepts from one society to another. The most obvious of these is related to language. For example, most of the literature we used had to be translated from English (or French and German) into Bulgarian, and trainees had to be able to read English to acquaint themselves with literature on art therapy, psychotherapy, group analysis, etc. This was seen as inevitable until sufficient experience had been gained for Bulgarian publications to be produced (such as the manual following the project's middle stage). We noted that problems of meaning had already occurred in the translation of Freud's work from German into English, and in transposing constructs which had been formed in the context of Austro-Hungarian or Swiss – those of Freud or Jung, respectively – bourgeois culture to therapeutic practice with, say, the British or Bulgarian working class. Indeed, the fundamental nature of psychoanalysis and its relationship to art therapy had to be considered in the context of a society which had for the past half century been structured on Marxist-Leninist economic theory.

The relationship between Marxism and psychoanalysis had been addressed in the 1920s and 1930s by various groups of Soviet and Bulgarian psychologists and German-speaking psychoanalysts who were interested in making psychoanalysis acceptable in the Soviet Union. Unfortunately the debate was cut short due to the rise of Fascism, which caused the majority of psychoanalysts to go into exile. Later, workers such as Marie Langer, a psychoanalyst who founded the Argentinian Psycho-analytical Association during the 1940s, had also addressed the problems involved in such a liaison. She and her colleagues had grappled with similar issues to ours in trying to establish a dynamically-oriented service in a socialist country (in her case Nicaragua). She always regarded practising psychotherapy as a political task, necessitating an understanding of social and ideological context. It was the combination of this, plus constitutional factors and early and later life experiences which she felt conditioned a person's resistance or fragility in the face of traumatic situations.

Langer (1989, p. 60) had noted in a talk given in Cuba in 1985, that the main criticism by Marxists of Freudian psychoanalysis was that it tended to exclude the external world and the notion of class struggle from any dialogue; and that Freud had biologised and psychologised the social. Yet as post-Freudian psychoanalysts such as Erich Fromm and members of the Frankfurt School, notably S.H. Foulkes, who did so much to establish group analysis in Britain, were to point out, psychoanalysis could and should consider the whole network of relationships in which the individual was involved (Foulkes 1938; Fromm 1962).

Following the changes in Bulgarian politics, psychoanalysis has become very popular and private practice is seen as a desirable goal. It remains to be seen if and how psychoanalytic thinking will be incorporated into the remains of the Bulgarian health care system.

Concluding thoughts

I wrote some notes in 1990:

One might ask, has psychotherapy or art therapy a role to play, given such a network? The answer seems to be Yes, provided it can be adapted to the needs of individuals and groups in the context of their society. The art object can, of course, be taken on many different levels and provides for the kind of indirect and guarded comments that can be accepted or denied according to the circumstances. Old customs and traditions are gradually disappearing and there is a rapid transition from agricultural-rural to industrial-urban. Tourism and exposure to the mass media have brought an influx of foreign ideas and ways of behaving. Since the political upheavals of last year, the country is severely traumatised and there is great anxiety about the future. Many Bulgarians are leaving home and will find themselves trying to adapt to a new way of life without their stable network and in the competitive maelstrom of Western-style capitalism.

Most of the work of the project has turned out to be a way of trying to create an avenue, not only for art therapy but for other psychodynamic interventions, to infiltrate the Bulgarian health service. In other words, the art therapy project helped to sensitise staff in three major centres to the possibilities of working in ways which involved the active participation of patients. It is likely that the 'group interactive' approach which developed during the training blocks was an appropriate one to use, as much importance was, and probably still is, placed on social interaction and the ability to work in a team. Also, as I have said, the model had to acknowledge that the 'network' of family and friends who supported and maintained each other in the face of the somewhat impersonal 'State' was essential to daily life. Even with the collapse of the 'State' such networks are liable to remain. No doubt they will change and re-form, now that so many families and friends are in open conflict about their political persuasions.

CONCLUSION

It is difficult to write a conclusion to a process which is still very much on-going, despite being interrupted in such a serious and dramatic manner. There is as yet no tidy report nor art therapy manual, as planned back in 1985. Participants have scattered, some have acquired high-level posts in the new system and some of these were actively involved in the art therapy projects. Many 'chiefs' in the psychiatric system have lost their jobs and been replaced by others with a more 'open' attitude to mental health care. Unfortunately, the framework for this care has disintegrated and needs to be rebuilt. There were several important things to be learned, though, which have been carried through to other projects. In summary, these are:

- The motivation of the trainees who undertake an art therapy programme and their expectations needs to be thoroughly explored.
- The motivation of institutions who 'send' or 'second' the trainees and their expectations must be taken into account and it is necessary to maintain constant dialogue with staff in the institutions where the trainees are working.
- The issue of 'role change' and subsequent perceptions of colleagues towards the trainee has to be discussed.
- The family and social networks which are vital to the trainees' emotional well-being have to be considered.
- It is necessary to be able to adapt psychodynamic models to take account of the previous point without losing the effectiveness of the model.
- It needs to be recognised that the development of art therapy in Britain and the USA, based as it is on art education and psychoanalysis, is particular to those countries. In many other places it is likely that trainees will have little or no art experience and this must be accounted for in their training: without the confidence that comes from being immersed in visual media for a significant period, an impoverished attitude towards image-making is likely to occur. This cannot be good for either trainee or patient. Working with so many groups where trainees have no practical visual art background has led me to conclude that it would be necessary to try to 'compensate' for this in any on-going training, lest the effectiveness of the process be reduced.
- The issues which arise when trainees or conductor are working in a

foreign language are essential to recognise and address. Working through an interpreter is certainly possible but it is better to know something of the language of the country where one is working, either as trainee or conductor. This may not always be practical, but in any case it has to be acknowledged that expressing deep emotions in a foreign language is extremely difficult and taxing.

• Art therapy appears to have been 'subversive' in Bulgaria in enabling the trainees to have a new means of indirect communication. At a time when it was rather risky to speak one's mind too openly, images gave a wonderful opportunity to be ambiguous.

• A project should not be too ambitious in its aims and objectives, especially when introducing a new element into a system. There are liable to be contradictions between the new model and the organisational model in which one is functioning and this must be continually addressed.

• Finally, and echoing the conclusion reached by Gheorghieva and myself in our article in *Inscape* (Waller and Gheorghieva 1990, p. 35), official projects in psychosocial interventions should be well timed; they should not be the first step to be made but should follow a more informal input, spontaneously initiated by self-organised teams.

REFERENCES

Cohen, L. and Manion, L. (1981) *Research Methods in Education*. Croom Helm, London.

Foulkes, S.H. (1938) Book review of Norbert Elias, *The Civilising Process*, in *International Journal of Psycho-Analysis* 19: 263–5. (Later published by Blackwell, Oxford, 1978).

Fromm, E. (1962) *Beyond the Chains of Illusion: My Encounter with Marx and Freud*. Abacus, London.

Langer, M. (1989) 'Psychoanalysis Without the Couch'. *Free Associations*. No. 15: 60–6.

Marinov, A. (1972) 'Psychopathology of Expression and Psychedelic Art'. *Inscape*. 5: 24–9.

Marinov, A. (1975a) 'Free Art Expression Produced by a Drug-addicted Male'. In: Jakab, I. (Ed.) *Transcultural Aspects of Psychiatric Art. Psychiatry and Art*. vol. 4. Karger, Basel.

Marinov, A. (1975b) 'Graphic Expression of Schizophrenic Anxiety'. *Inscape*. 12: 30–2.

Marinov, A. (1983) *Schizophrenia: Artistic Self-expression*. Psychiatric Hospital Press, Bela, Bulgaria.

Waller, D. (1983) 'Art Therapy in Bulgaria: Parts 1 and 2'. *Inscape*. April: 12–15; and October: 15–17.

Waller, D. (1993) *Group Interactive Art Therapy*. Routledge, London.

Waller, D. and Boyadzhiev, V. (1983) 'Art Therapy and its Relationship to Psychiatry in Bulgaria'. In: James, K. (Ed.) *The Institution*. Hertfordshire College of Art and Design.

Waller, D. and Gheorghieva, J. (1990) 'Introducing New Psychosocial Programmes into the Bulgarian NHS: The Case of Art Therapy'. *Inscape*. Summer: 26–35.

Brief bibliography of suggested reading on research

METHODOLOGY: GENERAL

Bell, C. and Roberts, H. (Eds) (1984) *Social Researching: Politics, Problems, Practice*. Routledge and Kegan Paul, London.

Bell, J. (1987) *Doing Your Research Project: A Guide for First-time Researchers in Education and Social Science*. Open University Press, Buckingham.

Cohen, L. and Manion, L. (1980) *Research Methods in Education*. Routledge, London, 3rd edn.

Moser, C.A. and Kalton, G. (1977) *Survey Methods in Social Investigation*. Heinemann Eduational Books, London.

Phillips, E.M. and Pugh, D.S. (1987) *How to Get a PhD: A Handbook for Students and their Supervisors*. Open University Press, Buckingham.

Quinn Patton, M. (1982) *Practical Evaluation*. Sage Publications, Beverly Hills.

Reason, P. (Ed.) (1988) *Human Inquiry in Action*. Sage Publications, London.

Reason, P. and Rowan, J. (Eds) (1981) *Human Inquiry: A Sourcebook of New Paradigm Research*. John Wiley and Sons, Chichester.

Selltiz, C. and Jahoda, M. (1965) *Research Methods in Social Relations*. Methuen and Co., London.

Silverman, D. (1993) *Interpreting Qualitative Data: Methods for Analysing Text, Talk and Interaction*. Sage Publications, London.

CLINICAL AND PSYCHOTHERAPY RESEARCH

Abbott, P. and Sapsford, R. (Eds) (1992) *Research into Practice: A Reader for Nurses and the Caring Professions*. Open University Press, Buckingham.

Aldridge, D. (1991) 'Aesthetics and the Individual in the Practice of Medical Research: A Discussion Paper'. *Journal of the Royal Society of Medicine*. 84: 147–50.

Aldridge, D. (1991) 'Single Case Research Designs for the Clinician'. *Journal of the Royal Society of Medicine*. 84: 249–52.

Barlow, D.H. and Hersen, M. (1978) *Single Case Experimental Design: Strategies for Studying Behavior Change*. Pergamon Press, New York.

Bloch, S. (1988) 'Research in Group Psychotherapy'. In: Aveline, M. and Dryden, W. (Eds) *Group Therapy in Britain*. Open University Press, Buckingham.

Bloch, S. and Crouch, E. (1985) *Therapeutic Factors in Group Psychotherapy*. Oxford Medical Publications, Oxford.

Gale, A. (1985) 'On Doing Research: The Dream and the Reality'. *Journal of Family Therapy*. 7: 187–211.

Gurman, A.S. and Razin, A.M. (Eds) (1977) *Effective Psychotherapy: A Handbook of Research*. Pergamon Press, New York.

Herbert, M. (1990) *Planning a Research Project: A Guide for Practitioners and Trainees in the Helping Professions*. Cassell Educational, London.

Kazdin, A. (1982) *Single Case Research Designs: Methods for Clinical and Applied Settings*. Oxford University Press, Oxford.

Krupnick, J.L. and Pincus, H.A. (1992) 'The Cost-effectiveness of Psychotherapy'. *American Journal of Psychiatry*. 149: 1295–1305.

Lewith, G. and Aldridge, D. (1993) *Clinical Research Methodology for Complementary Therapies*. Hodder and Stoughton, London.

Malan, D.H. (1976) *Toward the Validation of Dynamic Psychotherapy*. Plenum Press, London.

Milne, D. (Ed.) (1987) *Evaluation in Mental Health Practice*. Croom Helm, Beckenham.

Partridge, C. and Barnitt, R. (1986) *Research Guidelines: A Handbook for Therapists*. Heinemann Medical Books, London.

Sapsford, R. and Abbott, P. (1992) *Research Methods for Nurses and the Caring Professions*. Open University Press, Buckingham.

Strupp, H. (1973) *Psychotherapy: Clinical, Research and Theoretical Issues*. Jason Aronson, New York.

Sutton, C. (1987) *A Handbook of Research for the Helping Professions*. Routledge and Kegan Paul, London.

ART HISTORY AND MUSIC ANALYSIS

Bailey, D. (1992) *Improvisation: Its Nature and Practice in Music*. National Sound Archive, British Library, London.

Carrier, D. (1991) *Principles of Art History Writing*. Pennsylvania State University Press, Pennsylvania.

Cooke, D. (1959) *The Language of Music*. Oxford University Press, London.

Dean, R. (1989) *Creative Improvisation: Jazz, Contemporary Music and Beyond*. Open University Press, Buckingham.

Dean, R. (1992) *New Structures in Jazz and Improvised Music since 1960*. Open University Press, Buckingham.

Dunsby, J. and Whittall, A. (1988) *Musical Analysis in Theory and Practice*. Faber Music, London.

Ferretti, S. (1989) *Cassirer, Panofsky and Warburg: Symbol, Art and History*. Yale University Press, New Haven and London.

Gannt, L. (1986) 'Systematic Investigation of Art Works: Some Research Models drawn from Neighboring Fields'. *American Journal of Art Therapy*. 24: 111–18.

Nattiez, J.J. (1990) *Music and Discourse: Towards a Semiology of Music*. Princeton University Press, Princeton.

See also a series of papers, entitled 'The State of Research', on research in art history in *The Art Bulletin* 1986, 1987 and 1988, e.g. Haverkamp-Begemann, E. (1987) 'The State of Research in Northern Baroque Art'. *The Art Bulletin* LXIX: 510–20.

ART THERAPY AND MUSIC THERAPY

Aldridge, D. (1991) 'Meaning and Expression: The Pursuit of the Aesthetic in Research'. *Holistic Medicine*. 5: 177–86.

Gilroy, A. (1992) 'Research in Art Therapy'. In: Waller, D. and Gilroy, A. (Eds) *Art Therapy: A Handbook.* Open University Press, Buckingham.

Gilroy, A., Hoskyns, S., Jenkyns, M., Lee, C. and Payne, H. (Eds) (1989) *Proceedings of the First Arts Therapies Research Conference.* City University, London.

Henzell, J. (1978) 'Art and Therapy'. *Inscape.* 2.2: 3–11.

Henzell, J. (1980) 'Ambiguity, Art and Symptoms'. *Inscape.* 5.1: 21–6.

Hoskyns, S. (Ed.) (1988) *The Case Study as Research. Proceedings of the Fourth Music Therapy Research Conference.* City University, London.

Hoskyns, S. and Clarke, E.C. (Eds) (1987) *Starting Research in Music Therapy. Proceedings of the Third Music Therapy Research Conference.* City University, London.

Kersner, M. (Ed.) (1991) *The Art of Research. Proceedings of the Second Arts Therapies Research Conference.* City University, London.

McNiff, S. (1986) 'Freedom of Research and Artistic Inquity'. *The Arts in Psychotherapy.* 13: 279–84.

McNiff, S. (1987) 'Research and Scholarship in the Creative Arts Therapies'. *The Arts in Psychotherapy.* 14: 285–92.

Payne, H. (Ed.) (1993) *Handbook of Inquiry in the Arts Therapies: One River, Many Currents.* Jessica Kingsley, London.

Schmidt, J.A. (1984) 'Structural Analysis of Clinical Music'. *Music Therapy.* 4: 18–28.

See also *The Arts in Psychotherapy,* vols 20 and 21, 1993: both volumes devoted to research in the arts therapies.

Name Index

This index contains only personal names. All other names will be found in the Subject index

Subject index